Ning® For Dummies®

BESTSELLING BOOK SERIES

D1487240

Cheat Sheet

Interacting with Others in a Network on Ning

- Write a note on the Comment Walls of your friends.
- Say hi to new members that have joined your network.
- Embed a very cool video you found on YouTube.
- Start a new topic or write a blog post.
- Join a few groups you're interested in.
- Start your own group if you don't find any that you like.
- Share photos from your weekend trip.
- Leave a comment about someone else's photo, blog, or video.
- Add a new event and invite all your friends to it.
- Participate in a chat session with other members.
- Send a message to all your friends.

Reasons to Start a Network on Ning

- To reconnect with your high school or college classmates.
- To discuss favorite songs and share photos with other fans of a musical artist.
- To rally people around a political campaign.
- To offer support to patients with a chronic condition.
- To coordinate communications with your students.
- To raise awareness about an important cause.
- To network with professionals in your trade.
- To offer a space for online learning.
- To give conference attendees a place to connect.
- To discuss your favorite movies with others.

Customizing Your Network

- Give it a unique name and URL.
- Play with one of the existing themes.
- Add a logo to your network's header.
- Modify your network's navigation.
- Add RSS feeds to complement your own content.
- Customize your network's players.
- Use Text Boxes to include banners.
- Create categories in the discussion forum.
- Use CSS to jazz up your network.
- Rename things using the Language Editor.
- Add new pages to your network.
- Use a few JavaScript hacks to take things to the limit.

For Dummies: Bestselling Book Series for Beginners

Ning® For Dummies®

Enhancing Your Ning Network Experience

- Invite all your friends to join the network.
- Search for networks to join on Ning.com.
- Start and run a new group in the network.
- Add new friends and leave them comments.
- Upload your own videos to the network.
- Post comments on photos and videos.
- Visit your network on your cell phone.
- Volunteer to be an Administrator.
- Start your own network on Ning.
- Join the Network Creators network.

Promoting Your Network

- Tell everyone you know about your network.
- Ask your members to add a network badge to their Web sites.
- Ask your members to invite others to join.
- Ask bloggers to write about your network.
- Set up and promote Facebook applications.
- Syndicate your network's content on other sites.
- Offer unique, viral content.
- Distribute flyers at events.
- Optimize your network for search engines.

Things That You Can Make Private on Ning

- An entire network
- A group of members
- Videos, photos, and blog posts
- Your profile page

Features Your Network Should Not Be Without

- Forum
- Groups
- Photos
- Videos
- Chat

For Dummies: Bestselling Book Series for Beginners

Ning®
FOR
DUMMIES®

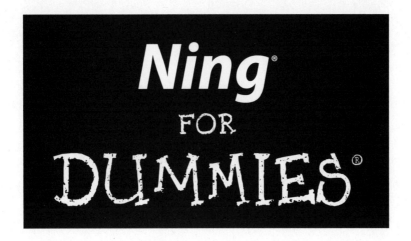

Ning® FOR DUMMIES®

by Manny Hernandez

WILEY

Wiley Publishing, Inc.

Ning® For Dummies®

Published by
Wiley Publishing, Inc.
111 River Street
Hoboken, NJ 07030-5774

www.wiley.com

For general information on our other products and services, please contact our Customer Care Department within the U.S. at 877-762-2974, outside the U.S. at 317-572-3993, or fax 317-572-4002.

For technical support, please visit www.wiley.com/techsupport.

Wiley also publishes its books in a variety of electronic formats. Some content that appears in print may not be available in electronic books.

Library of Congress Control Number: 2009924577

ISBN: 978-0-470-45317-9

Manufactured in the United States of America

10 9 8 7 6 5 4 3 2 1

WILEY

About the Author

Manny Hernandez is a social entrepreneur and a community strategist committed to connecting people touched by diabetes and raising diabetes awareness. He is the President of the Diabetes Hands Foundation (DHF), a nonprofit that runs the first two social networks for people touched by diabetes: TuDiabetes.com (in English, started in March 2007) and EsTuDiabetes.com (in Spanish, started in August 2007). Both social networks run on Ning.

In early 2008, Manny worked briefly as a Community Advocate for Ning, in Palo Alto, CA. Between 2000 and 2008, he worked in Web product management, online community management, content management, and search engine marketing in a number of companies, including Full Sail University, Quepasa.com, Earth911, and Pets911. From 1996 to 2000, Manny worked for Procter & Gamble in Venezuela.

In 1994, Manny earned his bachelor's degree in Electrical Engineering in Universidad Metropolitana, Venezuela, and in 1996 he earned his Master's degree in EE in Cornell University. While attending Cornell, the Web bug bit him, and it hasn't abandoned him since. Manny loves to listen to music, read, and spend time with his family. You can find him on Twitter at askmanny and blogging at www.askmanny.com.

Dedication

To my father, Manuel Adolfo (1928–2005): Even four years after your departure, you continue to be my biggest inspiration. Te echo de menos, Viejo. . . .

Acknowledgments

Above all, thanks to my wife Andreina and my son Santiago for being so patient and supportive during the times I was sitting in front of the computer writing, instead of being with them. I now go back to having a life!

Thanks to the folks at Wiley, in particular Nicole Sholly and Amy Fandrei, who made the book possible before and during the writing process. Thanks for making me sound smarter . . . or should I say dummier?

To all my friends at Ning: Mackenzie Cooper, Brad Mallow, Laura Gluhanich, Athena von Oech, Kyle Ford, Evan Goldin, Alex Fishwick, along with the entire Advocacy crew. Gina and Marc, thanks for creating such an incredible platform. Thank you also to everybody else I had the honor of meeting and working with while I was at Ning; this book is a testament to your hard work.

Thanks to the amazing team of Administrators in TuDiabetes.com and EsTuDiabetes.com for all you do every day to help create and maintain an incredible member experience for people touched by diabetes.

Last, thanks to all the members of TuDiabetes.com and EsTuDiabetes.com. You have become my extended family, and I am honored to be able to serve you.

Publisher's Acknowledgments

We're proud of this book; please send us your comments through our online registration form located at http://dummies.custhelp.com. For other comments, please contact our Customer Care Department within the U.S. at 877-762-2974, outside the U.S. at 317-572-3993, or fax 317-572-4002.

Some of the people who helped bring this book to market include the following:

Acquisitions and Editorial

Project Editor: Nicole Sholly

Acquisitions Editor: Amy Fandrei

Copy Editor: Virginia Sanders

Technical Editor: Jeb Banner, www.smallboxweb.com

Editorial Manager: Kevin Kirschner

Editorial Assistant: Amanda Foxworth

Sr. Editorial Assistant: Cherie Case

Cartoons: Rich Tennant (www.the5thwave.com)

Composition Services

Senior Project Coordinator: Kristie Rees

Layout and Graphics: Melissa K. Jester, Sarah Philippart, Christin Swinford, Christine Williams

Proofreaders: Kathy Simpson

Indexer: Potomac Indexing, LLC

Publishing and Editorial for Technology Dummies

    Richard Swadley, Vice President and Executive Group Publisher

    Andy Cummings, Vice President and Publisher

    Mary Bednarek, Executive Acquisitions Director

    Mary C. Corder, Editorial Director

Publishing for Consumer Dummies

    Diane Graves Steele, Vice President and Publisher

Composition Services

    Debbie Stailey, Director of Composition Services

Contents at a Glance

Table of Contents

Introduction

*O*nline social networks are part of modern life. Long gone are the days when MySpace, Facebook, and LinkedIn were a remote notion. Being a member of a social network has become an incredible way to connect (and reconnect) with other people who share your interests.

Until Ning was created, social networks offered members a space on the Internet that either looked all the same on every page (as in the case of Facebook or LinkedIn) or lent itself to a bit of a chaotic visual experience (as in the case of MySpace). Ning acknowledged the gap in between and started giving people the power and the platform to easily create, manage, and even make money running a social network dealing with any subject they want to share.

From school groups to scientists, from music fans to health patients . . . there can be a network on Ning for anything. You can either become a member of one or many social networks on Ning or start your own.

About Ning For Dummies

I wrote *Ning For Dummies* with two audiences in mind: members of social networks on Ning and Network Creators on Ning. The first two parts of the book are meant for anyone who is a member of a network on Ning and for people who are considering joining a network on Ning. Part III is for someone who is considering creating a network. Parts IV to VI are for anyone who wants to create a network and people who have already taken the leap and are running a network.

Here are some of the things you can do with this book:

- ✔ **Set up a profile to share about yourself with others.** You find out how to make your profile look good and tell enough about yourself. You also discover how to protect your privacy and limit access to your information to only those you care to share it with.

- ✔ **Connect with others that you have something in common with.** All social networks on Ning have an edge that makes them unique. Considering how many networks there are, there's a good chance that you can find a network you can join to meet other folks that are like you.

- ✔ **Create a social network and customize it as much as you want.** The management and customization tools built in to your social network on Ning are very well thought out and let you make your network look great. Your work goes mostly into getting new members to join and managing the network once it's running.

- ✔ **Extend your brand through a social network and monetize it.** You can extend your brand through the connections you develop in your social network. Ning also gives you the means to make money from your network.

Foolish Assumptions

In this book, I make the following assumptions:

- ✔ **You have Internet access and an e-mail address.** Ning is a service based on the Web, and you need an e-mail address in order to join or start a network on Ning.

- ✔ **You have a basic understanding of how to use a Web site.** I mean simple things like clicking links, selecting options from a drop-down list . . . nothing that's rocket science.

- ✔ **You get a kick out of connecting with others online.** If you would rather *not* leave comments to others, participate in a discussion topic, share photos, post in your blog, and so on, this book and Ning are not for you.

Conventions Used in This Book

By *conventions,* I mean a set of rules I've used throughout this book to present information to you consistently.

- ✔ When you see a term *italicized,* look for its definition, which is included so that you know what things mean in the context of Ning.

- ✔ Sometimes, I give you information to enter on-screen; in this case, I've used **bold** for what you need to type.

- ✔ Web site addresses and e-mail addresses are in `monofont` so that they stand out from regular text.

What You Don't Have to Read

This book helps you take the steps to eventually create and run your own social network for anything. It starts by introducing you to the basics of Ning and being a member of a network. If that's all you want to do, you don't need to read much else. If you already run your own network, you'll find the later chapters in the book particularly useful. All in all, the book is structured in a modular way, so you can read the chapters containing the information you need and nothing more.

How This Book Is Organized

Ning For Dummies is split into six parts. You don't have to read it sequentially, and you don't even have to read all the sections in any particular chapter. You can use the Table of Contents and the index to find the information you need and quickly get your answer. In this section, I briefly describe what you can find in each part.

Part I: An Overview of Ning

Part I covers the basics of Ning. What is Ning? Let me tell you right now that Ning is not a Chinese Web site or a style of martial arts. I introduce you to what Ning helps you accomplish and go through the process of setting up an account on Ning and joining your first social networks on Ning. Chapter 3 discusses how you can protect your personal information on Ning, so you can confidently participate in social networks on Ning.

Part II: Using an Existing Network on Ning

This part gives you the information you need to participate actively in a network on Ning while making the most of all its features. Uploading photos and videos, communicating with other members in the network, participating in the discussion forum, events, groups, and chat are all things you find out how to do in Chapters 4 through 6.

Part III: Creating and Managing Your Own Social Network

Part III takes your experience in Ning to the next level. You find out how to go about creating and managing your own social network. I show you how to set it up, tweak it to make it look the way you want it, and manage it as you go along. I also discuss the importance of enlisting the help of others along the way in order to keep up with the demands of running a successful social network.

Part IV: Promoting Your Network

After your network is set up, you need to promote it to make sure members start joining. This part is devoted to showing you how you can spread the word about your network to get more people interested in it. I also deal with the use of tools to help you learn from your members and what they do, so you can keep on improving the network for them. Last, I show you how to keep your members coming back.

Part V: Advanced Tips and Tricks

Part V is meant for people who want to really spend some more time going "under the hood" to fine-tune elements throughout the network. I discuss CSS and internal tools within your network, which you can use to customize the appearance, language, and features of the network. With a little effort, you can make your network match as much as possible what you had in mind when you first thought of it.

Part VI: The Part of Tens

The last part contains a chapter dealing with ten ways to help you make money from your network, ten hacks to make your network stand out even more and ten tools to help you run (or be a member) of a network on Ning. Complementing Part V, the last chapter offers a list of ten ideas for networks on Ning.

Appendix

The appendix contains a list of Ning resources you can go back to in order to stay current on the latest news and details from the Ning headquarters in Palo Alto.

Icons Used in This Book

What's a *For Dummies* book without icons pointing you in the direction of really great, super-helpful information? In this section, I briefly describe each icon I use in this book.

The Tip icon points out helpful information that is likely to make your job easier.

This icon marks an interesting and useful fact — something that you might want to remember for later use.

The Warning icon highlights lurking danger. With this icon, I'm telling you to pay attention and proceed with caution.

When you see this icon, you know that there's techie stuff nearby. If you're not feeling very techie, you can skip this info.

Where to Go from Here

If you want to get a feel for what Ning is and how to join a social network on Ning, go to Part I. If you already belong to a network on Ning and want to make the most of your experience on it, read the chapters in Part II. If you want to create your own network on Ning, jump to Part III. If you want to find out how to best promote your network, go to Part IV. Last, if you want to take your network to the next level, make sure to read the chapters in Part V.

Part I
An Overview of Ning

The 5th Wave   By Rich Tennant

"I think you're just jealous that I found a community of people on Ning that worship the yam as I do, and you haven't."

In this part . . .

By now you know that this is not a Chinese book or a book on martial arts. So you are in the right place! By the same token, if you're reading the introduction to Part I, I'm going to go out on a limb and assume that you want to start from square one.

Because Ning is such a huge place that can be different things to different people, in this part of the book I cover the basics to help ease you into things such as

- ✔ Understanding what Ning is and what you can do on it
- ✔ Getting started on Ning
- ✔ Finding your way around Ning
- ✔ Protecting your personal information on Ning

Chapter 1

Exploring Ning

*W*e all have different things that we're passionate about. You may be a life-long fan of your hometown sports team. You may enjoy buying and selling handmade crafts. You may have even seen your favorite band twenty times in concert.

Regardless of all the facets that make up your life, you are not alone in them: Thousands, most likely millions, of people out there have something in common with you. But until now it wasn't easy to find them or to connect with them.

Enter Ning. Ning exists to help people create their own social networks for anything. Inside social networks, people can connect and stay in touch with others they have a very specific connection with.

Nearly a million different social networks have already been created on the Ning platform. So depending on whether you choose to join one or more existing social networks or create your own social network, you may find yourself interacting with others in networks on Ning in a number of possible ways.

What Is Ning?

Ning is a platform for creating your own social network to interact with others in a niche social network that looks and feels unlike other social networks you may belong to. As a matter of fact, you can be a member of multiple social networks on Ning, and each network may be completely different, focusing on different topics and having an entirely different appearance.

The comparisons between Ning and other social networks such as Facebook, MySpace, and the like are inevitable. Yet Ning addresses a need that the others don't: It empowers individuals in a way that wasn't possible before because Ning allows you to create, customize, and run your own social network related to any topic.

The "Ning" name, according to co-founder Gina Bianchini, had a combination of being "short, sweet, and had good karma." Plus it helped that the URL was available, of course! And so Ning was born in October 2004, when Bianchini launched it with the help of Marc Andreessen of Netscape and Loudcloud fame. Nearly one million social networks later, it seems they had the right idea when they thought of it.

Since it first saw the light of day, Ning has become the best (and most afford-able) option available to create customized social networks focused on specific areas of interest, something that general social networks fall short on.

Over the years, Ning has gradually become a more complete and robust platform that keeps adding new networks by the thousands every week. A large number of those networks have several thousand members, and membership is also growing very rapidly.

What Can You Do on Ning?

When you first arrive on Ning.com, you can do quite a few things, as shown in Figure 1-1.

- **Sign up for a free Ning account or sign in with it.** I discuss the sign-up and sign-in processes in this chapter. This is different from actually joining a network. If you've already joined a network, you can sign in to Ning with the same credentials you used. If you haven't already joined a network, this is a good first step for getting your feet wet with Ning.

- **Create your own social network for anything.** You can find out how to create your own social network on Ning in Chapter 7.

- **Discover social networks on Ning.** I deal with finding networks to join them in Chapter 2.

So are you ready to start your trip through Ning? Ready or not, here we go!

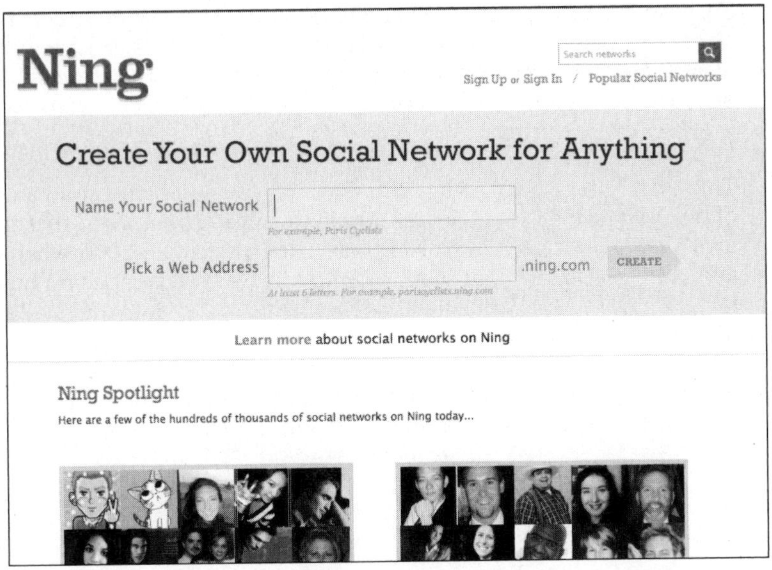

Figure 1-1:
The Ning.
com home
page lets
you do a
number of
things.

Sign up for a free account

When you click the Sign Up link on the Ning.com home page, you're taken to
the Sign Up page, as shown in Figure 1-2.

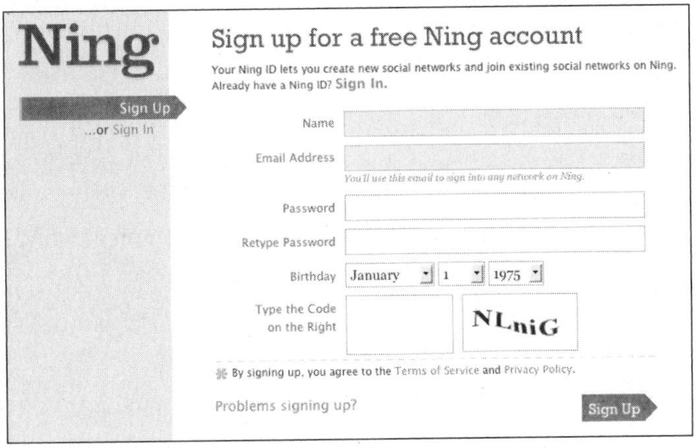

Figure 1-2:
The Sign
Up page
lets you
create your
free Ning
account.

On this page, you find the following elements:

✔ **Name:** You can enter your actual name or a nickname by which you want to be known in networks on Ning that you join or create.

✔ **Email Address:** You need to enter a valid e-mail address you have access to.

✔ **Password:** Think of something that isn't *too* obvious . . . you know, try avoiding things like your last name or the name of your dog.

✔ **Retype Password:** You need to retype the password to confirm that you entered it correctly.

✔ **Birthday:** Your date of birth is required to confirm that you're eligible to use Ning. After you join a network, if you choose to make your birthday visible, it can inform your friends on the network that you're having a birthday so they can congratulate you.

✔ **Type the Code on the Right:** This element is here to make sure you're a human and not a computer setting up an account on Ning.

✔ **Terms of Service:** This link takes you to the Ning Terms of Service page, which lists all the definitions, policies, licenses, and fun things you always read in detail when you sign up for a new service.

✔ **Privacy Policy:** This link takes you to the Ning Privacy Policy page, where you can become informed about the use Ning makes of personal information on the Ning platform.

✔ **Problems Signing Up?:** This links takes you to a page from which you can reset your password, identify some of the causes that may be preventing you from signing up, or go to the Ning Help Center for more troubleshooting information and support.

When you're done entering all these items, click the Sign Up button.

Establish your profile

When you click the Sign Up button, you're taken to your Ning Activity Feed. On top of it is a floating window (see Figure 1-3) prompting you to add your photo, enter your country and gender using the drop-down lists offered, and write a little bit about yourself. If you prefer to pimp out your profile at a later time, you can click the Skip link at the bottom. I discuss the details of setting up and making changes to your profile in Chapter 2.

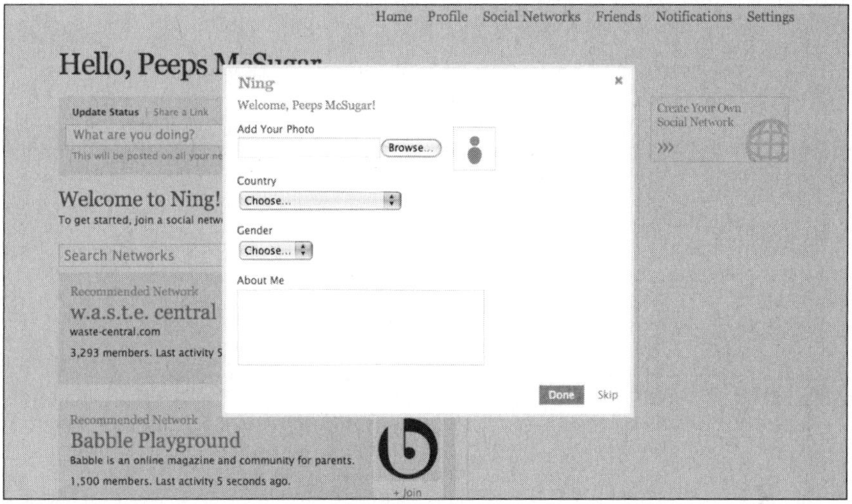

Figure 1-3:
You can
establish
your profile
information
now or take
care of it
later.

Sign in with your account

After you've set up an account on Ning or any network on Ning (as explained
in Chapter 2), you can sign in on the Ning.com home page. Clicking the Sign
In link takes you to the Sign In page, as shown in Figure 1-4.

Figure 1-4:
The Sign In
page gives
you access
to your Ning
Activity
Feed.

When you click the Sign In button, you're taken to your Ning Activity Feed,
just like you would after you're done signing up.

Join and participate in social networks

In Chapter 2, I give you the details of finding and joining networks. When you find a network you like and join it, you can start participating in the social network. For example, you can

✔ Give your profile page all the personality that you want.

✔ Maintain a blog.

✔ Leave comments to other members.

✔ Post videos from a recent activity or event.

✔ Participate in the discussion topics in a forum.

✔ Organize events and meet-ups with other members.

✔ Chat with others about topics of common interest.

✔ Create and join regional groups.

Before you dash off to start socializing on Ning, you might want to check out the next section, where I give you a full tour of the Ning Activity Feed.

Getting Around Ning

Your Ning Activity Feed is packed with information and navigation links. Everything you need to get around Ning is right there. All that information coming at you can be confusing, so in the following sections, I break down each bit of the Activity Feed and then describe each link that appears in the navigation bar across the top.

Exploring your Ning Activity Feed

Your Ning Activity Feed gives you lots of territory to explore: Through it, you can manage your participation in networks you're a member of and keep a tab on networks you created. Through it, you can also find out about networks you could benefit from joining. Take a look at some of it in Figure 1-5.

Status

Starting at the top, you can update your status, much you like you can do on Facebook or MySpace. This status not only appears on your Ning Activity Feed, but also gets updated in every network on Ning you belong to. As explained in Chapter 5, you can also update your status on a network-by-network basis.

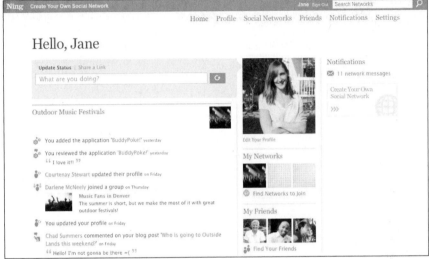

Figure 1-5:
Your Ning
Activity
Feed gives
you access
to all your
networks
and friends.

Latest Activity

Below the green status box, you find a stream that pulls information from several different places:

✔ Status updates from your friends across all networks on Ning.

✔ Latest Activity from all networks on Ning you belong to.

✔ Latest Activity from all networks on Ning you created or have administration rights to.

✔ Latest Activity from your friends across all networks on Ning. This includes things like videos they've added, photos they've posted, and friends they've made.

✔ Recommended Networks. Ning recommends networks intelligently based on what it judges to be your interests.

You can see in Figure 1-6 how another portion of the stream on the Ning Activity Feed looks.

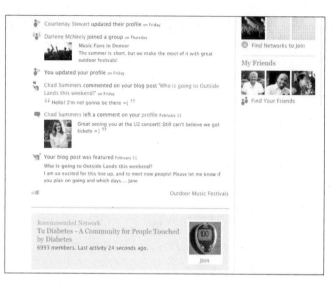

Figure 1-6:
Your Activity
Feed shows
Latest
Activity on
your
networks
on Ning,
recom-
mended
networks,
and friend
updates.

Profile photo

If you added a profile photo when you signed up, you can see it next to the green status box. Clicking it takes you to your profile page on Ning.com, discussed shortly. Clicking the Edit Your Profile link below it takes you to the My Settings page, also discussed in a bit. You can access the Settings page clicking the Settings link in the top navigation.

My Social Networks

Below the profile photo is the My Social Networks area . . . well, not *my* social networks, but *your* social networks! You know what I mean: the social networks on Ning that you're a member of. You can expand the number of networks you belong to by clicking the link Find Networks to Join directly below your social networks. Doing so takes you to the Social Networks page, which I deal with later on.

My Friends

Below your list of social networks is the My Friends grid, showing up to 15 of your friends across all networks on Ning you're a member of. You can see all your friends together by clicking the View All # Friends link below the grid, where # is the number of friends that you have across all social networks on Ning. When you click this link, you're taken to the My Friends page, which is covered later in this chapter. You can see the My Friends grid in Figure 1-7.

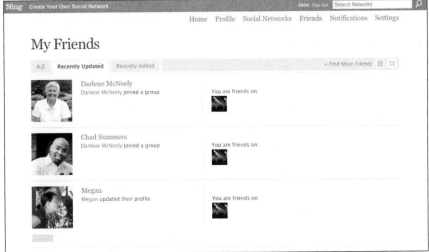

Figure 1-7:
You can see
your friends
across all
networks
in the My
Friends grid.

Notifications

In the right column of your Ning Activity Feed is a Notifications area, where you can see a summary of the notifications you have outstanding in connection with all networks you belong to. Notifications include

- ✔ **Network Invitations:** Messages you've received inviting you to join other networks.

- ✔ **Network Friend Requests:** Messages from others who want to be your friend in one of your networks. I talk more about friends in your network in Chapter 3.

- ✔ **New Messages:** Private messages you've received from others in your networks. Private messages are discussed in Chapter 5.

- ✔ **Group Invitations:** Invitations you've gotten to join groups in your networks. Groups are covered in Chapter 6.

- ✔ **Event Invitations:** Invitations you've received to attend events in your networks. Events are also covered in Chapter 6.

- ✔ **Application Alerts:** Alerts sent by OpenSocial applications you have set up in your networks. OpenSocial applications are discussed in Chapter 21.

My Links

Below Notifications, you can see the My Links section, containing links you can add and modify through your Settings page.

Create Your Own Social Network button

In the right column is the Create Your Own Social Network button. When you click it, you're taken through the steps involved in setting up your own network. I explain this process in detail in Chapter 7.

Navigating the Ning links

Across the top of your Ning Activity Feed, the navigation gives you access to the following pages: Profile, Social Networks, Friends, Notifications, and Settings. I discuss each of these pages in the following sections. All these pages also have a Home link in the navigation bar that takes you back to the Ning Activity Feed no matter where you are.

Profile

When you click the Profile link in the navigation, you're taken to your Profile page, as shown in Figure 1-8.

Your Profile page displays most of the same information contained in your Ning Activity Feed, along with a few extra bits of information, such as your location, the number of times your profile has been viewed, and whether you're online.

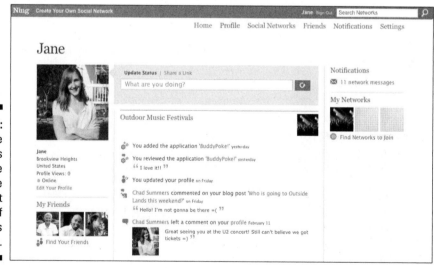

Figure 1-8:
The Profile page lets you share a bit more about yourself with others on Ning.

Social Networks

Clicking the Social Networks link in the navigation takes you to the My Social Networks page, shown in Figure 1-9.

Below the My Social Networks heading you can sort or filter the list of your networks in the following ways:

- ✔ **A-Z:** Displays all the networks you belong to in alphabetical order.

- ✔ **Recently Visited:** Sorts your networks starting with those that you've given more love to recently, expressed in the form of a visit to them.

- ✔ **Most Active:** Displays your networks starting with those that have exhibited the most activity recently.

- ✔ **Networks I've Created:** Shows all networks you've created on the Ning platform. You can also identify your own networks in the other views because they have a light green background (by default), which makes them stand out from the other networks listed.

Additionally, clicking the + Create a Social Network link lets you start a new network. Clicking the icon of stacked lines next to this link displays your networks using a list view (the default view of this page). Clicking the icon of four tiny squares displays your networks in a grid, letting you see more networks in less space.

Last, the Search Networks search box comes in handy if you're a member of a very large number of networks and need to find one quickly.

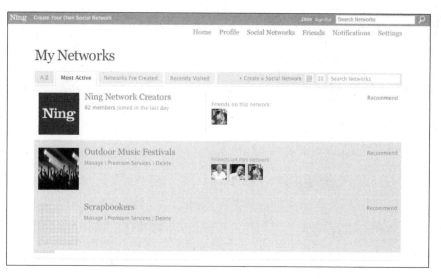

Figure 1-9: The My Social Networks page gives you a snapshot of activity in all your networks.

Friends

Clicking the Friends link in the navigation takes you to the My Friends page, which you can see in Figure 1-10.

By default, you see the results in the Recently Updated tab, starting with your friends who have updated their status most recently. Clicking the All tab shows all your friends, and clicking Recently Added shows your most recently added friends at the top.

You can also grow your list of friends by clicking the + Find More Friends link. This takes you to a page where you can find recommended friends based on your current friends: people you're likely to want to add as friends. As with social networks, you can also display your friends in a list view or in a grid view by clicking the appropriate button at the top right.

For each friend on the list view shown in Figure 1-10, you can see a photo, a name, and the friend's most recent status update along with how long ago it was posted. Also, you get to see which networks you're friends on and the Recommend a Network link on the right of each row. Clicking this link lets you invite that person to all the networks that you belong to but the friend does not.

Notifications

When you have an account on Ning, you receive notifications of many types: invitations to join a network or a group, invitations to RSVP for an event, requests from people to be your friends, messages from your friends, and many more such communications.

Figure 1-10:
The My Friends page lets you see your friends' last status and more.

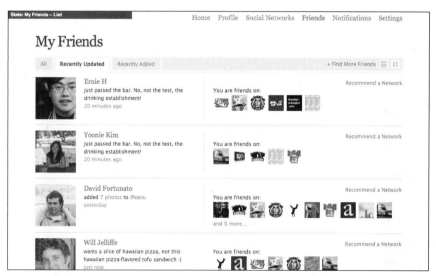

When you click the Notifications link in the navigation, you're taken to the Notifications page, as shown in Figure 1-11. This page combines all notifications you may get from all networks you belong to, which is particularly convenient if you're a member of several networks.

Settings

The last option in the navigation bar is the Settings link. Clicking it takes you to the My Settings page, shown in Figure 1-12.

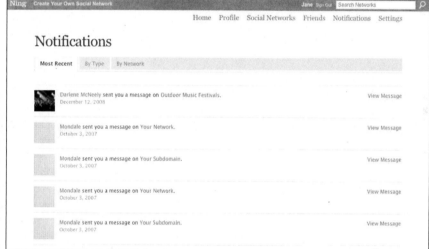

Figure 1-11:
The Notifications page combines all notifications you get from all networks.

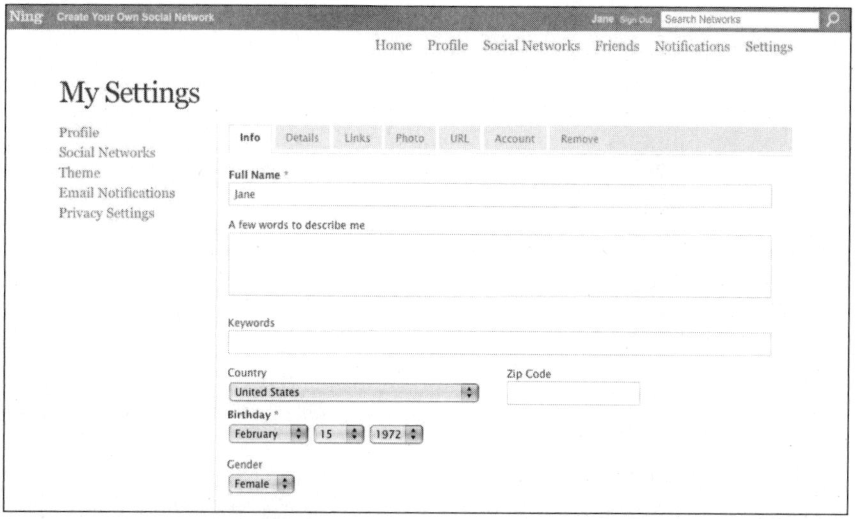

Figure 1-12:
The My Settings page lets you tweak your settings across all networks.

When you first get to My Settings, you can modify the details of your profile:

- ✔ **Info:** The information you entered when you created your profile.
- ✔ **Details:** More details about yourself for others on Ning.com to get to know you better.
- ✔ **Links:** Links to pages of interest that appear on your profile page, under My Links.
- ✔ **Photo:** The profile photo you may have added while setting up your profile.
- ✔ **URL:** The address you want for your profile page on Ning.
- ✔ **Password:** Changing your password across all networks you belong to.
- ✔ **Remove:** Removing your account on Ning.

Clicking the Remove link lets you remove your account on Ning. Doing this effectively deletes your member account on all networks you belong to, along with all content you've contributed to them (posts, photos, videos, and so on). Be very careful with this option, because you may lose a *lot* of information if you choose it.

On the left side of the page, the list of options lets you modify settings for the following things:

- ✔ **Social Networks:** This section of your settings (see Figure 1-13) lets you view general details about your profile and privacy for each of the networks you're a member of. It also lets you conveniently edit both, allows you to adjust the frequency of the updates from each network that you get on your Activity Feed, and even lets you leave the networks.
- ✔ **Theme:** This section lets you change the theme or color palette for your Ning Activity Feed. You pick a primary color, and the page gives you five options for secondary colors, all of which complement the primary color very nicely. This way you have control of how your home page looks, and it still looks very good.
- ✔ **Email Notifications:** You can choose what specific types of e-mail notifications you want to receive from the networks you're a member of. This section lets you set your default notifications when you join new networks. You can override these default settings in each individual network. Chapter 3 details what notifications you can expect from networks on Ning and how you can decide which ones to receive for each network.

  The section also allows you to control the e-mail notifications you receive for New Network Invitations and Ning Profile Friend Requests, as shown in Figure 1-14.

- ✔ **Privacy Settings:** In this section, you can decide who can view your Ning profile and your profile on each of your social networks. The Network Profiles privacy settings you choose become your default settings for any new networks you join. These can be overridden, as explained in Chapter 3, which has an entire section dedicated to the level of control over your privacy you have in networks on Ning.

Your options for Privacy Settings are

- *Ning Profile:* You can choose among Anyone, Friends and Members on My Networks, My Friends, and Just Me.

- *Network Profiles:* You can choose among Anyone, Members of the Network, and My Friends on the Network.

Figure 1-13: The Social Networks section of the My Settings page gives you a bird's-eye view of your networks on Ning.

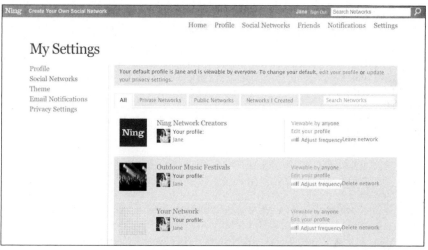

Figure 1-14: The Email Notifications section of the My Settings page lets you control which e-mails you get.

My Personal Journey with Ning

In late 2006, after working on Web sites for more than six years and living with diabetes for four years, I knew I wanted to create a social network about diabetes.

I spent the next few months searching for a platform that would let me spend as much time as possible facing the community members and not require me to spend too much time "under the hood." I'm an engineer, so this might sound odd, but as much as I love playing with programming code, I actually prefer facing people.

In early March 2007, a blog post I ran into made me aware of Ning. In less than 15 minutes, I had set up and launched my social network. I couldn't believe it. Ning allowed me to have a social network and to focus on creating a community for people touched by diabetes, and I didn't have to worry about things behind the curtains.

As impressive as the social networking platform was, I was equally impressed with how affordable it was. It cost me nothing to set up the social network! And when I was ready to tell people about it, I added a few premium services that cost me very little. It didn't take me long to know Ning was the right platform for what I had in mind.

Since then, through word of mouth in the blogging community, members of the network spreading the word, and media coverage, TuDiabetes.com (in English) and EsTuDiabetes.com (in Spanish) have grown and continued to help people touched by diabetes.

Both social networks run on Ning and continue to prove every day what the platform can do. I've seen the Ning platform evolve, providing more tools to enrich the experiences of the members so that they would keep coming back. Today, Ning empowers thousands of Network Creators worldwide with tools that are helping change the world.

Chapter 2

Joining an Existing Network on Ning

In This Chapter

▶ Finding a network to join

▶ Joining networks, both public and private

▶ Tweaking your profile

*W*hen you consider the volume of networks on Ning (more than a million of them at the time this book went to press), finding a network you really want may sound like a tough exercise. Don't lose hope! There are ways for you to find the network that suits your needs and interests.

In this chapter, I walk you through not only finding the network you're looking for, but also joining networks, so you can start connecting with others in a social network on Ning in no time. I also explain how to set up and customize your member profile once you join.

Finding a Network to Join

Ning has made it easy to find networks that may be of interest to you. When you go to Ning.com, you will see a search box, where you can enter topics or keywords that you're interested in. The results you get show you a list of networks that match your search, sorted by activity level (with the most active networks at the top of the list).

The Search Networks results page includes a Join link to the right of each entry listed. Clicking the link takes you directly to the Sign Up page for that network, bypassing the network's main page.

If you're signed in when you visit Ning.com, you're presented with information as explained in Chapter 1. In the stream below your status update box, you encounter featured networks and recommended networks. These entries in your stream also include a Join link.

Manny's Ten Favorite Networks on Ning

Ning has a network for everyone, no matter what your interests are. To give you a feel for the kinds of networks you can find and join on Ning, I've compiled a list of my favorite networks for you:

- ✔ **AlternativeEnergy.com** (http://alternativeenergy.com): Tightly integrated with lots of resources about green and renewable energy, this network has been named one of the top 100 networks for people who want to change the world.

- ✔ **ASPCA Online Community** (http://aspcacommunity.ning.com): This network is a thriving community that supports the objectives of the American Society for the Prevention of Cruelty to Animals.

- ✔ **Classroom 2.0** (www.classroom.com): This social network is aimed at those interested in Web 2.0 and collaborative technologies in education.

- ✔ **Firefighter Nation** (www.firefighternation.com): This is a vibrant professional and social network for current and former fire, rescue, and EMS professionals.

- ✔ **Im Saturn – u r 2** (http://imsaturn.com): This gorgeous-looking network is for Saturn drivers, employees, fans, and enthusiasts. The Saturn team runs regular contests such as Kiss My Astra and On The Road with Bon Jovi.

- ✔ **Ingles Verde Amarelo** (http://verdeamarelo.ning.com): This social network in Portuguese helps Brazilians learn English, connecting them with English speakers who are interested in learning about Brazil.

- ✔ **NAVY For Moms** (http://navyformoms.ning.com): This network is aimed at mothers who have sons and daughters in the U.S. Navy and for mothers with questions about life in the Navy for their kids.

- ✔ **The Spill.com** (http://my.spill.com): This network offers videos of movie reviews given by animated characters discussing the newest films. This network also provides a great space for movie buffs to exchange their thoughts about flicks old and new.

- ✔ **ThisIs50** (http://thisis50.com): Though I'm not a huge fan of the content on it, at more than 400,000 members, this social network is a testimony to the kind of growth that a social network on Ning can experience.

- ✔ **TuDiabetes** (http://tudiabetes.com): This network is a place for people touched by diabetes. (I am partial to this network, since I started it.) Many of the examples in this book are borrowed from my experience with TuDiabetes.com.

Joining a Network

Broadly speaking, you can find two kinds of networks on Ning:

- **Public networks** are visible to everyone, and anyone can become a member of them.

- **Private networks** are visible only to members. Some private networks are set up in a way that lets anyone become a member; others are set up to allow only invited people to sign up. In this case, only after you get an invitation from any member of the network can you create a member profile. See the "Joining a private network" section, later in this chapter, for more details.

The following sections give you step-by-step instructions for joining both types of network.

Joining a public network

In the following steps, I explain the process of joining a public network:

1. **Find the network you want to join, as described in the earlier section "Finding a Network to Join."**

    Public networks display a box in the top-right corner, giving visitors two options: Sign Up or Sign In, as shown in Figure 2-1.

2. **Click the Sign Up link.**

    You're taken to a page where you need to enter the information shown in Figure 2-2. This step is identical for all networks on Ning. By signing up, you agree to Ning's Terms of Service and Privacy Policy . . . you know, that fun and detailed fine print that you always read.

Figure 2-1:
Your first
step to join
a public
network is
to click the
Sign Up link.

Welcome to
Network For Dummies

Sign Up
or Sign In

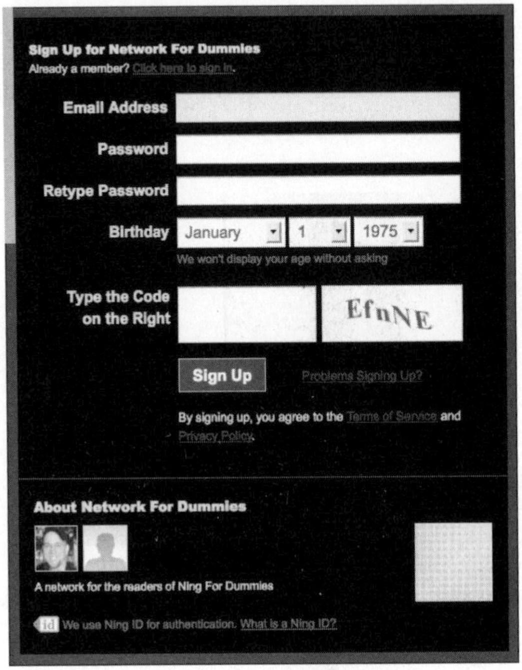

Sign Up for Network For Dummies
Already a member? Click here to sign in.

Email Address	
Password	
Retype Password	
Birthday	January ▼ 1 ▼ 1975 ▼

We won't display your age without asking

Type the Code on the Right [ ] EfnNE

Sign Up   Problems Signing Up?

By signing up, you agree to the Terms of Service and Privacy Policy.

About Network For Dummies

A network for the readers of Ning For Dummies

[Id] We use Ning ID for authentication. What is a Ning ID?

Figure 2-2:
On this page, you enter your e-mail address, password, birthday, and a super-secret code.

3. Enter the following information:

- *Email Address:* You need an e-mail address to sign up for (and, later, to sign into) networks on Ning.

- *Password:* You're required to enter and retype your password.

- *Birthday:* Your date of birth is required to confirm you're eligible to use Ning.

- *Type the Code on the Right:* This is required so that Ning can make sure you aren't a machine, but a human . . . you are a human, right?

If you have problems signing up, click the Problems Signing Up? link next to the Sign Up button. You're taken to the Problems Signing Up or Signing In page, which gives you the option to reset your password, details the system requirements to successfully sign up (or sign in), and gives you a link to the Ning Help Center (http://help.ning.com) in case you're still experiencing problems signing up.

Alternatively, to reset your password, click the Click Here to Reset Your Password link. The page you are taken to gives you a field to enter your e-mail address. After you do so, click the Reset Password button, and an e-mail is sent to you with a link that you can click to change your password.

4. Click the Sign Up button.

You're taken to the Create Your Profile page (see Figure 2-3), where you create your profile and complete any signup questions specific to the network you're joining.

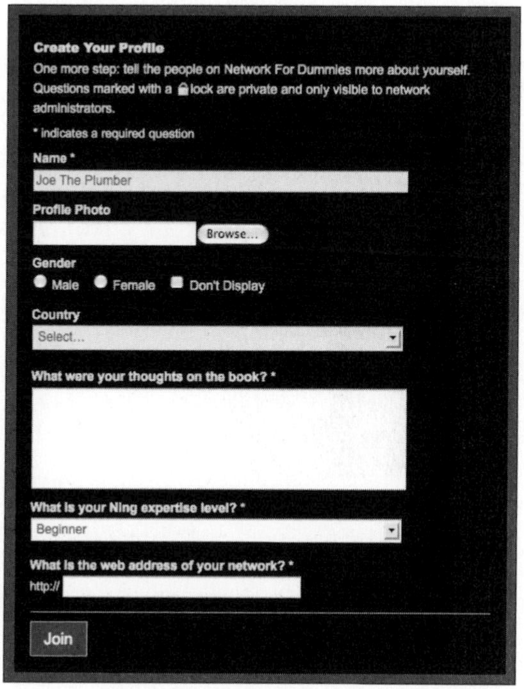

Create Your Profile

One more step: tell the people on Network For Dummies more about yourself. Questions marked with a 🔒 lock are private and only visible to network administrators.

* indicates a required question

Name *

Joe The Plumber

Profile Photo

[   ] Browse...

Gender

● Male   ● Female   ■ Don't Display

Country

Select... ▼

What were your thoughts on the book? *

[   ]

What is your Ning expertise level? *

Beginner ▼

What is the web address of your network? *

http:// [   ]

Join

Figure 2-3: The Create Your Profile page lets you create your member profile.

5. To create your profile, fill in the following fields:

- *Name:* This is a required field. Though you can enter anything here, I recommend that you type in something that will identify you as uniquely as possible in the network. In case you're wondering, you're allowed to have the same name as someone else who already is a member in the network.

- *Profile Photo:* You can choose to leave the default photo the network has for new members, but it's a very good idea to add one from your own crop. If you don't feel comfortable adding a photo showing your face, at least consider adding an image that distinguishes you.

To add a profile photo, click the Browse button. This opens a new window that lets you upload a new image from your computer.

- *Gender:* You can choose between Male and Female, and you can opt to not display your gender information by selecting the Don't Display check box.

- *Country:* When you click this drop-down list, you get a complete list of countries. When you choose any country besides the United States, a new text box opens below the drop-down list, letting you enter your City and State. If you choose the United States, you're prompted for your ZIP code. Your city, not your ZIP code, is the one displayed on your profile page once you are done signing up.

Following the profile questions are any signup questions specific to the network. For instance, in TuDiabetes, I ask members whether they have diabetes, what type of diabetes they have, when were they diagnosed, and what glucose meter they use, among other things.

Signup questions with an asterisk next to them are required. Questions with a lock next to them are private and visible only to you and the network's Administrators.

6. **Answer all the required questions and then click the Join button at the bottom of the page.**

   This takes you to your profile page. At this point, you can pat yourself on the back! You're officially a new member of the network.

Your profile is not set in stone. You can make changes to it, as I discuss later in this chapter, in the "Tweaking Your Profile" section.

Joining a private network

You know a network is private if you don't see the network's main page. Instead, when you enter the network's URL in your browser, all you can see is the network's Sign In page, as shown in Figure 2-4.

Private networks can be set up in one of two ways:

- **To allow anyone to become a member:** If this is the case of the network you want to join, you can simply join by clicking the Sign Up link and following the steps outlined in the previous section.

- **To allow only invited people to become a member:** If this is how the network is set up, the Sign In page is different — it has no Sign Up button. You can sign up only by clicking the link in the invitation e-mail you were sent by a member of the network. If you don't have an invitation . . . well, as the *Seinfeld*-ism goes, no soup for you!

Figure 2-4:
Private
networks
don't show
you the
network's
home page.
Instead, you
see only the
Sign In/Sign
Up page.

There's a special case, regardless of the network being public or private. The Network Creator may have set up the network to approve any new members before they can join. If this is the case, after you click the Join button, you're presented with a message informing you that your membership is pending approval. You have the option to withdraw the request to become a member by clicking the Withdraw Request link, as shown in Figure 2-5.

You receive an e-mail when your profile has been approved. If your profile is not approved, the network administrators can send you a personal message or contact you via e-mail, letting you know why. You can attempt to sign up again and make any necessary changes to your profile so the second time it gets approved.

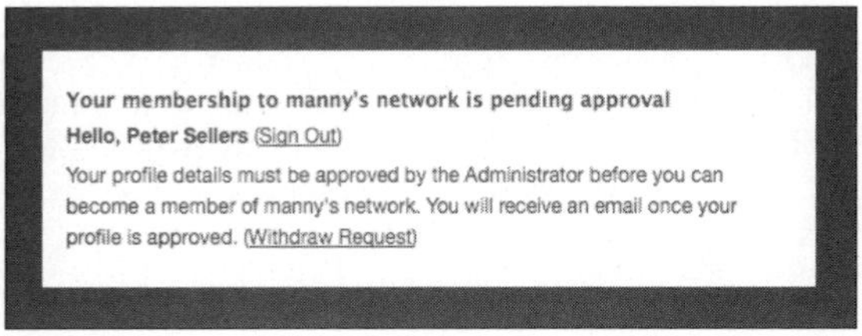

Figure 2-5:
Some
networks
are set up
to approve
new mem-
bers before
they can
join.

Your membership to manny's network is pending approval
Hello, Peter Sellers (Sign Out)

Your profile details must be approved by the Administrator before you can become a member of manny's network. You will receive an email once your profile is approved. (Withdraw Request)

Tweaking Your Profile

After you join a network, you can make changes to your profile as often as you need to. When you want to tweak your profile, the first thing to do is click the My Page tab on the top navigation, which brings you to your profile page. Some of things you can do on your profile are:

- ✔ **Change your theme.** Your theme is the way your profile page looks: background colors, font colors, font types, font sizes, and so on. As long as your Network Creator didn't disable this option, you can change your theme by clicking the My Page tab of the network and clicking the Theme link below your profile photo. The page you're taken to is almost identical to the one the Network Creator can use to change the network's theme, and so are the options available to you, so you can give your profile page as much personality as you want. Check out Chapter 8 for more details on how to do this.

- ✔ **Change the layout of your page.** You can move most of the boxes on your profile page around to your heart's content. Being able to do this and changing your theme are two great ways available for you to customize your profile page.

  To move boxes on your profile page around, position your mouse on top of the header of a box you want to move. The shape of your mouse's cursor will change to a hand, and a little box with four arrows pointing in four opposite directions appears (as shown in Figure 2-6) in the top-left corner of the box. When you see these appear, click the box's bar, drag it to where you want to place it, and drop it.

  Don't get frustrated if you can't move some boxes to some places on your profile page. For instance, OpenSocial applications (discussed in Chapter 21) and the Comment Wall can't be moved out of the middle column. And don't even dream of moving the profile photo and My Friends modules: They're locked where you see them.

- ✔ **Edit your Latest Activity.** When you click the Edit button at the top right of the Latest Activity box on your profile page, a panel opens up. In it is a drop-down list that lets you pick how many events you want to show in your Latest Activity box: 0, 4, 8, 12, 16, or 20.

- ✔ **Add an RSS feed.** If you have a blog, you may appreciate the ability to add an RSS feed to your page. For details on what RSS feeds are and how to add them to your profile page, refer to the section that discusses including RSS feeds on your main page in Chapter 9. Adding RSS feeds on your profile page works in very much the same way.

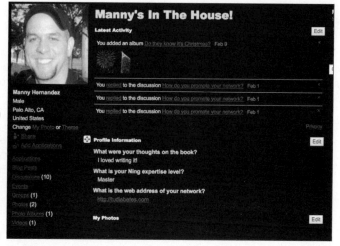

Figure 2-6:
You can conveniently move boxes around your profile page.

Chapter 3

Privacy, E-Mails, and Friends on Ning

*P*rivacy likely falls at the top of the list of your priorities when you go online — and if not, it should. Because sites require you to put so much of your personal information on the Web, it's important for you to feel safe about it. With any online service, you should be careful about the personal information you share, especially when entering sensitive information.

Ning helps protect your privacy online by requiring you to provide only an e-mail address to join a social network on Ning. Ning also provides a number of tools that ensure the information you're posting is visible only to those you care to show it to.

This chapter focuses on the elements that networks on Ning make available to you, so you can keep the privacy of your profile page and the items you share through the network out of the reach of people you don't want to be able to see them. Additionally, the chapter deals with the controls you have over the kind of e-mail notifications you receive from your network.

Before you dive into privacy on Ning, keep something in mind at all times: No privacy settings will protect you if you don't exert common sense while you participate in a network on Ning or any Web site. So be mindful of your choices and what you share about yourself when you're online.

Controlling Your Privacy Settings

In Chapter 2 I show you how to join an existing network on Ning. After you sign up, you're asked a few profile questions. The Network Creator adds these during the setup of the network. They may range from simply asking about the country you live in all the way to detailed questions about personal matters. Some of the questions may be optional, and some may be required. At all times, use common sense when answering questions during the sign-up process.

For example, writing the city where you live is probably okay; giving your full address is a bad idea. Adding a photo of yourself is perhaps not a big deal; exhibiting a less-than-glamorous picture of you and your friends after a party is a great recipe for losing points when applying for a job. You get the picture . . . no pun intended!

If something smells fishy . . .

If a profile question smells fishy, don't answer it! If it's a required question, try to type something to meet the requirement without giving away more information than you should.

In this case, it's best to stop the signup process immediately, go to `http://help.ning.com`, and report the network. The folks at the Ning Help Center will investigate the situation and take any necessary action.

Managing your profile

After you've signed up and answered all the registration questions, you can go back to modify the details in your profile at any time. You do this by clicking the Settings link at the top right of any page on the network. You're taken to the My Settings – Profile page, as shown in Figure 3-1.

This page is the first place where you can modify information that others see about you if you entered information when you signed up. If you make any changes to your profile, after you're done, scroll down to the bottom of the page and click the Save button.

Figure 3-1:
This page lets you edit your profile and your answers to the profile questions.

Here are some ideas of ways to keep your personal information more private in your profile:

✔ **Name:** This is how you're known in the network. You may feel completely comfortable using your actual name, but unless the network requires you to enter your full name as part of its terms of use, you may want to consider using only part of your name (such as Manny) or a generic username (like Manny_Mo) to keep your identity more private.

✔ **Birthday:** Your full birthday (month, day, and year) is not visible to anybody but the Network Creator and the Administrators. Your age in years is displayed on your profile, and your birthday gets displayed on the network (for others to congratulate you) unless you select the check box next to Don't Display My Age.

✔ **Gender:** In the same way as your birthday, if you don't select the check box next to Don't Display, your gender is displayed on your profile page. This may not be a big deal, but consider yourself informed about this.

Network Creators and Administrators don't have access to your password information unless you give it to them. Not even the folks at Ning have access to your password. Only you know your password, so keep it that way. It's in your best interest.

Your privacy in the network

Clicking the Privacy button to the left of the My Settings – Profile page (refer to Figure 3-1, earlier in this chapter) takes you to the Privacy page (shown in Figure 3-2). This page gives you extremely granular control over a number of things related to your contributions, your information, and even your actions and how others can reply to your actions in the network. There's so much going on in this page that it's worth covering in detail:

✔ **Who can view your profile page and friends?** This option gives you control over who gets a chance to view your profile page and your friends on the network. Your options are Anyone (all people in the network — and outside it, if the network is public), Members (all members of the network), and Just My Friends.

✔ **Who can view your photos, videos, and blog posts by default?** This option lets you choose Anyone, Just My Friends, or Just Me.

You can override this setting for any photo, video, or blog post at the time you're adding it, as explained in Chapters 4 and 5.

✔ **Who can comment on your photos, videos and blog?** This option also offers you the choices Anyone, Just My Friends, and Just Me, taking your control one level further. You can control not only who can view your contributions, but also who can comment on them.

✔ **Do you want to approve comments before they appear on your blog?** This option lets you choose between Yes and No. If you choose Yes, you have to approve comments before they appear on your blog. If you choose No, comments posted are published immediately. One good reason to approve comments on your blog (or elsewhere) is to avoid unwanted comments and spam.

✔ **Do you want to approve comments before they appear on your comment wall?** This option works on your Comment Wall the same way as the previous one operates on your blog. You can see all privacy options up to this point in Figure 3-2.

✔ **Who can view your events?** This option gives you control over who can view the events you create in the network. The options, again, are Anyone, Just My Friends, and Just Me.

✔ **Do you want to notify 3rd-party blog tracking services when you add a new post?** This option effectively sets off the equivalent of an announcement that gets sent to a number of services that operate by tracking people's blog posts. As a result, others are able to more easily find out when you've posted on your blog. If you would rather stay under the radar, deselect the check box next to the word Yes.

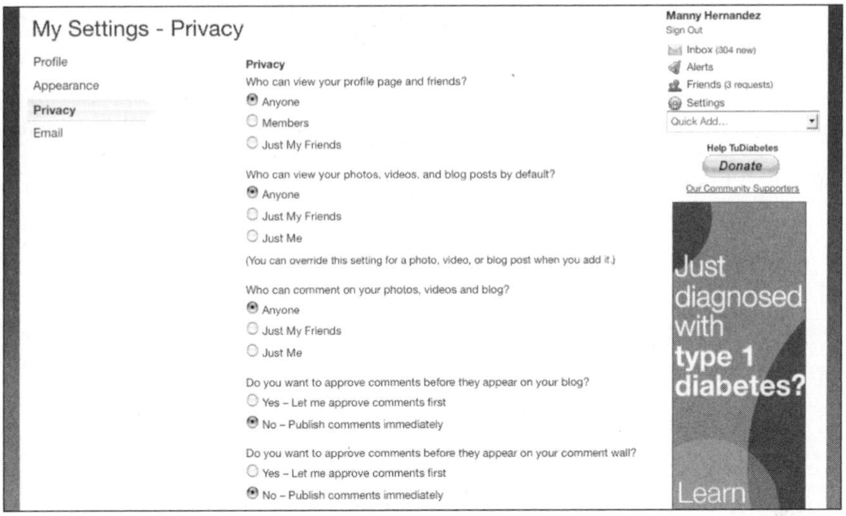

Figure 3-2:
The Privacy page gives you absolute control over your privacy.

✔ **Which of your actions should display on Latest Activity?** This option lets you choose what kind of information you want displayed in the Latest Activity section in your Profile page. By default, all actions are displayed. If you don't want a particular action to display on your Latest Activity, deselect the check box next to it. These are the actions you can choose to share, as you can see in Figure 3-3 (which shows the bottom half of the My Settings – Privacy page):

- *New content I add:* When you add a new photo, video, blog post, and so on.

- *New comments I add:* When you comment on someone else's content or reply to a forum thread.

- *New friends I add:* When you add a new friend. See the following Tip for details on what happens when you decline a friend request or de-friend someone.

- *When I update my profile:* When you make any changes to your Profile page, such as changing the theme or your photo, or adding a bit more meat to the box where you can brag a bit about yourself.

- *My events and my RSVPs:* When you create an event or make up your mind about attending an event.

Figure 3-3:
The bottom
half of the
Privacy
page
gives you
additional
controls.

In case you're wondering, there is no option to display when you send messages to others, when you visit other profile pages, when you decline invitations, when you de-friend or decline a friend invitation from someone, or when someone gets banned from the network. The reason for this is simple: They don't get displayed ever. So feel free to remove members from your Friends list if they become annoying. Nobody will be notified.

Controlling What E-Mails You Receive

E-mail is one of those mixed blessings. You have to be thankful for it, but it can be a disgrace when it's out of control. Thankfully, networks on Ning give you very fine control over what e-mails you receive.

To start managing notifications, alerts, and member activity, click the Settings link at the top right and click the Email button on the left of the page that appears. This takes you to the My Settings – Email page. Here, you have a large number of options that let you choose what network activity you want to receive an e-mail notification for. All options are selected by default. To stop receiving e-mails associated with a particular activity, you need to deselect the check box next to it, as shown in Figure 3-4. Your options are

✔ **Messages sent to me:** Your friends on the network can send you private messages in your inbox on the network. If you deselect this check box, you'll find out about private messages sent through the network only by checking your network inbox. I talk more about your inbox and private messages in the section on communicating with members in Chapter 5.

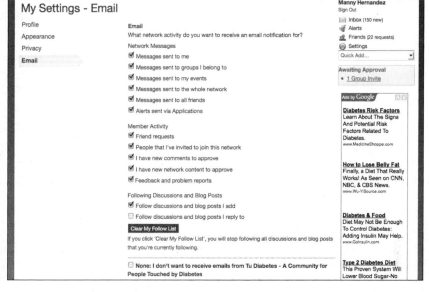

Figure 3-4:
The Email page lets you control which messages you get.

✔ **Messages sent to groups I belong to:** Some groups on the network may allow members to send messages to all the members in the group. All groups allow group creators and administrators to send broadcast messages to their group members. Deselecting this check box ensures that you don't get e-mails when messages are sent to groups you are a member of. You can discover a lot more about groups in Chapter 6.

✔ **Messages sent to my events:** The creator of an event can send a message to all event guests at any time. This is a great way for event creators to let guests know about changes to their events. You won't receive these messages if you deselect this check box.

✔ **Messages sent to the whole network:** Network Creators and Administrators have the option to send broadcast messages to all members. If you deselect this check box, you won't receive these e-mails when they're sent. Unless you're getting overwhelmed with broadcast messages from your network, I recommend you leave this check box selected because you may otherwise miss important communications from the network's head honchos.

✔ **Messages sent to all friends:** Occasionally, other members may choose to send a message to all their friends. These resemble a bit more the kind of messages you get from folks who have a question, a comment, or a joke they feel like sharing with a large group of people that you are part of. Again, deselecting this check box will stop these e-mails from reaching you.

✔ **Alerts sent via Applications:** Networks on Ning give you access to applications. These are third-party tools and services to add features and functionality to your profile on a network. Occasionally, there may be alerts sent via applications that you won't receive if you deselect the check box next to this option.

Certain activity by other members can also generate notifications that you receive via e-mail if you select the check boxes next to each of the following options:

✔ **Friend requests:** When someone in the network sends you a friend request. I talk more about this in the next section.

✔ **People that I've invited to join this network:** When someone you invited to the network becomes a member, you get notified.

To invite someone to a network, click the Invite link in the top navigation. You can invite others by various means: by entering people's e-mail addresses one by one; by inviting friends you may have from another network on Ning; by importing e-mail addresses from Web-based e-mail (Gmail, MSN, AOL, or Yahoo!); or by importing addresses from your Address Book application.

✔ **I have new comments to approve:** When someone posts a comment on your profile page or on any content you have added, and you have turned on comment moderation from the Privacy page in your network's Settings, you get a notification.

✔ **I have new network content to approve:** This is an option that applies only to Administrators.

✔ **Feedback and problem reports:** This one, too, applies only to Administrators.

Last, networks on Ning give you the option to follow discussions and blog posts:

✔ **Follow discussions and blog posts I add:** This option results in e-mails being sent to you when someone replies to a discussion or blog post you start.

✔ **Follow discussions and blog posts I reply to:** This option results in e-mails being sent to you when someone replies to a discussion or blog post you reply to.

If you're a very active person in the network, leaving this option on results in a potential flood of e-mails. If you find you're receiving too many notifications, it may be a good idea to turn it off.

From time to time, wouldn't it be nice if you could unplug yourself from all conversations that you have been part of until that day? Networks on Ning give you that option. If you click the Clear My Follow List button at the bottom of the Email page, you will stop following any discussions and blog posts you've been following until then. Handy, huh?

Last, at the very bottom of the Email page lies the None check box, which will result in your receiving no e-mails from the network at all. (It's a nuclear bomb of sorts that is second only to leaving the network altogether.) Selecting this option makes sense only if you feel overwhelmed by the sheer amount of messages you're getting from the network.

Managing Friends

Friends in social networks, as in real life, are the people you trust enough to tell them things you wouldn't share with others out there. Because of that, in networks on Ning, friends are also given special treatment:

- ✔ Only your friends can send you private messages in the network.
- ✔ You can set any content you post on the network so that only your friends can view it.
- ✔ You can also set content you post on the network so that only your friends can comment on it.

This section deals with friends: how you add them and how you accept friendship requests. I also tell you how you block messages from friends, how you decline friendship requests, and how you de-friend (unfriend, anti-friend?) someone.

Adding or accepting a friend

There are two ways to become someone's friend in a network:

- ✔ You add that person as a friend.
- ✔ That person adds you as a friend, and you accept.

You can add someone as a friend in a couple of different ways:

- ✔ **Click the profile photo of any member,** anywhere on the network. That takes you to the person's profile page. Below the person's image at the top left, click the Add as Friend link, as shown in Figure 3-5. This request then goes to the person, and she can accept it or ignore it. I explain later in this section how the request gets accepted (or ignored).

- ✔ **Click the Add as Friend link** above any discussion topic, blog post, photo, or video posted by another member. Figure 3-6 shows an example of how this looks like in the case of a photo. It looks exactly the same way with videos, discussion topics, and blog posts.

Figure 3-5: Asking another member to become your friend is easy.

Click to add this person as a friend

Finding new friends that meet a specific profile (such as living in your same area or enjoying the same things as you do) is easy thanks to the Advanced Member Search functionality. To perform an advanced member search, go to the Members page and then click the Advanced Member Search link next to the Search Members button. The page you're taken to gives you the option to select among a number of parameters directly related to members' answers to the profile questions during sign-up.

Also, you can become someone else's friend by accepting his request to become his friend. If your e-mail settings are set to notify you when someone sends you a friend request, you receive an e-mail when this occurs. The message you receive gives you a link that takes you to your My Friends page, as shown in Figure 3-7.

Click to add this person as a friend

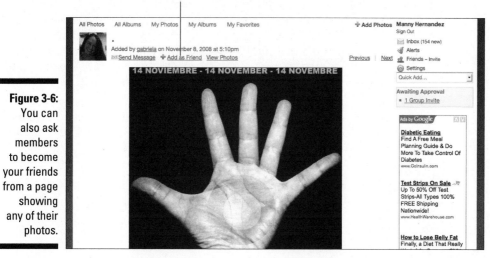

Figure 3-6:
You can
also ask
members
to become
your friends
from a page
showing
any of their
photos.

To accept the friend request, click the Accept button. That adds the member to your Friends list. To decline the request, click the Ignore button. The person won't be notified, so you don't have to worry about that.

Figure 3-7:
Below
each friend
request
are buttons
that let you
accept or
ignore it.

If you've chosen not to receive notifications about friend requests or if, for any other reason, you need to get to your My Friends page, click the Friends link in the top-right section of the network. Also, next to the Friends link you can click a link that shows the number of outstanding friend requests you have waiting for you to accept or ignore.

Blocking and removing friends

Occasionally, you may be annoyed by someone who is your friend in the network. There's a way for you to block her without removing her as a friend. To block messages from a friend, here's what you do:

1. **Go to the friend's profile page and then click the Block Messages link below her image, as shown earlier in Figure 3-5.**

   This opens a box asking you to confirm whether you want to block all future messages and invitations from this person.

2. **Click the OK button.**

   You will no longer receive all those messages, yet you will still be friends with this person: the best of both worlds!

Unfortunately, things don't always work out between friends: Friendships get tarnished, and at times you find out that the person you thought was your friend really isn't. Networks on Ning also let you handle these cases gracefully.

Directly above the link to block a member's messages is the Remove as Friend link (in the same place where the Add as Friend link appeared previously). If you click this link, you're prompted to confirm whether you're sure that you want to remove the person as a friend. If you click the OK button, this removes the person from your list of friends, with the following implications:

✔ She will no longer be able to send you private messages in the network.

✔ She will no longer be able to view the content you set as being for friends to view.

✔ She will no longer be able to comment on the things you set as being for friends to comment on.

Fortunately for you, blocked and removed friends don't get notified when you take these actions. They may still yell at you when they see their messages unanswered, but that will be up to you to deal with.

Part II
Using an Existing Network on Ning

The 5th Wave   By Rich Tennant

"You ever notice how much more streaming media
there is than there used to be?"

In this part . . .

There isn't much point in setting up a profile in a social network on Ning and not joining the fun. Social networks give you (as a member) the means to easily add multimedia content and to communicate with other members in a more individual way as well as tools to interact with many other members at the same time.

This part of the book gives you the information you need to participate actively in a social network on Ning while making the most of all its features.

Chapter 4

Adding Multimedia Content to the Network

*M*ost people love looking at photos, watching videos, and listening to music. It's just how people are. Photos bring back memories, videos make you laugh or think, and music wakes up the singer you have hidden inside of you — even if it's just while you're taking a shower!

So it's no surprise that photos, videos, and music are among the most popular content you can add or check out on a network on Ning. As soon as you join a network on Ning (which you read about in Chapter 2), you can start adding multimedia content to it.

In this chapter, you discover how you can add some photos, videos, and music from your own crop to a network you're a member of.

Photos

If you're old enough to remember what life was like before the Web, you probably remember that photos used to be printed in labs where rolls of film were developed. This was not only expensive, but also inconvenient because you had to wait anxiously to check out your photos, only to find out too late that the "amazing" shot you took of the Grand Canyon during your vacation was out of focus.

Fortunately, digital cameras have made these photo nightmares a thing of the past, and you can now take tons of pictures until you feel happy with the result.

With the advent of digital photography and more people taking more photos than ever before, new Web sites began to appear that allowed people to share their photos. Some good examples of these sites are Flickr, Photobucket, and Picassa.

As a member of a network on Ning, you can browse through the photos that others have added to the network, or you can add your own photos by using a number of convenient features. The next few sections walk you through the details involved in viewing, adding, and editing photos and albums on your network.

Viewing a network's photos

When you click the Photos tab in the top navigation of your network, you land on the Photos page. You're sure to discover a lot about your fellow network members and the topic of your network simply by checking out the photos in this section.

On the Photos page, you can view all photos that other members are okay with you viewing. You can also view all the albums that any member has created. You can also access your own photos (if you've gotten started with your photo-sharing frenzy), your own albums, and the photos that you may have marked as Favorites.

At the top of the page, you can see photos that have been featured by an Administrator of the network. Below the Featured Photos section, under the All Photos heading (see Figure 4-1), you can view all photos in the network and search for photos by typing a name or keyword in the text box and clicking the Search Photos button.

You can also sort photos by using the Sort By drop-down list on the right. Your sorting options are

- ✓ **Latest:** Shows the latest photos. (This is the way photos are shown by default.)
- ✓ **Top Rated:** Shows the top-rated photos. (Photo rating is explained in Chapter 5.)
- ✓ **Most Popular:** Shows the most popular ones (those that have been viewed the most).
- ✓ **Random:** If you're feeling a little adventurous, you can simply view photos at random.

You can view the network's photos in a slideshow by clicking the View Slideshow link on the left, under the All Photos heading.

Figure 4-1:
The Photos page lets you search and view photos and sort them in multiple ways.

You can mark any photo or video as a Favorite by clicking the photo or video to view it and then clicking the Add to Favorites link below it. You can later view the items you've marked as your Favorites by going to the Photos page or the Videos page and clicking the My Favorites link at the top.

Viewing the photos added by others can be fun, but adding your own photos is even better. Networks on Ning allow you to add photos in many different ways. If you're viewing photos and you start getting an itch to share your own, check out the following two sections, which cover two ways to add photos.

Using the bulk photo uploader

Commonly, as a good digital photographer, you will have a bunch of photos to upload. The folks at Ning have made it easy for you to do this by simply dragging and dropping them much like you would while moving files around your own computer.

You can upload photos that are up to 10MB. Photo formats supported by networks on Ning are `.jpg`, `.gif`, and `.png`.

By using the bulk photo uploader page, you can upload up to 100 photos at a time. To add photos with the bulk photo uploader, follow these steps:

1. **Click the Add Photos link at the top of the Photos page.**

   The first time you use the bulk photo uploader, you see a pop-up window asking whether you want to trust this applet, as shown in Figure 4-2. The applet that the pop-up asks you about is the Java applet that allows you to copy photos from your computer to your network.

Figure 4-2:
Click the
Trust button
to use the
bulk photo
uploader.

2. **Click the Trust button.**

   You see two panels: one on the left, containing a list of folders in your hard drive, and one on the right, originally empty.

3. **Double-click the folder where the photos you want to add to your network can be found.**

4. **Select the photos you want to add and then drag them and drop them into the panel on the right, as shown in Figure 4-3.**

   If you decide you don't want to add a particular photo, you can drag it and drop it outside the right panel to remove it.

5. **When you're done selecting photos to add, click Next.**

   You'll be able to enter details for each photo as well as apply them to all photos you have uploaded, as shown in Figure 4-4.

Figure 4-3:
The bulk
photo
uploader
allows you
to drag and
drop photos
from your
computer
into your
network.

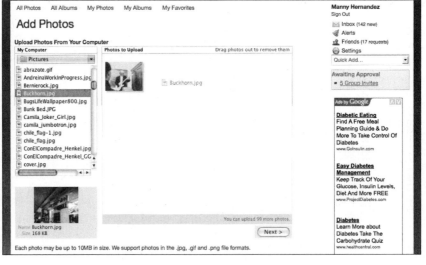

6. **Enter the title, description, and tags for each photo.**

   Adding a title will help others get an idea of what the photo is about, before they click it. The description isn't as critical, but it helps provide more context for the viewer. Tags are like keywords that describe the photo in general terms (for example, "Empire State," "building," "skyscraper," and so on).

7. **(Optional) Designate whether each photo can be viewed by anyone in the network (and outside it, if the network is public); by just your friends; or by just you.**

   This is a good example of how you can control the privacy of the content you submit to the network.

8. **(Optional) Apply the same info to all photos you're uploading by clicking the Apply This Info to the Photos Below button, as shown in Figure 4-4.**

9. **Click the Upload button.**

   You're taken to your Photos page when all the photos you've added have been uploaded.

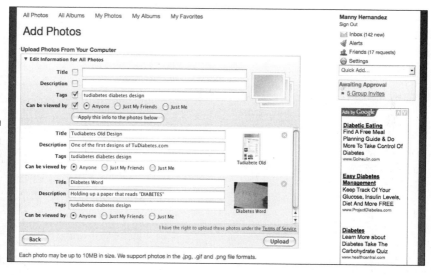

Figure 4-4:
Adding info to your photos helps people find them when they search for photos.

Adding photos one by one

If you have only a photo or two to upload or if you're having problems with the bulk uploader, you can use the simple uploader. With the simple uploader, you can browse to find photos one by one and then add them to your network all at once by clicking the Add Photos button. It lets you upload up to eight photos at a time. In Figure 4-5, you can see the simple uploader.

Sending photos by phone or e-mail

If you're one of the many people who have a camera included in your mobile phone, chances are good that you take photos with your cell phone while you're on the move. To add photos to your network from your phone or via e-mail, go to the Photos page and click the Add Photos link. Then click the link labeled . . . By Phone or Email (located under the More Ways to Add Photos . . . heading).

The page you land on gives you an e-mail address that you can use to e-mail your photos. You can send only one photo per e-mail. The subject you type becomes the title of the photo, and the body of the e-mail becomes the description.

Assuming that you can send e-mails from your phone, this may very well be the easiest way you can add photos to your network.

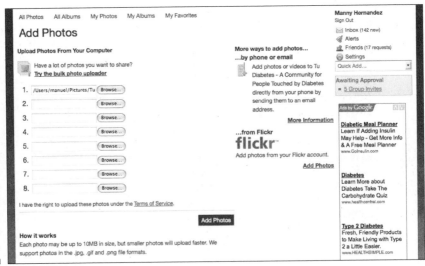

Figure 4-5:
The simple uploader lets you upload photos one by one.

Importing photos from Flickr

If you have an existing Flickr account, you'll appreciate the convenience of importing your Flickr photos straight to your network, which means you won't have to upload them a second time. To add photos from your Flickr account to your network, click the Add Photos link below the Flickr logo.

You land on a new page where you get to choose what photos to upload. You have four uploading options, which you can choose by clicking the circle next to each:

- ✔ **Most recent photos:** This option lets you get your 10, 20, 50, or 100 most recent photos.

- ✔ **Get photos from a set:** This option lets you chose among the Flickr sets of photos you have created.

- ✔ **Get all my photos tagged:** This option lets you choose the photos that match a certain tag or keyword.

- ✔ **Get all of my photos from Flickr:** This option, as you would expect, allows you to bring all your pics from Flickr . . . just hang on tight while the upload happens.

Before you get the photos, you can also choose to get the descriptions and the full-size versions of the photos. This is accomplished by selecting the Get All of My Photos from Flickr and/or Get All of My Photos from Flickr check boxes above the Get Photos button.

However, if you plan on importing 20 photos or more, getting the descriptions and full-size versions will significantly add to the time the import process takes. So think well or go have a nice meal before you import all the pics you took during your most recent vacation . . . or, if you don't mind the time, go fix yourself a cup of coffee while you wait.

At the time this book was written, Flickr is the only photo-management Web site that networks on Ning support for photo importing.

Before you can import your photos from Flickr, the Network Creator needs to set up Flickr importing. You can find out how to create a network on Ning in Chapters 7 and 8. After you've selected what photos you want to get and what information you want to get them with, click the Get Photos button. Your photos are imported, and you're taken to the My Photos page, where you can click any of them and edit any details as you see fit.

Editing a photo

Regardless of the method you used to add a photo, you may feel compelled to change something about it.

First off, if you don't want to have the photo up on the network anymore, you can delete it. To do this, just click the photo you want gone from the Photos page and click the Delete Photo link below the photo.

If you don't want to delete the photo, you can edit it. To edit a photo, click the photo you wish to affect from the Photos page and then click the Edit Photo link below it. As you can see in Figure 4-6, you can do a number of things when you edit a photo:

- ✔ **Change the title:** You know . . . give it a little more personality beyond that `IMG00988.jpg` filename.

- ✔ **Add or modify the description:** This can help others find your photo when they're searching.

- ✔ **Edit the tags:** You can also do this without having to edit the photo. Simply click the Add Tags link below the photo.

- ✔ **Modify the photo's privacy settings:** Under the Who Can View This Photo? question, you can choose who gets to view the photo. You can make your photo available for viewing by Anyone, Just My Friends, or Just Me.

- ✔ **Add or modify the location of the photo:** It can be a ZIP code, a city, a venue, you name it.

- ✔ **Rotate the photo:** This feature comes in handy if you took the photo sideways! It can also be done without having to edit the photo by clicking the Rotate Photo link below the photo.

Figure 4-6:
You can edit lots of things about your photos.

When you're done editing your photo, click the Save button. Or, if you decide you don't want to submit your changes, click the Cancel button.

The page you see when you edit a photo has the same options and fields that you get when you're using the simple or bulk photo uploader after the photo has been uploaded.

Creating an album of photos

Albums in a network on Ning work in similarly to real-life albums: They let you group photos that are part of the same event or occasion. But creating an album is far easier on Ning!

1. **Go to the Photos page by clicking the Photos tab in the top navigation.**

2. **Click the All Albums link or the My Albums link at the top.**

   Both links give you the option to create an album.

3. **Click the Add an Album link at the top.**

   The page you're taken to shows your photos by default. If you want to create albums from the photos by other members, select the Everyone's Photos option next to the words Choose From, as shown in Figure 4-7.

4. **Drag the photos you want to add to the album from the box on the left to the box on the right, as shown in Figure 4-7.**

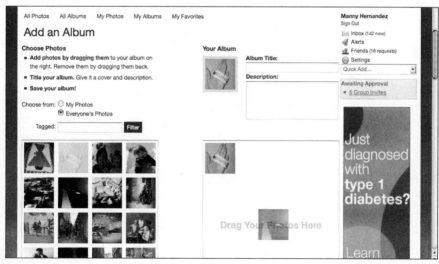

Figure 4-7:
If moms only knew how easy it is to create a photo album in a network on Ning....

5. **In the text boxes provided, type a title for your album and add a description.**

6. **(Optional) Rearrange the order of the photos as you need to by dragging and dropping them.**

7. **(Optional) Change the cover of the album (by default, this is the first photo in the album) by dragging a new photo into the box next to the album title.**

8. **Scroll down and click Save and — voilà! — you have an album.**

Sharing photos

As with photos, you can edit and delete albums if you need to. But with albums, you also have the option of viewing them as a slideshow, and you can even link to them or embed them as a slideshow in another Web site.

You can obtain the code for embedding the slideshow from the album page itself:

1. **While you're on the album page, click the Get Embed Code link, located on the left side of the page.**

   Clicking this link gives you a couple more options, allowing you to conveniently share the album on MySpace and Facebook.

2. **Copy the code in the text box labeled HTML Embed Code, as shown in Figure 4-8.**

Figure 4-8: Albums in a network on Ning are best savored when you embed them in another Web site, but you can enjoy them on your network, too.

3. **Paste the code in the Web site where you want to share the video.**

4. **Save the changes on the Web site.**

You can also obtain the embed code directly from the slideshow:

1. **Click the View Slideshow link on the album page.**

2. **Click the Embed button at the top right of the slideshow.**

3. **Select the code shown in the middle of the screen and click the Copy to Clipboard button.**

4. **Follow Steps 3 and 4 from the preceding list.**

Another way to share photos and all other content from your network is by clicking the Share link below them. (See Chapter 15 for more details on sharing items with members.)

Videos

Online video is everywhere. Most likely you've already had your first encounter with online video: Maybe you were catching an embarrassing moment by a celebrity on YouTube or a brilliant viral video spreading like wildfire through the Funny or Die site. Each day, more and more sites not only offer videos for you to watch, but also give you the option to embed video on your own Web site, and networks on Ning are no exception to this.

Through your network, you can conveniently upload your own videos or embed videos from other sources, such as YouTube. In the following sections, you find out how you can share videos with other members of your network and beyond.

Watching the videos on the network

Clicking the Videos tab in the top navigation of your network takes you to the Videos page.

On the Videos page, you can find all the videos uploaded by members of the network that they don't mind you watching. (I explain about privacy settings in the section titled "Uploading videos using the bulk video uploader," later in this chapter.) You can also access your own videos and other members' videos that you have enjoyed and designated as your Favorites.

Starting at the top of the Videos page, shown in Figure 4-9, you encounter the Featured Videos heading. Below this heading, you find the All Videos heading, which lists all the videos in the network. The All Videos section also includes a search box, which you can use to find a specific video, and a Sort By drop-down list, which you can use to sort videos by the following criteria:

- ✔ **Latest:** This option sorts videos based on the date they were uploaded, starting with the most recent ones.

- ✔ **Top Rated:** This option sorts videos based on their average star rating, starting with the ones with the highest rating.

- ✔ **Most Popular:** This option sorts videos based on how many times videos have been viewed, starting with the ones viewed the most.

- ✔ **Random:** This option shows videos in no particular order.

Figure 4-9:
The Videos page allows you to access videos uploaded by all members in the network.

When you click any of the thumbnails on the Videos page, you land on the page that houses that video on the network. If the video is playing back from another Web site (YouTube, Vimeo, and so on), it won't starting playing automatically: You have to click the Play button for the fun to begin.

If the video file was uploaded directly to the network, it will start playing as soon as it starts loading, so be mindful of this and make sure to keep your speaker volume down if you want to avoid having the rest of your office figure out that you're procrastinating while you should be working.

If you like the video you're watching, make sure to let the other member know by adding a comment in the text box under the video and then clicking the Add Comment button. You can see an example of a comment on a video in Figure 4-10.

Figure 4-10: Don't forget to show some love for your fellow members when you like a video they've posted: Leave a nice comment or give it a good rating.

Embedding videos on another Web site

If you find a video to be particularly enjoyable or useful, you may feel compelled to share it with others elsewhere, such as on your own blog or another Web site. Networks on Ning make it very easy for you to do this. These are the steps you need to follow:

1. **While you're on the video page, click the Get Embed Code link, located below the video.**

2. **Copy the code in the text box labeled HTML Embed Code.**

3. **Paste the code in the Web site where you want to share the video.**

4. **Save the changes on the Web site.**

If the video was uploaded directly to the network (not embedded from YouTube or another Web site), it becomes another way for your network to get visits (which will be appreciated by the Network Creator) because people clicking the video land on the page that contains the video in your network.

Getting ready to upload a video

Just like with photos, watching other people's videos is only half the fun: The real thrill comes with sharing your own videos for others to watch, rate, and comment on.

To rate a video or a photo, go to the video or photo page, look for the blank five stars below it on the right, and click the star that designates the rating you want to give.

Before you rush to start uploading videos, keep these things in mind to save time and avoid frustrations:

- ✔ Video files uploaded have to be 100MB or smaller.
- ✔ Networks on Ning support .mov, .mpg, .avi, .3gp, and .wmv formats.

Even if you stick to the supported formats when creating a video to upload to your network, once in a blue moon you may encounter an error message after you attempt to upload the video. This is a direct result of the kinds of algorithms used by your computer to generate the videos from the raw footage: Sometimes movie files that have the same extension (WMV files are a good example) aren't compatible and therefore may not result in a successful upload.

If you're struggling with your video and your network doesn't seem to want to cooperate, don't blame it. Simply convert the movie file to a format that will result in an error-free upload process. To do this, Ning recommends using one of two applications, depending on what platform you use:

- ✔ **If you're a Mac user,** you can convert your video files using a program called iSquint. You can download it for free at www.macupdate.com/info.php/id/19769/isquint.
- ✔ **If you're a PC user,** you can accomplish the same thing by using a program called Videora. It's available for free at www.videora.com/en-us/Converter/iPod/download.php.

Even if you use iSquint or Videora to ensure that your video doesn't conflict with Ning when it's being uploaded, make a habit out of playing it back using QuickTime or some other video player before you upload it. If the conversion process was not successful for any reason, you may save yourself some precious time and the frustration of getting an error message after a while.

Uploading videos using the bulk video uploader

If you're serious about producing videos, you'll love the bulk video uploader. It lets you upload up to 30 video files at a time.

Like the bulk photo uploader, it lets you drag and drop files from your computer's hard drive into the network. To add videos through the bulk video uploader, follow these steps:

1. **Click the Add Videos link at the top of the Videos page.**

   The first time you use the bulk video uploader, you see a pop-up window asking whether you want to trust this applet, just like the one that appears the first time you use the bulk photo uploader.

2. **Click the Trust button.**

   You see two panels: the one on the left, containing a list of folders in your hard drive, and the one on the right, originally empty.

3. **Double-click the folder where the videos you want to add to your network can be found.**

4. **Select the videos you want to add and then drag them and drop them into the panel on the right.**

   If you change your mind about adding a video or add a file by accident, you can drag it and drop it outside the right panel to remove it.

5. **When you're done selecting videos to add, click Next.**

   The following page lets you enter details (title, description, and so on) for each of the videos, as shown in Figure 4-11.

6. **As with photos, enter the title, description, and tags for each video.**

   I explain more about adding this sort of info in the earlier section, "Using the bulk photo uploader."

7. **(Optional) Designate whether each video can be viewed by anyone in the network (and outside it, if the network is public); by just your friends; or by just you.**

   This option gives you control over the privacy of your video, effectively letting you designate who can watch it. You can choose Anyone, Just My Friends, or Just Me.

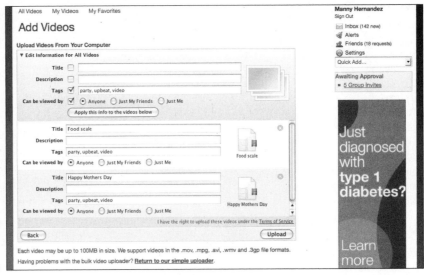

Figure 4-11:
The bulk video uploader can be a real time saver, letting you automatically copy the same information for multiple videos at the same time.

8. **(Optional) If you want to apply the same info to all photos you're uploading, you can do so by clicking the Apply This Info to the Videos Below button, as shown in Figure 4-11.**

9. **Click the Upload button.**

You're taken to the Videos page when all the videos you've added have been uploaded.

The upload process for videos takes significantly longer than the process for photos, due to the size of the movie files. Make sure to maintain the browser window through which the upload process is being conducted. If you need to conduct other business while this happens, open a new window or a new tab in your browser. If you navigate away from your upload page, you'll interrupt the process and lose your work.

Adding videos one at a time

If you have a single video to upload or can't get the bulk uploader to cut the video mustard for you, the simple video uploader will always come to the rescue.

To switch to the simple video uploader from the bulk video uploader, click the link at the bottom of the bulk video uploader page.

Like its cousin the simple photo uploader, the simple video uploader (shown in Figure 4-12) lets you upload videos one at a time.

Figure 4-12:
The simple video uploader can come in handy if the bulk video uploader is causing trouble or you don't need to upload multiple videos.

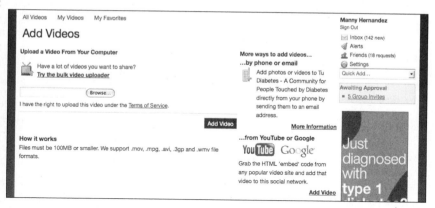

Sending videos by phone or e-mail

You can add videos to your network one at a time by sending an e-mail for each of them. To add videos to your network via e-mail, click the Add Videos link to get to the Add Videos page. From there, click the link . . . By Phone or Email (located beneath the heading More Ways to Add Videos . . .).

The page you land on gives you an e-mail address that you can use to e-mail your videos. (It's the same address you use to send your photos.) You can send only one video per e-mail. The subject you type becomes the title of the video, and the body of the e-mail becomes the description.

Assuming that you can send e-mails from your mobile phone, this method also lets you add videos to your network from your cell phone.

Adding videos from other video sites

Just as you can conveniently import photos from Flickr, you can easily add videos to your network from YouTube, Google Video, and just about every other video Web site you run into. To add a video from another site to your network, follow these steps:

1. **On the page where you found the video you want to add, find and copy the HTML embed code for it.**

   For example, in the case of a video on YouTube, the HTML embed code can be obtained from the box labeled Embed to the right of the video.

2. **Return to your network on Ning and click the Videos tab in the top navigation.**

   This takes you to the Videos page. From there, click the Add Videos link at the top of the Videos page.

3. **Click the Add Videos link beneath the heading Add Videos from YouTube or Google.**

   You're taken to the Add Videos page.

4. **In the provided box, paste the HTML embed code you copied in Step 1.**

5. **Click the Add Video button.**

Editing a video

In the same way that you can do with photos, you can delete any of the videos you've added. To delete a video, click the video icon on the main Videos page and click the Delete Video link below the video.

You can also edit all the details about a video you have uploaded. The only thing you can't edit about the video is the video itself (that is, you can't change the video file). To edit a video, click the video icon from the Videos page and click the Edit Video link below it. Figure 4-13 shows the Edit Video page and all the details that you can edit about a video:

✔ Change the title.

✔ Add or modify the description.

✔ Edit the tags.

✔ Modify the privacy settings.

✔ Add or modify the location of the video.

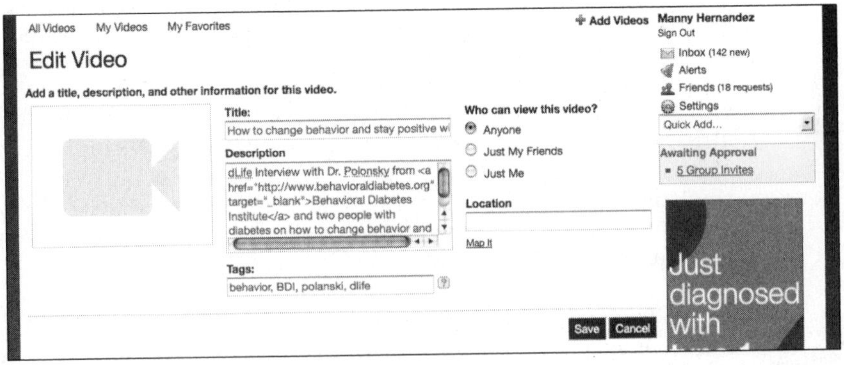

Figure 4-13: Editing a video allows you to add or modify all the details about it.

Music and Audio Podcasts

Listening to music and downloading songs are two of the most popular activities online. Nowadays, services like iTunes, Amazon, Lala, eMusic, and Last. FM (which are actually my favorite ones, in case you're wondering) let you tap into your favorite music and either download it to your computer or play directly online (also known as *streaming* the music track).

Audio podcasts have also become staples of online life in recent times. As opposed to straight-up music tracks, audio podcasts typically contain interviews and spoken commentary. You can encounter podcasts about every topic under the sun, from politics to sports, from technology to business, from comedy to news. (I mean, news shows can be the complete opposite of comedy these days.)

It's no surprise that networks on Ning give you the option to upload music and audio podcasts and listen to the ones you and other members have added. In the following sections, you find out all about the Music Player option and how to use it to share audio tracks.

Listening to the tracks on the Music Player

All the music and audio podcasts in the Music Player are part of a *playlist*. The playlist determines the order in which the tracks are listed for playback. The Music Player lets you listen to the tracks on its playlist in a number of places in your network:

 ✔ To listen to a specific track, you can click that track and click the Play button directly on the Music Player in the main page of the network.

 ✔ You can also open a pop-up window by clicking the Open Popup Window button in the Music Player in the main page, as shown in Figure 4-14. Playing tracks from within the pop-up window allows you to continue navigating the network.

You can also embed the Music Player on another Web site. To obtain the HTML embed code for the music player, click its top-right corner. This "flips" the Music Player around, exposing the code. Copy the code and paste it within the HTML code for your Web site, and give your Web site visitors the chance to also enjoy your network's Music Player.

Depending on how the network has been set up by the Network Creator, you may or may not be able to download the tracks that have been uploaded. If downloading is not allowed, you still can stream the tracks just fine; you just can't copy them into your hard drive.

As soon as you begin playing a track, the top portion of the Music Player gives you the option to rate the track by clicking the number of stars you want to give it (which is the same way you can rate photos and videos).

You can also click the Add to My Page link directly below the playback information on the Music Player. Doing this adds the track to the My Music box on your profile page, effectively adding the track to your own playlist.

Adding tracks to your playlist

The Network Creator sets up the network's playlist, but you can create and manage your own playlist. You can add tracks to your playlist by choosing from the music in the network's playlist or by adding your own.

To add tracks from the network's playlist:

1. **Double-click a track in the Music Player on the network's main page.**

2. **When the track is playing, click the Add to My Page link above the Play button.**

   This appends the track at the end of your playlist.

To add new tracks:

1. **Go to your profile page.**

2. **Click the Add Music link below the My Music box.**

   This takes you to the Add Music page. The Add Music page lets you upload audio tracks from your computer, as shown in Figure 4-15.

3. **Add tracks using either the simple uploader or the bulk music uploader:**

- The simple uploader for the Music Player works just like the simple uploader for photos and videos. (See the earlier section "Adding videos one at a time.")

- The bulk music uploader works just like the bulk uploader for photos and videos. (See the earlier section "Uploading videos using the bulk video uploader.") By default, the bulk music uploader appears when you click the Add Music page. The bulk music uploader lets you upload 62 songs at a time.

Networks on Ning support only the .mp3 file format. You can upload up to 100 MP3 files in total. Each file may be up to 20MB.

Another way to add tracks to the Music Player involves clicking the Edit Playlist link below the My Music box that's located on your profile page. Then click the Add Music link below the . . . From Another Website heading.

As shown in Figure 4-16, this method takes you to a page where you can enter up to four URLs of audio tracks in text boxes. Then you simply click the Add Songs button. As a result, the Music Player establishes a link to the external MP3s you add.

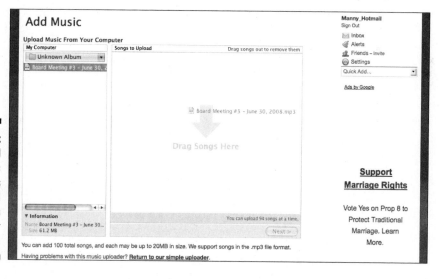

Figure 4-15: The Add Music page lets you upload audio tracks from your computer.

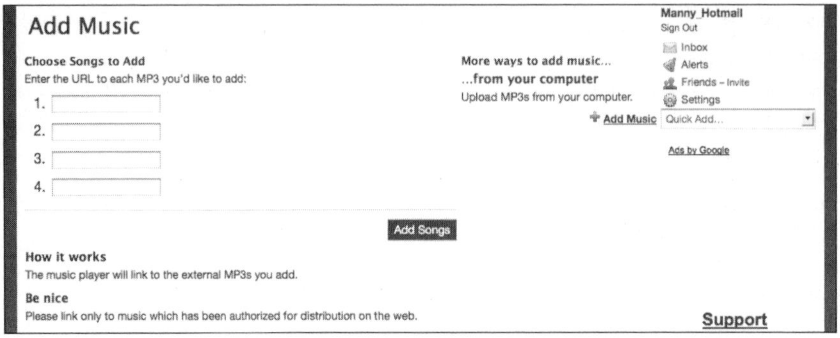

Figure 4-16:
If you enter
the URLs
to external
MP3s, the
Music
Player links
to them.

Managing your playlist

Your network's playlist can be managed in a number of ways. To manage your playlist, click the Edit Playlist link below the My Music box on your profile page. You're taken to the Edit Playlist page. As you can see in Figure 4-17, on that page, you can do all of the following things:

- **Play tracks:** You can play any of the tracks on your playlist by clicking the little button to the left of the track name.

- **Reorder tracks:** You can drag and drop tracks to change the order in which they are played.

- **Delete tracks:** You can delete tracks by clicking the Delete link to the right of the track you want to remove.

- **Edit tracks:** You can edit lots of details about each track by entering or editing the information in the appropriate field after clicking the Edit link beside the track name:
  - The title of the track
  - The artist
  - The album name
  - The album artwork
  - Enable the download link for the track
  - Allow another member to add the track to the My Music box on his or her member profile page
  - More: Genre, Year, Label, Artist Site, Hosting Site, Label, whether the track has Explicit Lyrics, Label Site, License, License Name, and License URL

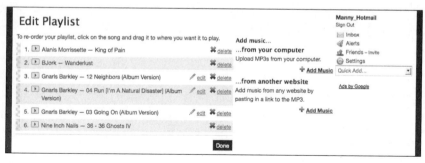

Figure 4-17:
The playlist
page lets
you play,
reorder,
edit, add,
or remove
tracks.

A Word or Two about Copyright

Just because you *can* upload music or add videos and photos to your network, that doesn't mean it's okay to upload a track by your favorite artist or post a skit from a popular TV show for others to enjoy. In case you missed the news, that's I-L-L-E-G-A-L, and it can get you in trouble.

When you upload any kind of media to your network, you're basically agreeing that you either have permission from the creator of the media or the copyright holder. (Maybe you are the copyright holder yourself.) In case you were wondering, here are the facts:

- ✔ Having paid for a CD or a few MP3s does *not* mean you have the right to distribute it.

- ✔ Renting or buying a movie doesn't mean you can capture a portion of it and share it with your friends in the network. The same goes for TV shows you record with your DVR.

- ✔ That amazing pic by an Associated Press photographer that you saw on the home page of *The New York Times* . . . you guessed it: It's protected by copyright laws!

Don't kill the messenger: Those are just the rules.

So what can you do with this fantastic Music Player, you may be wondering? What can you do with it if you can't upload any of that good music you have sitting on your hard drive? Here are three examples (far from a comprehensive list) to get your creative juices flowing. If you have specific doubts about a copyright matter, better get your checkbook ready so you can run them past an intellectual-property attorney.

✔ **If you're an up-and-coming artist:** You have no record deal, and you essentially own all the music you have written and recorded. A network on Ning can be a great channel for you to use to share your music with others (not unlike what many bands and artists do through their pages on MySpace, for example). Before you do this, make sure to check with the Network Creator to verify that this is an acceptable practice in your network.

✔ **If you're great with words:** You may have in your hands a great podcast. You just sit in front of that microphone and hit the ground running, talking about the topic that makes you an interesting person to listen to. Sharing the podcasts you record is another great use for the Music Player. You can discover more about the world of podcasts by reading *Podcasting For Dummies,* 2nd Edition, by Tee Morris, Chuck Tomasi, and Evo Terra (Wiley Publishing, Inc.).

✔ **If you need records of your meetings:** Some groups that have networks on Ning have conference calls with their members that they record for the convenience of others who were unable to participate in them. The Music Player is a great solution to help share these meeting archives in cases like these. (Granted, this isn't the kind of stuff you would be tapping your feet to, but it's helpful.)

Clearly, the same criteria apply for photos and videos. You have a world of photos you can upload: You simply have to have taken them yourself or have permission from the person who took them. Same with videos: Make sure that you're not only the talent on the screen, but also the one with the rights to the video. Otherwise, you may find yourself dealing with some unnecessarily uncomfortable situations.

Chapter 5

Communicating with Others on the Network

*T*hey say that those who find a friend find a treasure (or something like that, but you know what I mean). Communication, whether by private message or with a group in a chat room, is the backbone of your friendships on a social network.

This chapter delves into how members of a network can communicate with their friends and other members on the network. I talk about ways to do this privately and openly. You discover ways you can control the comments that others leave for you. You look at the ways that you can evaluate members' contributions, and you go over the details of writing a blog on your network.

So buckle up and get ready to start connecting with others in the network. May you uncover many new treasures through your social network on Ning!

Communicating with Members

You talk to people on the phone, and you chat when you're in a gathering. These are two examples of ways in which you communicate with others. One is fairly private and direct, just between you and the other person. The second one is more open, letting many people hear what you're saying and also comment back to you.

Just like you can talk on the phone or chat at a party, you can communicate privately or publicly with other members in a network on Ning. The following sections go over the tools that you have at your disposal to communicate with others in a network.

Sending private messages

In a network on Ning, you can exchange private messages only with two groups of people: your friends and the Administrators (including the Network Creator).

Private messages give you an ideal way as a member to communicate with other members in the network without everybody finding out about it. Because of the importance that private messages have for a social network, Ning has placed links to let you send private messages to other members in multiple places:

- On the member's profile page, the Send a Message Link appears below the person's photo, as shown in Figure 5-1.

- On pages for photos, videos, blog posts, and forum posts contributed by the member, the Send a Message link appears next to the member's icon.

Figure 5-1: A member's profile page is only one of the places where you can find a link to send a message to that member.

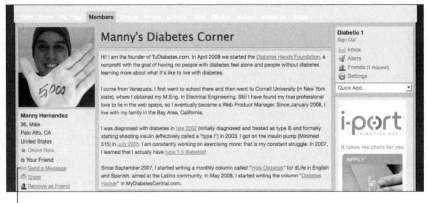

Click to send a private message

When you click the Send a Message link in any of these places, you're taken to a page that will remind you of your e-mail, as shown in Figure 5-2.

As with e-mail messages, you have room for three pieces of information:

- **The recipient:** Next to the To header appears the name of the recipient as a link back to the person's profile page.

- **The subject line:** This is an optional field, but it's a good practice to write something to give the recipient an idea of what the message is about.

- **The message itself:** You can enter only text in this box. Messages in networks on Ning do not currently support HTML or any kind of formatting.

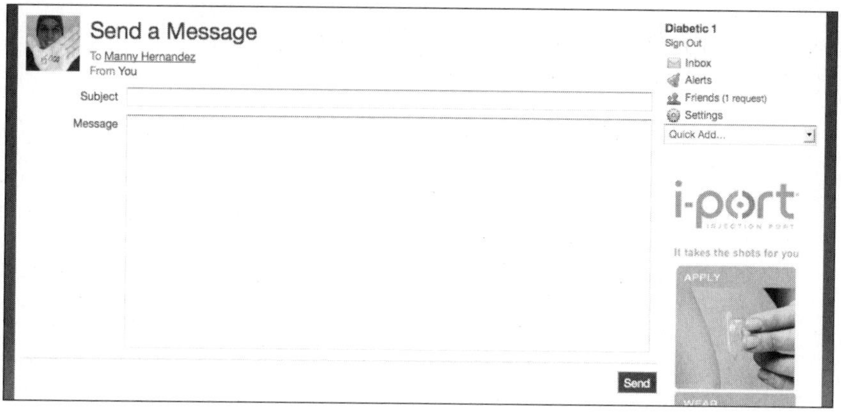

Figure 5-2:
A private
message
looks a
lot like an
e-mail
message

After you finish writing your private message, click the Send button, and after a brief confirmation message, off it goes. You get another brief confirmation message indicating that the private message has been sent, and then you're sent back to the page where you clicked the Send a Message link.

Controlling private messages

All this sounds great, right? You can click the Send a Message link anywhere in the network to get a private message to anyone without any limitations? Wrong! This is where privacy kicks in, and Ning has thought of ways to prevent people from contacting you if you don't want to be messaged privately. Here are some restrictions, so you may feel more comfortable:

- ✔ **Only your friends (and the Administrators) can send you private messages.** I mean your friends on the network, so that gives you a first level of control because only you can add friends or approve friend requests being sent your way. Administrators, which include the Network Creator, need to be able to message you for obvious reasons: They run the network.

- ✔ **Even if you're friends with someone else in the network, you can choose to block messages from that person.** Go to the profile page of the person you want to block. Among the links below the person's profile photo is one that reads Block Messages. Click this link, and after you confirm your decision (you're prompted to do so), you will no longer receive messages from this member.

- ✔ **You can remove a person from your friends list.** Go to the profile page of the person you want to remove as a friend and click the Remove as Friend link. After you confirm your action, this member will no longer be your friend and, therefore, will no longer be able to message you.

TIP

If a person in your social network continues to try to contact you (through your Comment Wall, for instance) after you've blocked him or her, that person needs to be reported to the Administrators. To do this, use the Report an Issue link at the bottom of any page in the network.

Managing your messages and alerts

Just like your e-mail service, your network gives you a place where you can conveniently access, read, and delete all the messages you've received or sent.

You can read all your messages by clicking the envelope-shaped icon in the bar at the very top of your network or by clicking the Inbox link at the top right of any page. This takes you to the Messages section, defaulting to the Inbox tab.

As you can see in Figure 5-3, your network inbox starts by showing your received messages. Messages that you haven't yet read are designated by a small dot to the left of the row that contains the message details. For each message, you see the date, sender, subject, and a few words that serve as a preview.

When you click any of the messages, the entire message gets displayed, giving you an opportunity to reply to the sender (Reply), reply to all persons who received the message (Reply All), forward the message to others (Forward), archive the message in the Archive folder of your network's inbox (Archive), delete the message (Delete), and block messages from the sender (Block Messages).

Figure 5-3:
Your network Messages section looks a lot like your e-mail inbox. You can compose a new message by clicking the Compose link.

Besides reading messages you've sent or received through the network, in this section you can also review the alerts sent to you by applications you or your friends have added. I discuss these in more detail in Chapter 21, which is dedicated to OpenSocial applications. For now, all you need to know is that the Alerts tab to the right of the Inbox tab contains these messages.

If you click the Sent tab to the right of the Alerts tab, you can see the messages you've sent through the network. If you click the Archive tab to the right of the Sent tab, you can access the messages you've marked to be archived using the Archive link contained in them.

You can also compose a new message from within the Messages section by clicking the Compose link at the top right. This opens a page that looks quite a bit like the one shown earlier in Figure 5-2, except that it lets you choose the recipients from among your friends on this network or your friends in all networks, or you can enter one or more e-mail addresses, as shown in Figure 5-4.

Figure 5-4: You can send messages to your friends or e-mail recipients outside the network.

Leaving messages on a Comment Wall

Work with me on this memory exercise: You're back in college, living in the dorms, and you have a bulletin board on the door of your room. People can leave you notes letting you know to meet them at such-and-such place or telling you that they came looking for you and missed you. . . . Does this sound familiar?

Fast-forward to the present day, and turn to your network. You have a Comment Wall on your profile page (like the one shown in Figure 5-5), where other members can leave you messages in the same way. It lets members write something to you, include a link to another Web site, embed video from the network (as discussed in Chapter 4) or other sites, or post a photo for you to check out.

Moderating Comment Wall messages

Anybody in the network can leave you a message on your Comment Wall: People leaving messages don't have to be your friends.

However, Ning provides you the means to control what appears and what doesn't on your Comment Wall. If you click the Settings link at the top right and click the Privacy link on the left, you find an option on that page that asks "Do you want to approve comments before they appear on your comment wall?" Essentially, if you select Yes, you set up your Comment Wall so that you have to approve all comments before they're displayed. This is shown in Figure 5-6.

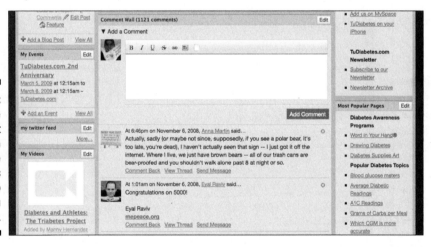

Figure 5-5: The Comment Wall on your profile page allows members to leave you messages.

If you choose to moderate comments before they appear on your Comment Wall, every time a comment left is by a member, the right column displays a notification indicating the number of comments to be approved. The notification provides a link, which takes you to a new page where you can view the comments (see Figure 5-7). This page lets you approve the comment or reject it if you don't want it to appear on your Comment Wall. You can also view comments that are pending your approval by going to your profile page and scrolling to the Comment Wall section.

Figure 5-6:
The Privacy
section
in your
Settings
page lets
you control
whether
Comment
Wall mes-
sages
require your
approval
before
they're
displayed.

Figure 5-7:
You can
approve
or reject
comments
posted
by others
on your
Comment
Wall.

Click to accept the comment.

Click to reject the comment.

Evaluating Members' Contributions

Remember that song by The Beatles that went "I get by with a little help from my friends"? Or the one that said "All you need is love"? This was true back in the '60s and holds just as true today in social networks on Ning.

Everyone likes being loved and getting appreciated for contributions. In a social network, the contributions are in the form of photos and videos, among other ways to share. One of the subtlest but nicest things you can do in a network is evaluate somebody else's contribution by rating it, adding it as a Favorite, tagging it, or making a comment about it.

In the following sections, I discuss all these ways to evaluate the contributions made by other members.

Rating photos and videos

Rating things seems to be human nature. It's everywhere: from the Olympics to *American Idol,* from YouTube to Digg. People like rating things, and because of that you can rate items on Ning. You're given the option to give a rating of one to five stars to every photo and every video on your network.

To rate a video or a photo, simply go to the video or photo page, look for the blank five stars below the item on the right next to the word *Rate* (see Figure 5-8), and click the star that designates the rating you want to give.

As ratings get submitted, the average rating is displayed below the item on the left. It's fun sometimes to just sit back and look at the average ratings that videos and photos get.

Adding an item as a Favorite

You can designate a photo or a video as a Favorite by clicking the Add to Favorites link below it.

You can later view the items you have marked as Favorites by going to the Photos page or the Videos page and clicking the My Favorites link at the top.

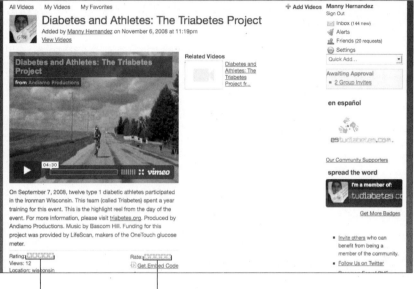

All Videos   My Videos   My Favorites

Diabetes and Athletes: The Triabetes Project
Added by Manny Hernandez on November 6, 2008 at 11:19pm
View Videos

Figure 5-8:
Rating
videos and
photos is
very easy in
a network
on Ning.

On September 7, 2008, twelve type 1 diabetic athletes participated in the Ironman Wisconsin. This team (called Triabetes) spent a year training for this event. This is the highlight reel from the day of the event. For more information, please visit triabetes.org. Produced by Andiamo Productions. Music by Bascom Hill. Funding for this project was provided by LifeScan, makers of the OneTouch glucose meter.

Rating:
Views: 12
Location: wisconsin

Click a star to rate the video.

These stars show the video's average rating.

Tagging items

Tagging is a new term that became popular with the start of the Web 2.0 movement a few years ago as Web sites such as Flickr (a photo-sharing service) and del.icio.us (a social bookmarking service) came about. Tagging entails assigning keywords (or key phrases) to an item — whether it is a photo, video, or bookmark — to help describe it.

For example, if you add a photo of the Empire State Building, you can assign tags like *newyork*, *building,* and *skyscraper* to it. If you need to add multiple word tags to an item, you need to surround the words with double quotes (as in *"new york"*). Otherwise, they get treated as two separate tags: *new*, *york*.

Tags can be added to photos, videos, forum topics, blog posts, and events by the person who adds them, either as they're being uploaded or by editing them later. This is explained in more detail in Chapter 4.

Tags make searching for items on your network easier in two ways:

✔ Items that are tagged with a certain keyword will appear in searches for that keyword that are performed in the network. So if you type **New York** in the main search box of the network (at the top right of the page), the Empire State Building you posted will appear. It will also appear if you type **New York** in the search box on the main photos page.

✔ Tags for an item are found below its rating, in the form of links. The tag links act as paths to help you find more items that also have the same tag. So if you click the *newyork* tag for the now-famous Empire State Building photo, you're taken to a page that contains all other photos with the tag *newyork*. Tags provide a very convenient way to search for related items, as shown in Figure 5-9.

Tagging events

Tags in events are not called *tags,* but *event types.* But at the end of the day, they're still tags: If you tag an event as *party,* whenever there's a general search for the term *Party* or a search in the Events page using the term *Party,* the events that are tagged this way appear in the results.

Also, the event types you add to an event become clickable and lead to a page showing all other events that are of the same type. For example, Figure 5-10 shows all the events with the event type Fundraiser. The power of tags in action!

Figure 5-9:
All the photos in this network that are tagged "newyork."

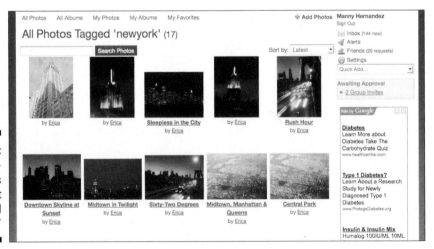

Commenting about contributions

You can leave comments on blog posts, events you have given an RSVP to, photos, and videos, as shown in Figure 5-11. Your comments may include the same elements as a comment you would leave on a member's Comment Wall: pure text, links to other Web sites, and embedded videos and/or photos.

To leave a comment, type it in the comment box. To apply bold, italic, underline, and strikethrough format to the text, click the B, I, U, or S button, respectively. If you want to turn a portion of the comment you leave into a link, select the text, click the chainlike button, and enter the URL of the page you want to link to. If you want to add an image to the comment, click the colored rectangular button. Last, if you want to insert a file into your comment, click the white document-shaped button.

If you want to, you can embed HTML code in the comment box, including embedding videos.

After you've left a comment anywhere in the network, you can delete it by clicking the little x symbol next to it. You can't edit it, but you still can delete it and post a new comment the way you want it to come up.

Leaving sincere and useful comments on other people's contributions will help earn you the trust of other members in the network.

Blogging in Your Network

Unless you've been hiding under a rock the past few years, you've heard of *blogs,* which are online journals of sorts: virtual containers for stories people write about themselves and others, on which readers can leave comments.

Quite possibly you have your own blog already. (If that's the case, check out Chapter 9 to find out how to syndicate the content from your blog on your profile page through the use of RSS feeds, which is a great thing.) One of the great things about your network on Ning is that it lets you write your own blog. This is another way in which you can communicate with others.

Adding a new post from your blog page

You can start a new blog post in the following three ways:

- ✔ Go to your profile page and click the Blog Posts link below your photo. If this is your first blog entry, you're taken straight to the Add a Blog Post page. (See the steps in this section for details on writing and posting a blog entry.) After you write blog entries, clicking the Blog Posts link takes you to your blog page, where you click the Add a Blog Post link to write more entries.
- ✔ Click the Blogs link in the navigation of the network. Once you're taken to the Blogs page, click the Add a Blog Post link.

✔ Click the Quick Add drop-down menu that appears at the top right of every page. Select Blog Post from the options, as shown in Figure 5-12. I explain the Quick Add method in the next section.

If you want to add a blog post that you can format and add tags to, follow these steps:

1. **Click the Add a Blog Post link on your blog page.**

   You're taken to a page that lets you add the title and the body of the post.

2. **(Optional) Add a title.**

   If you choose to not add a title, the first few words of your post will become the title of the post. I recommend that you add a title.

3. **Type your blog entry.**

   If you're unable to finish writing your blog post, you can click the Save as Draft button, which saves the current version of the post for you to later finish and publish.

4. **Format your blog entry as desired.**

   To make life easier, at the top of the text box where you enter your post, there are buttons to help you easily boldface, italicize, underline, and strikethrough words, as well as insert a link or an image or attach a file to your post. You can see this in Figure 5-13.

   At the bottom of the Add a Blog Post page (see Figure 5-14), you can find other blog posting options.

Figure 5-12:
The Quick Add option lets you easily add new blog posts, discussions, events, photos, videos, and notes to the network.

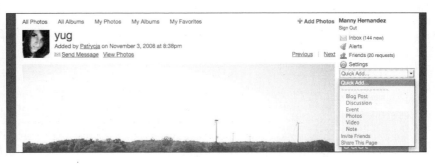

Figure 5-13:
The new blog post text box offers you a convenient way to format your post.

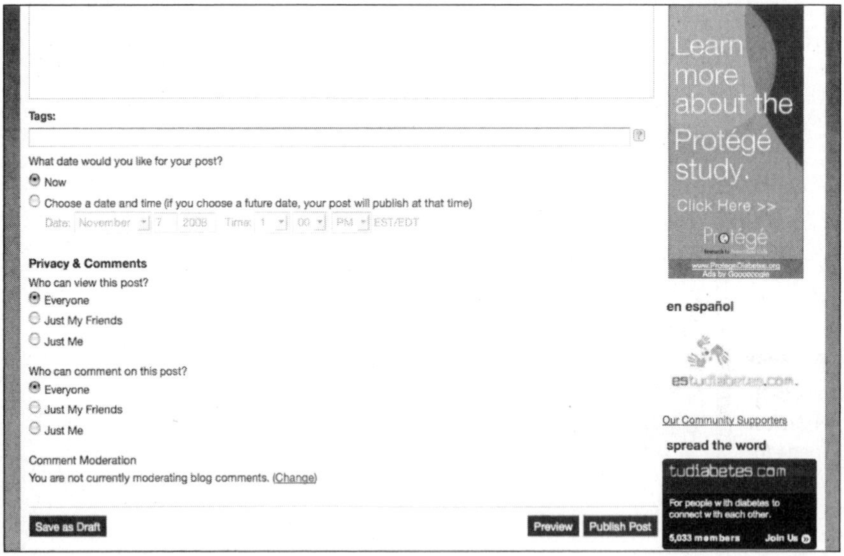

Figure 5-14:
Add tags and choose when to post your blog.

5. (Optional) Add keyword tags.

This is the field where you can add tags to help describe the nature of your blog post and make it easier to find, as explained earlier in this chapter.

6. **Choose a publishing date and time.**

   You can just select Now if you want to keep it simple. Alternatively, select Choose a Date and Time and then set the date and time. For instance, you could use this feature to synchronize announcements you may want to make at times you won't be in front of your computer.

7. **Control who can view the post and who can comment on the post.**

   Your options are Everyone, Just My Friends, or Just Me.

8. **(Optional) Change your moderation settings on your privacy page by clicking the Change link.**

   This opens the My Settings – Privacy page in a new browser window (or tab). After making and saving your changes, simply go back to your blog post, which is open in its original window.

9. **Click the Preview button to see how your post will look after it has been published.**

10. **If you like what you see, click the Publish! button (see Figure 5-15) to make the post visible to others based on the privacy settings you selected.**

    You're all done! If, instead, you need to make any changes, go to Step 11.

11. **Click the Back button to make any necessary corrections or additions.**

12. **When you're ready to show your blog post to the world, click the Publish Post button, and voilà — you're done!**

Figure 5-15:
The Preview page for your blog post lets you see how it will look before it gets published.

Adding a new post through Quick Add

When you add a blog post using the Quick Add drop-down list, instead of being taken to a new page, you're presented with a floating box that allows you to enter the post title and entry of the post.

The box doesn't offer any formatting tools (that's why it's called Quick Add, in case you were wondering), but it gives you the option to go to the full-featured page (shown in Figure 5-13, earlier in this chapter) if you prefer the convenience of the formatting buttons. To switch to the full-featured format, click the More Options link in the floating box. When you're ready with your post, click the Publish Post button.

Managing and editing your blog posts

Inspired bloggers are bound to write lots of blog posts. If this describes you, over time you'll find the blog management page handy. To access this page, visit your profile page and click the link to your blog posts. On the page that appears, click the Manage Blog link below the header Admin Options.

The Manage Blog page shows the basics of all blog posts — date, time, title, and number of comments — along with all the means for you to edit or delete any of them (as shown in Figure 5-16):

- ✔ **Edit a blog post by clicking the Edit link next to the post's title or clicking the title itself.** Doing so takes you back to a page that's identical to the one you get while you're creating a post. The difference is that it contains the title and the body of the post you chose to edit.

- ✔ **Delete a blog post by selecting the check box next to the post's title and clicking the Delete button at the bottom.** You can also delete a post from within the blog post itself by clicking the Delete Post link on the right side of the post.

- ✔ **Preview draft posts.** Another important use of the Manage Blog page is that it gives you access to any drafts of posts you may have saved in the past. By clicking them, you can edit, preview, publish, or delete drafts of blog posts shown on this page.

Moderating comments on your blog

On the Privacy page in your Settings, you're given the option to moderate the comments posted by others on your photos, videos, and blog posts. If this is your case, the Comments tab on the Manage Blog page allows you to approve or reject comments posted by others. As long as you set up your Email Settings to notify you when you have new network content to approve, you get a notification every time there's a comment for you to review.

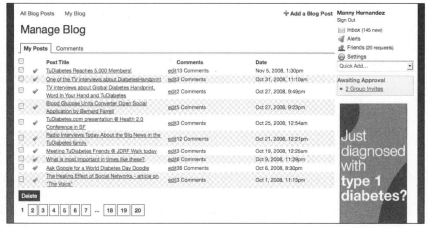

Figure 5-16: The Manage Blog page gives you convenient access to all past posts you have written.

You can set up your blog, photos, and videos so that you can moderate comments before they're displayed. Visit the Settings page (link on the top right) and click the Privacy link on the left. Make sure you answer Yes to the question "Do you want to approve comments before they appear on your blog?"

If your blog isn't set up to moderate comments, the Comments tab on the Manage Blog page shows you all the comments that have been posted by others on your blog posts. You can delete any of them if you so choose to by clicking the check box next to them and then clicking the Delete button.

Updating Your Profile Status

Last but by no means least, among the things you can do to communicate with others in the network is update your profile status.

In Chapter 1, I show you how you can do that from your Ning Activity Feed. When you update your status in your Ning Activity Feed, the new status is applied to all networks you are a member of.

You can also update your status on a given network by going to your profile page, typing your new status in the text box at the top (using 140 characters or less), and then clicking the button next to it.

Chapter 6

Interacting with Others on the Network

*T*he key word in *social network* is the word *social,* and everyone has a very good idea of what that means. It involves people. Can you imagine a social network of one person? Not too exciting, huh?

Social networks come to life as their membership grows. Social networks on Ning become even more interesting as more and more people who have a common interest — whether it's having gone to the same school or being fans of the same band — sign up and start participating and interacting.

When members start participating in the network, Ning offers many crossroads where they can interact with one another. This chapter is dedicated to these crossroads: the discussion forum, events, groups, and network chat.

Having Fun with the Forum

Discussion forums have been around as long as people have been connecting online (which, by the way, was before the advent of the Web as it's known today). Forums lie at the heart of just about any successful online community that you can think of. Even more so, many successful online communities hover strictly around just a discussion forum because the forum gives participants plenty of room to interact.

Considering the history of online discussion forums and their popularity, it's no wonder that the forum lies at the heart of most networks you can join on Ning. In the following sections, I tell you a bit more about the forum and how it can help you interact with others in your network.

Starting a discussion

Hopefully the Administrators of your network have created different categories to help group discussions (existing and future) into neatly separate buckets. Forum categories help you explore the content on the forum before you get busy creating a fantastic discussion topic . . . only to later find out that somebody else had already created it. If you're an Administrator or you're simply curious about how it's done, I discuss how to set up forum categories in Chapter 11.

You get to the Discussion Forum page by clicking the Forum link in the navigation of your network. Even if there are no categories in the forum and all discussions in the network live together on the main Discussion Forum page, shown in Figure 6-1, you can do a cursory search using the search box to find out whether anyone else has already brought up the topic you're thinking of. If you don't find anything, don't worry too much over it: It's totally possible that your topic is an original one, so get started with the new topic.

Figure 6-1:
The main
Discussion
Forum
page in a
network,
showing
featured
discussions
and some
categories.

To start a new discussion topic, click the Add a Discussion link at the top right from anywhere in the forum. This link takes you to a page, shown in Figure 6-2, where you can craft the first post of what will hopefully turn into a fruitful discussion. The elements that you need to fill in for a new discussion topic are

✔ **Discussion Title:** A title is needed to start a new topic. Spend a little time thinking of a good title, something indicative of what the topic is about. ("This is amazing!" would be a poor title choice, for instance.) Also consider making the title as engaging as possible. (For example, "Are you in favor or against X?" would sound inviting to many people.) Last, try including keywords in the title in order to help make the topic easier to find through search engines.

✔ **Post:** This is the bread and butter of the topic. Make sure to elaborate your topic in the body of the post so the other members have access to enough information to understand your point.

Figure 6-2:
Adding a
new topic is
simple, but
try to think
of a good
title and
give others
some con-
text so you
can spark
a good
discussion.

If needed, you can take advantage of the formatting capabilities that are available (bold, italics, and underline). Including a link to a reference, if you have one, might also come in handy.

Pictures speak a thousand words. So why not save yourself some typing by embedding an image as you're creating the topic? To add an image, click the colored icon on the formatting toolbar above the Post text box. This opens a window, shown in Figure 6-3, where you can either find an image file on your computer or include the link to an existing image elsewhere and embed it in your new discussion. Click the Add button to finish the job: The needed HTML code is inserted into the text for you.

You can also embed a video in your discussion topic. Just follow the same steps I cover in Chapter 4, using the HTML embed code, which you can get either from your network or from another video site.

Figure 6-3:
You can either browse through your hard drive or enter the URL of an existing image to insert an image as part of your topic.

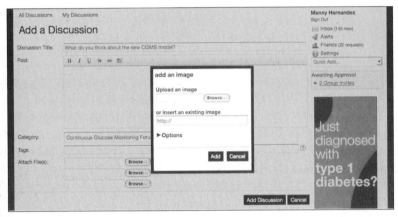

Figure 6-3: You can either browse through your hard drive or enter the URL of an existing image to insert an image as part of your topic.

- ✔ **Category:** If your discussion forum has categories into which it is divided, you have the option to select where, among the different categories, you want your new discussion topic to be included.

- ✔ **Tags:** You can add tags to your discussion topic, to make the topic easier to search. You can think of tags as keywords that describe the topic.

- ✔ **Attach File(s):** To upload a file, click the Upload Files link below the text box for the post. This opens a panel that lets you find the file in your computer to attach to your post. You can attach up to three files to any discussion topic or reply to a topic.

When you attach a file to a discussion topic, you can link directly to it from anywhere else. This can be useful if you want to reference the file outside the context of the discussion where you included it.

When you have all the ingredients ready, click the Add Discussion button and let the replies roll in.

Unless you change your e-mail settings, you automatically follow all discussions that you start or reply to. This means you will get an e-mail notification every time someone replies to your discussion: If your discussion becomes very popular, you may find yourself getting a few too many e-mails. You can avoid this e-mail backlog by clicking the Stop Following link at the bottom of the discussion, after it has started. You can also disable notifications through the Settings section: Click the Email link and deselect the Follow Discussions and Blog Posts I Add option and/or the Follow Discussions and Blog Posts I Reply To option.

Replying to an existing discussion

If your idea for a new discussion topic isn't as new as you thought or if you find an existing topic that you feel compelled to participate in, you can easily join in the discussion.

If you want to reply to the topic that the discussion started with, just type your comment in the text box directly below it. You can format (using bold, italics, or underlining) and enhance your reply (with photos, videos, or attached files) in the same way that I describe in the preceding section. When you submit your reply, it appears in chronological order below any other existing replies to the main topic, and the left margin of your reply is aligned with the original post.

If you want to reply to someone else who has already replied, click the right-pointing arrow next to the words *Reply to This* and enter your response. Depending on how your network's forum is set up (threaded style or flat style), the text box for you to reply appears indented to the right below the post you replied to or in the text box below the original post that started the topic, quoting the post you're replying to. The two kinds of forum setup are discussed in Chapter 11.

You can see the two kinds of replies in Figure 6-4. This figure shows replies in a forum set up with threaded style.

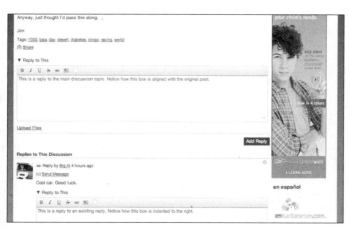

Figure 6-4:
You can reply to the main topic or to someone else's reply.

Participating in Events

When you think of the word *social,* the word *event* naturally comes to mind too: Events, after all, are part of your social life. Whether you're referring to events taking place outside your computer (you know, in the real world, where most stuff happens) or you're talking about chats, webinars, and other forms of online events, networks on Ning give you resources to RSVP for an event, create your own events, and invite others to attend an event.

Finding an event

You can find all the events that have been created on your network through the Events page. You can access this page by clicking the Events tab in the navigation at the top.

When you land on the Events page, you see at the top the events that have been featured by the Administrators. Directly below them are all the events existing on the network, as shown in Figure 6-5. Each event listing contains enough information to help you make up your mind about it. Listings also show your RSVP information for each event.

Figure 6-5:
The Events page offers a summary of all the events in the network. You can access any event to learn more and RSVP.

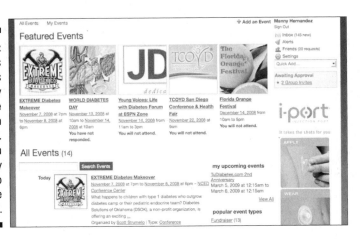

If you can't find an event you're looking for and you think you know what it's called or know a keyword that adequately describes it, you can search for it using the search box on the Events page. The results page contains a listing with all the events that match your search, arranging them in a similar way to the events on the Events page.

You can also find the event you're looking for by navigating through the calendar that's shown in the bottom right. The calendar shows the current and next months and offers Last Month and Next Month links to let you go back or forward in time and find more events.

Days on which there's at least one event scheduled appear as clickable on the calendar, and clicking any of the days takes you to a page that looks like the one shown in Figure 6-6.

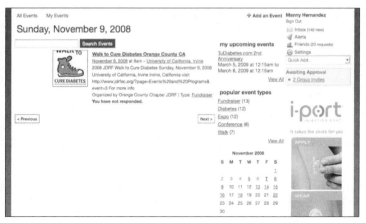

Figure 6-6:
You can display all the events scheduled for a particular day by clicking that day in the calendar.

RSVP-ing for an event

So you've found that conference you were looking for or that party you want to attend. Next, you have to RSVP for the event so that the organizer can get the right amount of drinks, food, and goods for all attendees — and also so your network friends know you're going. To RSVP for an event, click the event you're interested in attending on the Events page. You're taken to a page that shows you the details about the event, as you can see in Figure 6-7. Some of these details are optional for the event creator to supply, so they don't necessarily appear in all events.

 ✓ **Event name:** This information is shown at the top of the event in big letters — you can't miss it!

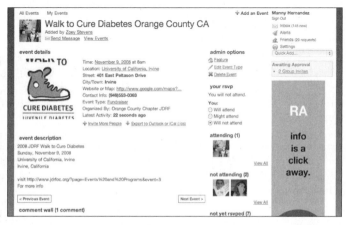

Figure 6-7:
An event page lets you learn more about the event, RSVP for it, and invite others to it.

- ✔ **Event time:** This field shows you when (date and time) the event is set to start.

- ✔ **Location:** This field displays the venue where the event will take place.

- ✔ **(Optional) City/Town:** The name says it all.

- ✔ **(Optional) Website or Map:** This field can include a Web site where you can get more information about the event or a link to a map page showing you how to get there.

- ✔ **(Optional) Phone:** This field can contain a phone number you can call for more information.

- ✔ **Event Type:** This field describes the event in general terms. Possible event types are party, conference, fundraiser, and meeting. Popular event types are shown on the right of the main Events page.

- ✔ **(Optional) Organized By:** This field can show the person or organization responsible for putting together the event.

- ✔ **Latest Activity:** The date shown in this field indicates the last time that someone added a comment on the event or gave an RSVP for it.

- ✔ **Invite More People link:** If you've responded for an event, you can invite others to it — even if you're not the event creator. See the following section for more details.

- ✔ **Export to Outlook or iCal (.ics) link:** This link lets you export the event details to your favorite calendar application so you can have it as part of your schedule. Just click the link, and the necessary information is brought over to your Outlook or iCal program.

- ✔ **Event Description:** This description appears below the event details block, and it contains as much detail as the event creator added about it. The description is followed by two buttons that let you navigate back to the previous event in the calendar or forward to the next one — yet another way to find out about more things going on in your network.

- ✔ **Comment Wall for the event:** This Comment Wall works just like the Comment Wall for the members on the network. In case you're wondering, no notifications about comments posted on the event page are sent to event attendees when other members leave a comment on the event's Comment Wall.

- ✔ **Your RSVP:** When you've given your RSVP, your RSVP shows up. Until you enter a status, your RSVP appears as You Have Not Responded. After you find out all you need to know about the event, you can RSVP for it. If you're unsure whether you'll be able to attend, select the Might Attend option. If you know you'll be attending, select the Will Attend option.

- ✔ **Guest List:** Unless the event creator chose to hide the guest list, below Your RSVP appears the list of attendees, followed by the list of those who might attend and those who are not attending the event.

After you RSVP for an event, that event appears in the My Events list. You can access your events in the following ways:

- ✓ Go to the Events page and click My Events at the top.

- ✓ Go to the Events page and view the items below the heading My Upcoming Events. This section will list the two next events that you've responded for. You can click the View All link below them to land on a page that contains all events you're scheduled to attend.

- ✓ Go to your profile page and find your My Events list as one of the boxes.

Inviting people to an event

You don't need to be the organizer of an event or the creator of the event in the network to be able to invite others to it. All you need to do is RSVP for the event. To invite others to an event, after you've given your RSVP, click the Invite More People link below the event details. You're taken to a page like the one shown in Figure 6-8.

The Invite page gives you the flexibility to invite other members or people outside the network to an event. You can do this in a number of different ways:

- ✓ **Enter Email Addresses:** You can manually enter e-mail addresses of people you want to invite, separated by comas.

- ✓ **Invite Friends:** You can choose among your friends to send an invitation to the event.

- ✓ **Import from Web Address Book:** You can import contact information from Yahoo! Mail, Hotmail, Gmail, or AOL Mail, simplifying the process of sending e-mail invitations.

- ✓ **Import from Address Book Application:** You can import contact information by uploading your address book data in `.csv` or `.vcf` format from your Microsoft Outlook or Apple Address Book.

In addition to these options, Administrators are able to invite all members of the network to the event through this page. Regardless of the option you use to invite others to the event, you can include an optional message to go along with the invitation.

Creating an event

In this section, I show you how you can create your own event. For you to be able to create an event, the Network Creator has to set up the network's privacy so that members are allowed to create events.

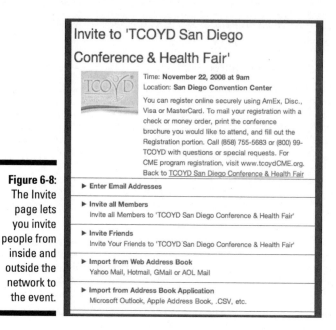

Figure 6-8:
The Invite
page lets
you invite
people from
inside and
outside the
network to
the event.

To create an event, follow these steps:

1. **Click the Add an Event link at the top of the Events page or any particular event.**

   You're taken to a page like the one shown in Figure 6-9.

   Event creation is a short process that involves filling out the details about the event and optionally sending invitations to the event.

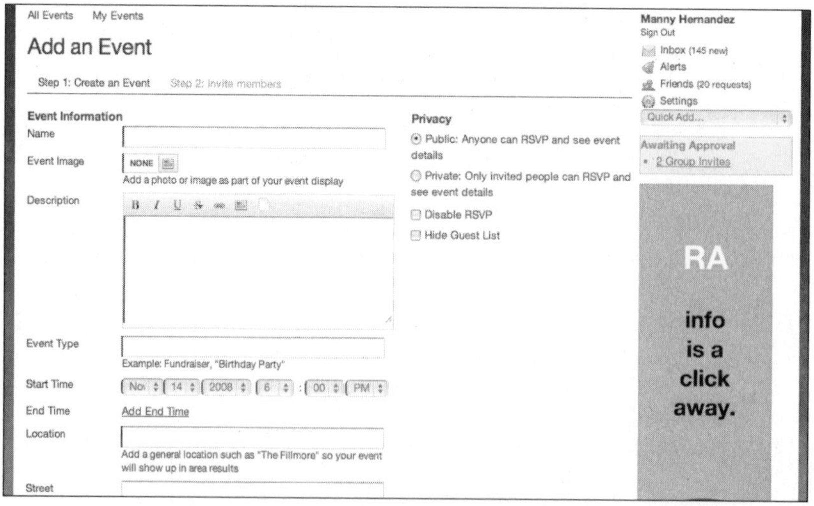

Figure 6-9:
To create
an event,
you need
to enter a
minimum
amount
of event
details and
an event
image.

2. **Fill in the event information, which includes the following details:**

- *Name:* This is a required field.

- *Event Image:* This is a required field. It may seem like something complicated, but it doesn't need to be. If you're holding a cookout, a photo with some food ingredients in it would work; if you're holding a birthday party, a picture of a birthday cake gets the message across. All you really need is to find an image you can use to illustrate your event, which you can do using Google Images or other image search services. Just be sure you have permission from the copyright holder to use the image you choose.

- *Description:* This is a required field. It lets you format the information you enter using bold, italics, underline, and strikethrough. You can also add links, images, and files to go along with it.

- *Event Type:* This is a required field. This is the equivalent of tagging the event.

- *Start Time:* This is a required field. It lets you choose the date and time of the event. The minutes field gives you 15-minute increments, so you can set up only events starting at :00, :15, :30, and :45.

- *End Time:* This is an optional field. If you want to add an end time, click the Add End Time link.

- *Location:* This is a required field.

- *Street:* This is an optional field.

- *City/Town:* This is an optional field.

- *Website or Map:* This is an optional field.

- *Phone:* This is an optional field.

- *Organized By:* This is an optional field. By default, it shows your member name. If you're creating the event on somebody else's behalf, you can enter that person's name in this field.

3. **Manage the event's privacy setting.**

Essentially, this privacy setting enables you to determine who will be able to see the details about the event and RSVP for it. You have two options:

- *Public:* If you choose the Public option (the one set by default), everyone in the network will be able to see the event details and RSVP for it.

- *Private:* If you choose the Private option, the event details will be visible only to those invited. These members will be the only ones who will be able to RSVP for the event.

4. **(Optional) Select the Disable RSVP check box.**

   Select this check box to disable the RSVP option. This may come in handy in the case of announcements that don't involve space limitations or require planning for food or other amenities.

5. **(Optional) Select the Hide Guest List check box.**

   Select this check box to hide the guest list. This prevents people from peeking to find out whether some member they highly like (or dislike) is going to be in attendance (or not). Sorry, lurkers: no fun for you!

6. **When you're done adding all the details about your event and defining the privacy settings for it, click the Add Event button.**

   You're taken to a page that looks a lot like the one that you use to invite folks to an event (refer to Figure 6-8, earlier in this chapter).

7. **Invite people to your event. (See the preceding section for the details.)**

   This is a step you can skip if you want to, but clearly it's in your best interest to invite others to your event; otherwise, you're leaving it to chance that people will out about the event on their own.

   When you're done sending out invitations, you land on your brand-spanking-new event page, showing all the details about the event. How do you feel now? Better hurry up to get the place ready for all those guests!

Going Gaga for Groups

No matter how narrow the focus of a network on Ning is, there are always smaller niches that people are going to be interested in. Members of a firefighters' network (FirefighterNation.com is a good example) may want to connect with other firefighters in their state, firefighters who share their love for music, or firefighters who are experts on a particular kind of situation or equipment. The possibilities are, quite honestly, endless.

You can start your own network on Ning to focus on these subniches, but there's a quick way to cater to most of the basic needs that a group of members in your network may have: groups!

Groups on Ning give their members a number of tools that they enjoy in the network at large in order to help them connect and share with other members of the same network. The following sections are devoted to covering the elements that make groups such a valuable element in your network.

Finding and joining a group

The Groups main page can be the place "where it's happening" in many networks on Ning. Each group listed on it can be a hub of activity and discussion about some extremely specific topics. To get to the Groups page, click the Groups tab in the top navigation. Figure 6-10 shows a typical Groups page.

On the Groups page, you can

✔ **Find featured groups listed at the top:** This is a recurring theme in all sections of a network on Ning, showing any featured items for that section up top.

✔ **Find other groups listed below the featured ones:** Depending on how active members have been creating groups, you may find anywhere from a handful to thousands of groups that range from a few members each to a ton of people participating in them.

✔ **Search for a group:** Performing a search for a group you may be interested in joining may be a useful first step. You can do this using the search box at the top of the All Groups section.

✔ **Sort the groups:** Another good idea is to change the way groups are sorted, to have a different view of them. When you first land on the Groups page, you're presented with the most active groups. But you can change this to show you the ones with the latest activity, the ones with the most members, and the most recent ones (the "baby" groups in the network, if you like).

Figure 6-10:
The Groups page in a network on Ning lets you join and participate in existing groups, as well as create and manage your own.

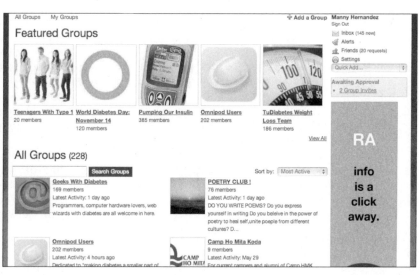

TIP

The most active groups are those with the most members, forum threads and replies, and so on. The ones with the latest activity will be those with the most recent comment on the Comment Wall, thread or reply in the forum, membership change, and so on.

Below the search box and the sorting drop-down list, you can find the listing of groups. Each group sports an image, its name, number of members, latest activity date, and a short description explaining its focus.

By clicking a group that interests you, you land on the group page. If the group has been set up as public (essentially, allowing any member to join it), you can join the group by clicking the Join link at the top right, as shown in Figure 6-11.

Figure 6-11:
A group page lets you join (and leave) a group as well as interact with the group members.

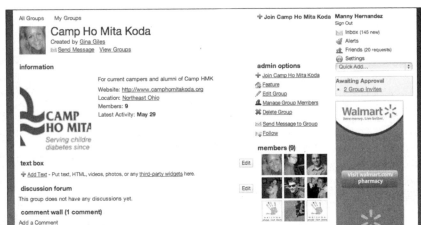

If the group has been set up for moderated membership, you're presented with an option to request access to the group. This request needs to be approved by the group creator or a group administrator before you can join the group and take part in it. Figure 6-12 gives you a feel for how a request to join a private group looks.

After you join an open group or get approved as a member of a private group, as long as your e-mail settings allow it, you receive a notification via e-mail, confirming your membership.

Participating in a group

Joining a group is really only the start of the fun (just like joining a social network on Ning is only the beginning of your interaction with other members). Groups can develop an incredible life of their own, and they offer all kinds of nifty benefits to their members. Groups can contain RSS feeds pulling head-lines and summaries of articles from another Web page. For example, a group of saxophone enthusiasts could pull saxophone-related news using an RSS feed from an outside site, thus giving members another reason to come to the group: They can get the latest news about the topic they care about. Groups give their members tools (as shown in Figure 6-13) — some informative and some interactive — that give meaning to their membership:

✔ **A Comment Wall:** The Comment Wall allows for back-and-forth conver-sation among members of a group in a very nonstructured way, just like you can do on another member's Comment Wall. The kinds of comments that can be posted can include formatted text; links; and embedded media, such as images and videos.

✔ **A discussion forum:** The discussion forum option in a group offers pretty much the same options that are available in the network's main forum. The main difference is that there are no categories available for you to assign new discussion topics to. Besides this, the discussion forum becomes an excellent resource for people to engage in topic-specific discussions.

✔ **A group message option:** You can message the members of a group. If the group creator has set up the group so that members can send mes-sages to the entire group, above the members list you can find the Send Message to Group link. This gives group members a convenient means to get the attention of their fellow group members, effectively turning the group into a mailing list of sorts.

Groups can turn into very busy spots in a social network on Ning. If you don't want to miss a thing, you can choose to follow the activity in the group. By default, when you join a group, you're notified every time someone new joins the group and when any new discussions or comments are posted in the group.

Figure 6-12:
Private
groups
require that
your mem-
bership be
approved
before
you can
participate
in them.

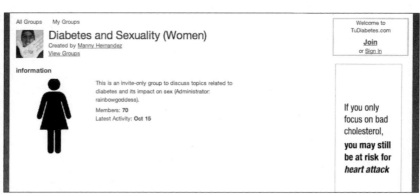

If you no longer want to receive notifications related to the group, click the Stop Following link at the top right of the group page. (You can still change your mind and opt in for notifications by clicking the Follow link at any time.)

If you decide that a group you joined is not for you anymore, click the Leave Group link at the top right of the group page, and you will no longer be among its members.

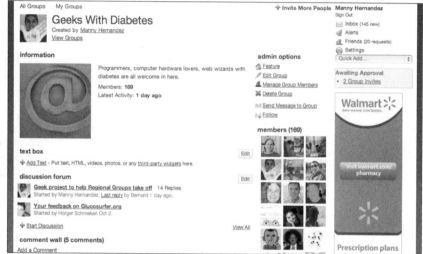

Figure 6-13: Groups are another way to be involved in a network.

Creating and managing a group

Starting a new group is one of the coolest things you can do in a network on Ning. It's almost like starting your own network. As a matter of fact, it can be great practice for you to eventually start a new network with a tighter focus on a topic that may be too specific for your current network.

As I discuss in the previous sections, groups can offer a number of options for their members. Which of those options are made available to members is a decision that you, as the group creator, get to make.

Before you can create a group, the Network Creator must have set up the network to allow members to create groups. Also, the Network Creator has the option to approve groups before they're displayed to other members.

If the network is set up to allow you to create groups, you can find an Add a Group link at the top right of the Groups page. When you click that link, you're taken to the Add a Group page (shown in Figure 6-14), which requires that you enter the group information, choose among the features it will offer, decide on the privacy level, and determine whether you'll allow members to message one another. The following list describes the different elements:

✔ **Group Information:** First, you get to enter the details that describe the group:

- *Name:* You need to give the group a name. Try to make the name distinctive enough to differentiate your group from the myriad other groups it will coexist with.

- *Image:* You have to add an image to go along with any new group. This is a good thing: Visuals help people make a connection more easily, so try to find an image you can use that relates to the topic of the group.

- *Description:* This is an optional field but one that is important to take advantage of, even if you write only a single sentence. This description accompanies the group's basic details in the listing shown in the main Groups page, so you can elaborate a bit more beyond the group name here.

- *Group Address:* This field is required, and it constitutes the only part of the URL of the group page that you have control over. For example, if you choose as group address the word *fantasticgroup,* and your network on Ning is `http://yournetwork.ning.com,` the URL for the group page will be `http://yournetwork.ning. com/group/`*fantasticgroup.* As you type the group name, this field will become automatically populated, but you can change the address as you see fit while you're setting up the group.

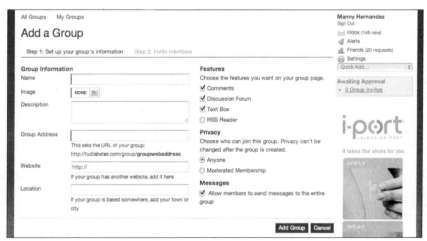

Figure 6-14: Setting up your group's information.

- *Website:* This is an optional field that gives you the opportunity to include a link to another site, in case the group has another Web site.

- *Location:* This is an optional field that allows you to localize the group if your group is based in some local area.

✔ **Features:** After the information is complete, you choose the features you want to add to the group:

- *Comments:* This feature adds a Comment Wall to the group.

- *Discussion Forum:* This feature adds a discussion forum to the group.

- *Text Box:* Adding this feature lets you include a text box below the group information, allowing you to include more details, images, videos, and so on.

- *RSS Reader:* Adding this feature gives you the opportunity to include an outside RSS feed that will give group members another reason to come back to it, such as getting the latest news about the topic dealt with in the group by adding an RSS feed of news about the topic to the group.

✔ **Privacy:** You have two options to choose between, which you cannot change after the group has been created,

- *Anyone:* Selecting this option gives anybody in the network the ability to join the group at will.

- *Moderated Membership:* Selecting this option makes the group membership a moderated process, giving you more control over who joins.

✔ **Messages:** This option allows your members to send messages to the entire group, which gives the group parts of the functionality of a mailing list.

After you add the group information and choose the features and settings, click Add Group to go to the next step, which involves inviting other members to join the group. This is an optional step. (The page you'll see at this point is similar to the invitation page for events shown in Figure 6-8, earlier in this chapter.) If you prefer, you can choose to invite members later by clicking the Skip link.

Two elements of the group creation process cannot be changed after the group has been created: the group address and the privacy setting. Make sure to choose these two wisely, because the only way to change them after you set up the group is to delete the group altogether and create a new one.

Managing a group

After you've set up your new group, you can make small adjustments to the main page. To edit the details of each feature in the group, click the Edit button at the top right of each of them. When you click Edit, you see options for modifying the feature. Figure 6-15 shows the discussion forum selected for editing. When you're done applying any changes, click the Save button. The following list describes the group features that you can edit:

Figure 6-15:
You can edit how things appear on your group page.

✔ **Text Box:** The Text Box on your newly created group page works like the Text Box on your profile page. It gives you a space to add formatted text, links, images, and files.

✔ **Discussion Forum:** When you click the Edit button, you're able to modify the following options:

• *Display:* You can choose between Detailed View and Titles Only. Detailed View shows the titles of the discussions along with a few lines of the post that opened the discussion. The Titles Only option, as you would guess from the name, displays only the titles of the discussion topics.

• *From:* This option determines which kinds of discussions are displayed. You can choose Latest Activity (includes new discussions along with new replies), Newest Discussions (includes only new discussions), Most Replies (shows the discussions with the most replies), Featured (as the creator or administrator of a group, you can choose to feature discussions in the group — more on this later), or Group Admin Discussions (discussions that the group creator or admins of the group have started).

• *Show:* This option lets you choose how many discussions topics (0, 1, 2, 3, 4, 5, 10, or 20) are shown under the Discussion Forum header.

✔ **Add RSS:** To add an RSS feed to your group, you need to click the Edit button next to the Add RSS link. This action opens a panel inside which you can enter the following items:

• *Title:* This will be the title displayed at the top of this box.

• *URL:* This is the address for the RSS feed that you want included in the page.

- *Display:* Like the Discussion Forum option explained earlier, this option lets you choose between Detailed View and Titles Only.

- *Show:* This option lets you choose how many items from the RSS feed are shown on the group page.

Managing discussions in a group

When you create a group or if you're a group administrator, you have administrative options you can use to control things in your group. Every discussion topic in your group shows the following options (see Figure 6-16), shown below the Admin Options header in the top right:

- ✓ **Feature:** Clicking this link features the discussion. If you choose to display featured group discussions on the group page, this option makes this discussion topic show up on the group page. Also, featuring the discussion displays the topic below the Featured Discussions header when you click the View All link at the bottom of the Discussion Forum section on the main group page.

- **Edit Discussion:** Clicking the Edit Discussion link takes you to a page where you can edit the discussion title, the post, the tags, and any attached files. After you're done making any edits, you can save them by clicking the Save button.

- ✓ **Close Discussion:** Occasionally you may find it necessary to close a discussion, either because it has derailed from its original purpose or because it's no longer timely. Clicking Close Discussion lets you put a stop to replies on the discussion topic.

- ✓ **Add Tags:** Clicking this link lets you add tags to the discussion topic to make it easier to find it through a search later on.

- ✓ **Delete Discussion:** If you need to remove a discussion topic from the group's discussion forum, this is the way to do it. There is no way to undo this action, so double-check before deleting any discussions in a group.

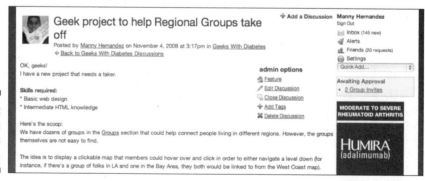

Figure 6-16:
Managing
discussions
in a group.

Managing group members

Just like a network on Ning, groups in a network can grow to a decent size. If that is the case, and you find yourself needing help from others, you can promote other members to group administrators. To do this, click the Manage Group Members link under the Admin Options heading on your group's main page.

When you land on the group Members page (see Figure 6-17), you can choose among the members by selecting the check boxes next to their names. After you've selected the members you want to promote to group administrators, click the Promote to Administrator button at the top left. (Note that you can also demote someone from group administrator.) Promoted members can help you with group administrative matters.

Group administrators cannot do a few things: delete the group, ban the group creator from the group, and promote or demote other members to group administrators.

Note that group administrators are different from network Administrators, whose role is explained in detail in Chapter 13.

Another thing you may find yourself needing to do once in a blue moon is ban people from your group. To ban a member from your group, click the check box next to the member's name and click the Ban from Group button at the top center. If the reason for the ban changes, you can unban a previously banned member.

Make sure to read Chapter 17 to find out how to work with group administrators and deal with banned members. Though the chapter deals with network Administrators and members of the network at large, some of the concepts can also be applied in a group.

Figure 6-17: You can promote, demote, ban, and unban members of a group.

Geeks With Diabetes Members (169)

← Back to Geeks With Diabetes

Manny Hernandez
Sign Out

Inbox (145 new)
Alerts
+ Invite More People Friends (20 requests)
Settings

Members (169)

| Promote to Administrator | Demote from Administrator | Ban from Group |

Search Show All   Quick Add...

Group Administrators have a similar level of control to the Group Creator.

Awaiting Approval
• 2 Group Invites

	Name	Email	Status	Date Joined
	Manny Hernandez		Group Creator	Jul. 19, 2007
☐	Bernard		Member	Jul. 19, 2007
☐	Chuck Lin		Member	Jul. 19, 2007
☐	jamiet		Member	Jul. 19, 2007
☐	Nicole		Member	Jul. 19, 2007
☐	craig620		Member	Jul. 19, 2007
☐	Anthony Davis		Member	Jul. 19, 2007
☐	Rachel B		Member	Jul. 19, 2007
☐	John Mignault		Member	Jul. 19, 2007
☐	beth		Member	Jul. 19, 2007
☐	Raven		Member	Jul. 19, 2007
☐	Mike Mullins		Member	Jul. 20, 2007
☐	Scott K. Johnson		Member	Jul. 20, 2007
☐	Tim		Member	Jul. 20, 2007
☐	dara rochlin		Member	Jul. 20, 2007
☐	Dan		Member	Jul. 20, 2007
☐	Jeff Rochlin		Member	Jul. 20, 2007
☐	Lili		Member	Jul. 20, 2007
☐	Gabe		Member	Jul. 20, 2007

i-port
INJECTION PORT
It takes the shots for you

APPLY

WEAR

Chatting with Members

Chatting is what people do, isn't it? It's what you do when you're on a long and boring plane trip, and it's what you do when you run into someone who seems to have some interesting story to tell. You chat. Nowadays *chat* seems to also be equated with exchanging instant messages with other people using AIM, MSN, Google Talk, or Yahoo! Messenger. But in the context of a network on Ning, chat is another element that lets you interact with multiple members.

The most unique thing about chat is that all participants in a chat session need to be "there" (in the chat page) at the same time for the interaction to take place. "Duh! I knew that," you may argue, but this actually makes chat an activity that's completely different from all the other activities I talk about in this chapter. None of the other activities requires participants to be in the same place at the same time.

Now that this little bit of philosophical debate is out of the way, you can get down to discovering chat in a network on Ning. Chatting on Ning is incredibly easy through the Chat bar at the bottom of every page on the network, as shown in Figure 6-18. You basically click either one of the arrows on the Chat bar to open up the Chat window.

Figure 6-18:
The Chat bar appears at the bottom of all pages in the network.

Chatting with multiple members

The Chat window shows you how simple chatting with other members can be. A typical Chat window is shown in Figure 6-19. (Before the chat session starts, the Chat window is a blank slate.) To the left, below the Main tab, you can see the messages posted by each member, and each message is preceded by a member icon and a time stamp.

Before you can chat with others, you need to make sure your status is set to Online through the little buddy-shaped icon next to the green or red circle in the bottom right of the Chat bar or (if the Chat window is open) at the top right of the Chat window. When you're online, the light is green, and the Chat bar shows you how many other members are online. When you're offline, the light is red, and on the Chat bar, instead of the number of members online, you see the message (Disconnected).

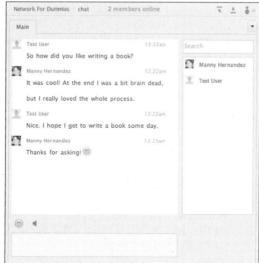

Figure 6-19:
Chatting on
Ning really
can't get
any easier.

When you're online, when you open the Chat window, you appear on the right, in the list of members currently participating in the chat session. Other features of the Chat window include

✔ **A search box:** This allows you to search for a specific member in case the list of members chatting is long.

✔ **The text box:** At the bottom, on the left side of the window, is the text box that you use to type your own messages as part of the chat. Above the text box is a handy panel with two buttons:

  • *The smiley button:* Click the first button to show a number of smileys you can include in your message. Clicking a smiley inserts the right code in the message box to give your posts a little bit of flavor. ☺

  • *The speaker-shaped button:* The second button enables you to un-mute and mute the chat. If it is un-muted, whenever someone posts a comment in the chat window, you hear a subtle yet audible beep alerting you to the fact that someone replied.

✔ **Hide:** At the top right of the Chat window, to the left of the buddy-shaped icon, you can click the downward arrow to hide the Chat window. Hiding the window doesn't take you offline: It simply hides it from view so you can go about browsing the rest of the network conveniently.

✔ **Detach:** To the left of the downward arrow is a diagonal arrow pointing to the top left (also available on the Chat bar, when the Chat window is hidden). If you click this icon, the Chat window becomes detached in a new browser window.

If you click the diagonal arrow and the Chat doesn't appear in its own window, most likely your browser is blocking pop-ups. Simply disable pop-up blocking for your network if you want to chat in the convenience of your own pop-up window.

Chatting with another member

Occasionally, you may want to chat privately with another member, as you can see in Figure 6-20. To do this, click the member icon in the chat window or on the listing of online members. You're presented with a window showing you these options:

✔ **Private Chat:** Clicking this link opens a new tab next to the Main tab, where you can chat with the other member privately.

✔ **View Profile:** Clicking this option opens a new window where the member's profile page will be loaded.

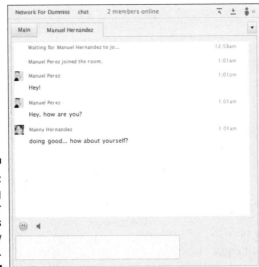

Figure 6-20:
Chatting
with another
member is
also very
easy.

Part III

Creating and Managing Your Own Social Network

The 5th Wave   By Rich Tennant

"This should unstick the keys a little."

In this part . . .

*I*f you think being a member of a network on Ning can be a great experience, wait until you set up your own network. There are so many options for you to play with that you can truly make your social network on Ning unique:

- ✔ You can choose how your network looks.
- ✔ You can select which features to add to it.
- ✔ You can polish it with Ning's premium services.

This part gives you the tools to go out there and get your own network started. You also find out how to manage the members in your network and how they interact and communicate with each other.

Chapter 7

Setting Up a Network on Ning

*Y*ou are not alone. I really, really mean it: You are not alone in thinking about setting up a network on Ning. By the time you read this, there will be well over a million networks powered by Ning. Don't be intimidated by that big number. This chapter deals with the steps leading up to the setup of a network on Ning, from preparing for it (including learning from other networks), through the creation process, to the point when you click the Launch! link and show your master creation to the world. Hang on tight!

Planning before You Start

I know, I know . . . planning is the boring part, but give me a few paragraphs of your time to share with you a few ideas that may come in handy.

Knowing your competitors

It's easy to set up a network on Ning, so there's a good chance you will find a good number of networks focused on the exact same topic you chose. (Yep, that brilliant idea that woke you up in the middle of the night.)

How do you find out who your competitors are? Go to Ning.com and enter a search term that matches your topic of interest in the Search Networks box at the top right of the page, as shown in Figure 7-1.

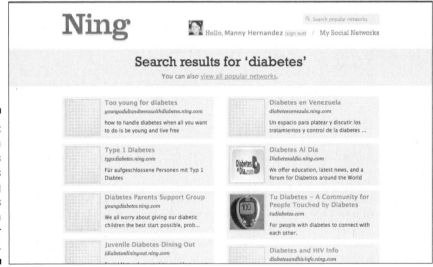

Figure 7-1:
The Ning.
com home
page is the
starting
point to
search and
create
networks.

To give you an idea, when I launched TuDiabetes (a network for people touched by diabetes), there were more than 15 networks about diabetes on Ning. At the time I'm writing this, there are more than 15 *pages* of networks, and each page has 20 networks listed on it, so you do the math. Figure 7-2 shows some of the current results when you type **diabetes** in the Search Networks box.

Figure 7-2:
The Search
Results
page shows
the existing
networks
about a
particular
topic.

What's happened? On one end, Network Creators have started networks with narrower and narrower focus, zeroing in on subniches that were untouched just a few months ago. So, going back to the diabetes example, you now have networks about type 1 diabetes, type 2 diabetes, gestational diabetes, teenage diabetics, parents with diabetes, parents of children with diabetes, and so on.

Also, there are unique niches coming up all the time: new networks centered on cities and neighborhoods; colleges, schools, and graduating classes; new artists and new political candidates; new technologies; and new games. Opportunities for Network Creators to start new networks are waiting around every corner.

Were you beaten to the punch? Why do I give you the "bad" news up front? Because you have an advantage! You have this book (which is awesome, I know), and even more important than that, having lots of other networks out there gives you the opportunity to look at what others have done, what has worked for them, and what hasn't. When you use that knowledge to your advantage, your network will be as good as it can be. Here are some things that you can look at and learn from in other networks:

- ✔ **Features to add:** See what features each network makes use of. You may notice a pattern. For example, the Music Player may be a hit for the kind of network you have in mind, or it may be a true headache and a distraction from the main goal of the network.

- ✔ **Public or private:** Making your network public or private is a decision that you can always revert, but you can't always revert the consequences of making the "wrong" choice.

- ✔ **Questions to ask:** Knowing what questions to ask new members is important. It helps you and other members learn more about the new members, how they found out about your network, how they relate to other members, and so on.

- ✔ **Main page layout:** See how the networks distribute the features on the main page. A good layout can help make the network great, just as a less-than-optimal layout will break it.

This list is not comprehensive, but it gives you an idea of what to pay attention to as you're looking at other networks. The first three items in the preceding list are discussed in more detail in this chapter. I talk more about main page layout in Chapter 9.

Before moving on to create your own network, consider one last thing: If lots of other networks are doing the same thing you thought of doing, make sure you have a very compelling reason to start another one. I'm not saying you can't, but it's important for you to have a good way to differentiate yourself, a nice marketing budget, or both. Otherwise, you may find yourself running a pretty lonely network.

Seeing the big picture

Throughout the rest of this chapter, I lay out the process of creating your own network on Ning. Instead of providing one giant step list for you to follow, I've broken down the process into four smaller processes:

1. **Sign in and describe your network.**

2. **Choose features for your network.**

3. **Choose a theme.**

4. **Define profile questions.**

Step 1 is the only step you must complete entirely to officially have a network up and running. You can complete the other three steps all in one sitting, but you can also come back to them at a later time. It's up to you.

Signing In and Getting Started

I recommend that you create a new e-mail address, sign up on Ning with it to create your new network, and use that e-mail account only for that purpose. The downside to this is that you won't have all your networks on Ning (those you belong to and those you are the creator for) conveniently accessible through Ning Activity Feed.

If you choose to create a network using the same e-mail address you use as a member or as a Network Creator on other networks, and one day you want to transfer ownership to someone else, you can do so by following the instructions on this page: http://tinyurl.com/ningfordummiesnewowner.

To create your own network, go to Ning.com (just like you do when you're searching for other networks) and then follow these steps:

1. **Sign in to your Ning account by clicking the Sign In link at the top of the Ning.com home page.**

   When you do so, you're prompted to sign in with your Ning ID — the e-mail address and password you used when you signed up — as shown in Figure 7-3. (For details on how to set up an account, check out Chapter 1.)

   After you're done signing in, there are only two steps that are absolutely required to set up your network on Ning: You must name your network and choose a Web address for it. Both of these steps are done on the Ning.com home page.

Figure 7-3:
You have
to sign in
before you
can create
a new
network.

Ning

Sign in with your Ning ID
No Ning ID? Sign Up.

Sign Up
...or Sign In

Email Address

Password

Forgot your password?

Problems signing in?

Sign In

2. **Fill in the Name Your Social Network text box.**

   You can change this name later, so don't worry too much if you misspell it or change your mind about it.

3. **Enter a Web address in the Pick a Web Address text box.**

   The characters you enter are appended in front of .ning.com and turn into your network's Web address. For example, if you enter **networkfordummies** (without spaces), your network's address becomes http://networkfordummies.ning.com.

   The Web address must contain only letters, numbers, or dashes. It cannot contain spaces.

   Think before you pick a Web address. After you've created your network, you CANNOT change it.

   To illustrate the rest of the steps involved in setting up a network, I've created a new network called Network For Dummies and entered **networkfordummies** as its Web address.

4. **Click the Create button and wait for a few seconds.**

   You're taken to the Describe Your Social Network page, shown in Figure 7-4. At this point, your network is still not available to others. You need to launch it for others to be able to join it.

   The next thing for you to do is enter information about your network, which I describe in some detail in the coming steps.

5. **Choose a network name.**

   You have the opportunity to change the name you chose in Step 2 when you created the network. If you don't want to touch it now, you can still change it later through the Manage section of your network.

6. **Choose a privacy setting.**

   You have two options you can choose between: Public – Anybody Can See or Join It; and Private – Only Invited People Can Join and See It. If you have limited time to set up your network, I recommend you set it up as private until you're able to complete the setup process so that others can't see it until your masterpiece is ready for the world. You can later change your network's privacy through the Manage section on your network.

After your network has been launched, you have more granular privacy controls available. To access the controls, click the Manage link in your network's navigation and click the network Privacy option. This leads you to the page shown in Figure 7-5.

Figure 7-4:
The Describe Your Social Network page.

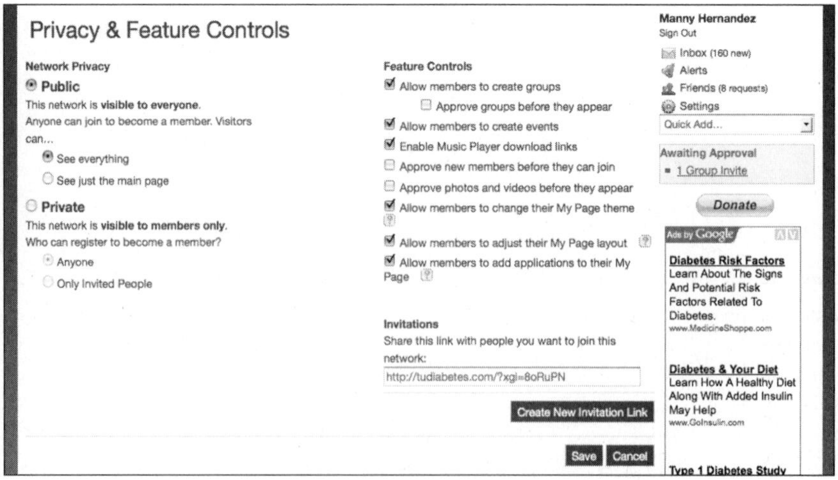

Figure 7-5:
This page lets you control your network's privacy and language, among other things.

Within the Public section, you have the option to let visitors see everything on the network or see just the main page. If you want to ensure that search engines are also able to find every bit of content on your network, make sure the See Everything option is selected.

Within the Private section, you have the option to let anyone become a member or only invited people. The former is useful if you want to make sure the content is not visible to people who are not members. The latter comes in handy if you want to have absolute control over who can join your network.

If your network is going to be used within a private organization, a school, or a family, it may be a good idea to leave it as a private network. Otherwise, if you want the network to be found by search engines and crawled all the way to the last corner, make sure to set it up as public.

7. **Enter a tagline, which is the text that will appear in the header of your network.**

    For Network For Dummies, I entered the tagline "A network for the readers of Ning For Dummies."

8. **Add a description of your network.**

    The description is limited to 140 characters. The text you enter in this box will appear in a number of places. It will appear in the Description box, if you add this feature to your network's main page. You'll also see the description in the entry for your network when it comes up in the Search Results page on Ning.com.

    The description also appears in every Google search result where the main page of your network appears. In Figure 7-6, you can see an example of this with TuDiabetes, where the description text is "For people with diabetes to connect with each other."

9. **In case your network's name, tagline, and description don't contain some keyword that you want to have associated with your network, enter some keyword terms, separated by commas.**

    Including relevant keywords makes it easier for people to find your network when they're searching on Ning.com.

Figure 7-6: Google search results also show your network's description.

10. **From the Language drop-down list, select a different language for the interface of your network, if the default English (U.S.) isn't the best option for your members.**

    From Polish to languages that I can't even attempt to pronounce correctly, your network can be offered in more than 20 languages, and new ones are being added frequently.

11. **At this point, you can launch your network or further tweak it.**

    If you want to launch your network (which makes it available to others besides yourself), click the Launch! link, as shown in Figure 7-4, earlier in this chapter.

    If you want to tweak your network some more, you can do so by clicking the Next button on the Describe Your Social Network page. Clicking Next gives you the option to select what features to add or remove from your network and lets you customize the way your network looks.

    So I definitely encourage you to click the Next button!

If you need to leave halfway through the network creation process, fear not. You can come back later and type in your network's Web address. If you're signed in to Ning, you're brought back to the same point you were in the creation process. If you aren't signed in, you're taken to a page indicating that the social network is still being set up, giving you the option to sign in to pick up where you left off.

Selecting Features for Your Network

If you click the Next button on the Describe Your Social Network page (refer to Figure 7-4, earlier in this chapter), you're taken to the Add Features to Your Network page, shown in Figure 7-7. This page lets you drag and drop all the features for your network's main page into the places where you want them to appear.

The features available appear on the left side under the Features heading. You can drag them to the right, inside one of three boxes: the left one, the middle one, and the small one in the bottom right.

If you change your mind about the placement of a feature, you can drag it and drop it wherever you want it to go. Piece of cake! Do the same if you want to remove it: You can drag a feature and drop it into the box labeled Drag Here to Remove Feature.

You see only the most popular features listed when you first land on this page: Description, Activity, Members, Videos, Blog, Forum, Events, and Groups. If you want to see the entire list, click the View All Features link at the bottom of the Features list. For starters, it isn't a bad idea to limit your-self to the most popular features: You can remove them or add to them later, as I discuss in Chapter 9.

Again, at this point you can click the Launch! link, or you can click the Next button (shown in Figure 7-7) to continue on and customize your network's appearance.

Figure 7-7: On the Add Features to Your Network page, you can add features and move features around your network's main page.

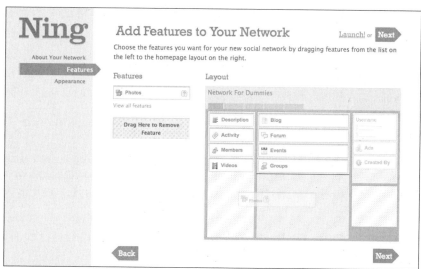

Choosing a Theme

One of the nicest things about running your network on Ning is that you don't need to be a very accomplished designer to make it look like a million dollars! The folks at Ning have taken good care of that and offer you more than 50 great-looking templates (they call them *themes)* that you can use with mini-mal effort.

If you click the Next button on the Add Features to Your Network page, you're taken to the Customize Appearance page, the last step before the launch of your network, as shown in Figure 7-8. From there, follow these steps:

1. **Choose a theme.**

   Doing this is as simple as scrolling using the scroll bar on the right (as shown in Figure 7-8) until you see a theme you like. Then simply click the theme.

Figure 7-8:
The
Customize
Appearance
page is the
last step
before you
launch.

2. **Scroll down the page and then tweak the theme to make it look the way you want it to.**

Under the heading Now, Make It Uniquely Yours, you can adjust the theme settings to a degree that will serve almost all your customization needs, as shown in Figure 7-9.

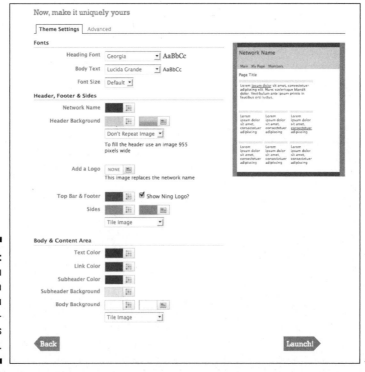

Figure 7-9:
After you
choose a
theme, you
can cus-
tomize its
settings.

I delve into great detail about how you can change your network's appearance in Chapter 8, so if you can live with the default settings of the theme you chose until then, I promise the wait will be well worth it.

3. **When you're done choosing a theme and customizing your network's appearance, click the Launch! button.**

Once you click on the Launch! button, you're taken to your network's main page. At this point, you can sit back and contemplate your network: It's finally up and running!

Defining Profile Questions

Now that your network has been launched, one of the first things to do is to define the questions for your members to answer during their sign-up process. Thinking of the questions will probably take longer than adding them to the network.

When you've thought up your questions, follow these steps to define your profile questions:

1. **Click the Manage link in your network's navigation.**

   This step takes you to the Manage page of your network, a page that you'll visit any time you need to make administrative changes to the network. You can see how this page looks in Figure 7-10.

Figure 7-10: The Manage page lets you make most of the admin changes to the network.

2. **Click the Profile Questions icon in the Your Members section.**

   You're taken to the Profile Questions page, shown in Figure 7-11.

   By default, the Profile Questions page includes gender and location questions, as shown in Figure 7-11. You can leave these as they appear or remove them by clicking the Remove link.

   You can add other questions for your members to answer by clicking the Add Another Question link, as explained in Step 6 of this step list. For each question (new or existing), you need to complete the following fields:

   - *Question Title:* The text you enter in this box is presented to the member during the sign-up process and will also be presented as the heading above the respective answer in the member's Profile Information section on the profile page, as shown in Figure 7-12. The gender and location questions prepopulated by Ning can't have their titles changed.

   - *Answer Type:* This drop-down list gives you several options: One Line Answer (ideal for asking things like "Profession" and "How did you find out about us?"), Longer Answer (suited for questions that require more space to answer), Multiple Choice (whether you want members to be able to choose only one or more than one of many options), Date (to ask for birthdays and other dates), and Website Address (to ask for URLs of Web sites).

     If you pick Multiple Choice as the Answer Type, the space below the drop-down list expands to make room for a new text box titled Choices, as shown in Figure 7-13. If you pick Multiple Choice, check out Steps 3 and 4, but if not, you'll skip those steps.

   - *Required:* Selecting the Required check box makes the question mandatory for members. This means a member trying to sign up won't be able to complete the registration process without answering the question.

   - *Private:* Selecting the Private check box makes the answer to the question visible only to the member, the Network Creator, and the Administrators on the member's profile page.

   - *Add to Advanced Search:* Selecting the Add to Advanced Search check box makes the profile question available among the search criteria in the Advanced Search page for Members.

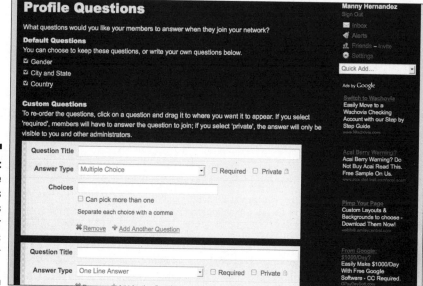

Figure 7-11:
The Profile Questions page lets you enter questions to ask your members.

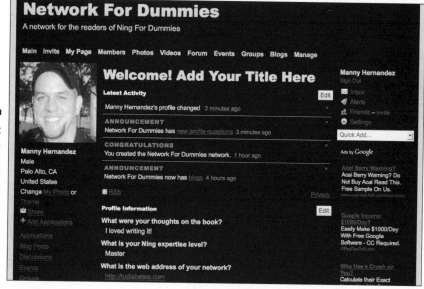

Figure 7-12:
The answers to the profile questions appear in the member's Profile Information section.

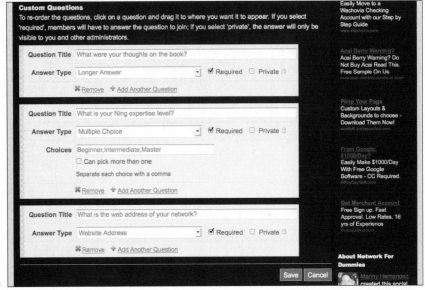

Figure 7-13:
Adding
Multiple
Choice
profile
questions
requires
a little bit
more work.

3. **(Optional) Enter all the choices you want to make available to your members, separating choices with a comma.**

   For instance, if the two options you want to offer are "Slime and Snails" and "Sugar and Spice," enter **Slime and Snails, Sugar and Spice**.

4. **(Optional) If you want to allow your members to pick more than one choice, select the Can Pick More Than One check box.**

5. **(Optional) Reorder questions by clicking any question and dragging it where you need it to appear.**

6. **(Optional) Add or remove questions.**

   You can add another question anywhere by clicking the Add Another Question link above the position where you want the new question to appear. You can also delete any questions by clicking the Remove link for the question.

   Any changes you make to profile questions, such as changing a question itself or removing a question you previously had, have a retroactive effect applying to all members who have signed up to the network up to that point. If you want to preserve their member data, make sure to export it, as explained in Chapter 10.

7. **When you're set with all your profile questions, click the Save button at the bottom of the page.**

   You see a Success! message confirming that your changes have been successfully saved.

Chapter 8

Changing Your Network's Appearance

In This Chapter

▶ Modifying fonts

▶ Modifying the header, footer, and sides

▶ Modifying body and content areas

▶ Managing tabs

In Chapter 7, you discover how to set up your network on Ning, and I touch on choosing your *theme* — the name Ning gives to your network's look and feel. I also mention that I would tell you more about how to modify your theme to match the network you dreamed of — well, as close to that as possible.

In this chapter, I show you how to change the colors, fonts, and backgrounds of your network. I also show you how you can give your network a sexy look with the inclusion of a logo. Last, I cover your network's navigation, how you can reorder its tabs, and add new ones if you need to.

To illustrate the changes you can make to your network's theme and navigation, I try to make the network resemble the cover of a *For Dummies* book. The closest theme I found among the 50+ Ning offers was Dark Slate. If you could see this theme in glorious color, you would notice that the original colors in the theme do not quite match the gorgeous yellow-and-black beelike theme featured on the covers of all *For Dummies* books. But fear not, readers: When you finish this chapter, your network will sport a *For Dummies*-worthy theme. Well, my network will; I imagine you'll want yours to look a bit different.

Modifying the Fonts in Your Network

To modify your published network's appearance, click the Manage link in the navigation and choose the Appearance option in the Your Network section.

Doing so opens the Appearance page, as shown in Figure 8-1. This page looks like one you see during the creation of your network, but it has the theme you chose for your network applied to it.

Figure 8-1: The Appearance page in your network lets you edit your network's theme.

The focus of this chapter is on the Theme Settings tab below the Now, Make It Uniquely Yours heading. Most of the changes you make to the theme settings are reflected in the small preview shown at the bottom of Figure 8-1, in the box where the words *Network Name* appear. However, image changes are not visible through the preview and require you to click the Save button at the bottom of the page.

Set up a private secondary network where you can play with changes to the theme and any other large-scale modifications. This way, you can make sure everything looks well on the secondary network before you apply the changes to your main network for all members to see. Check out Chapter 7 if you need a refresher on how to set up a network.

The first settings you see on the page affect the fonts in the network:

✔ **Heading Font:** You can choose from a drop-down list of standard Web-safe fonts. The font family you choose is applied to the *heading* of the network — that is, the name of your network. Next to the drop-down list are a few letters (AaBbCc) meant to help you preview your font changes before you save them.

  ✔ **Body Text:** You have the same font choices for the body text in the net-
     work. You can also preview the font change next to the drop-down list.

  ✔ **Font Size:** You can choose Small, Default, and Large from the drop-down
     list. The font size you select affects all the text in the network. Sticking
     with the default option works in most cases.

Modifying the Header, Footer, and Sides

Below the Fonts section, the Header, Footer & Sides section gives you a wide
range of options to tweak, as shown in Figure 8-2. (The title "Header, Footer
& Sides" was cut off the top of Figure 8-2, but you can see it at the bottom of
Figure 8-1, earlier in this chapter.)

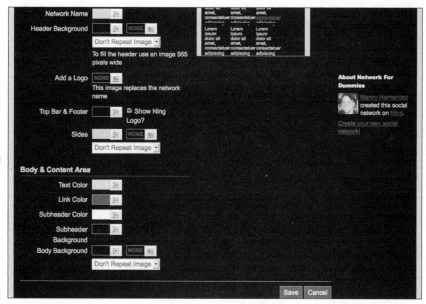

Figure 8-2:
The bot-
tom of the
Appearance
page gives
you more
customiza-
tion options.

This list describes the options shown in the upper portion of Figure 8-2:

  ✔ **Network Name:** This option lets you choose the color for your network
     name. When you click the colored button next to the rectangle, a small
     box appears (see Figure 8-3) where you can pick among a number of
     common colors or choose a specific color by entering its hexadecimal
     code (also called a *hex* code). After you choose the color your network
     name will appear in, click the OK link.

A good Web site for referencing color hexadecimal codes is `www.web monkey.com/reference/Color_Charts`.

✔ **Header Background:** This option allows you to change the background for your network's *header* — the area that contains the network's name, tagline, and navigation. You can modify the background color and/or add a background image.

- *Background color:* To modify the background color, click the colored button next to the first rectangle, make a color selection within the box that appears (refer to Figure 8-3), and then click the OK link.

- *Background image:* To add a background image, click the little picture button next to *NONE*. Doing so opens a box that lets you upload a photo from your computer (see Figure 8-4). Browse for the image on your hard drive, select it, and then click the Done button. If you want to remove an image, select the No Image option and then click Done.

To better understand how the header background image works, think of it as a rectangular hole cut into the page, with your network name left in place, floating on top of the image. If the image you use is at least 955 pixels wide (the width of the header background area), that many pixels of the image will show through the hole. If the image you upload is less than 955 pixels wide, you have the following options (illustrated in Figure 8-5):

- *Don't Repeat Image:* This option aligns the image you upload against the top-left corner of the header background area. The remaining area, from the edges of the image to the edges of the header background area, is filled with the background color you choose.

- *Tile Image:* This option tiles the image, filling the entire space in the header background area.

- *Repeat Vertically:* This option repeats the image vertically to the bottom edge of the header background area.

- *Repeat Horizontally:* This option repeats the image horizontally to the right edge of the header background area.

✔ **Add a Logo:** Hands down, adding a logo one of the coolest things you can do to give your network an identity. In essence, this option lets you upload an image that replaces the network name. Therefore, adding a logo lets your network header sport the same professional look as, say, your corporate Web site or the logo your graphic designer created for your business.

To add a logo, click the little picture button next to *NONE*. Follow the same steps I gave you to upload a header background image.

Your logo image needs to be 955 pixels wide to make sure that the entire image displays and no part of the header background color or network name shows.

✔ **Top Bar & Footer:** This option lets you change the color for the top bar and the footer of your network. The *top bar* gives you convenient access to your Members page, your inbox, and your Friends list. The *footer* displays the copyright notice for the network and other fun things, such as links to the Help page, the Privacy Policy, and the Ning Terms of Service.

- *Color drop-down list:* To change the color, click the colored button next to the rectangle and follow the earlier instructions to change the color for the network name and header background. The color you choose for the top bar is applied to the network footer.

- *Show Ning Logo? check box:* If you want to hide the Ning logo from the top bar, leave the check box unselected.

✔ **Sides:** This option works exactly like the Header Background option, except that it applies to the two vertical (empty) columns on the sides of the network. You can either choose a solid color for them or upload an image to display in the background.

The background images you upload to the sides of the network don't need to be photos. For a cool use of the Sides option, create a 1-pixel-wide image that is as high as you want to make it. Using image editing software, apply a gradient effect to this thin strip. When you upload the image as the background for the sides, choose the Tile Horizontally option from the drop-down list. The result is two neat sides that have a gradient effect as you scroll down your network.

Figure 8-3:
To pick a color, use the box that looks like this one.

Figure 8-4:
To upload an image, use the box that looks like this one.

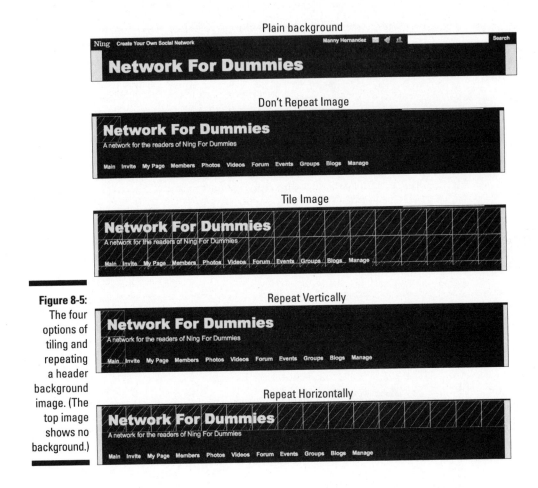

Plain background

Don't Repeat Image

Tile Image

Figure 8-5:
The four options of tiling and repeating a header background image. (The top image shows no background.)

Repeat Vertically

Repeat Horizontally

Modifying the Body & Content Area

Last but not least among the Theme Settings on the Appearance page is the Body & Content Area section. (Refer to the options visible in the lower portion of Figure 8-2, earlier in this chapter.) This is where you fine-tune and tweak the last remaining details of your network's appearance. The first four options in the following list operate the same way as the Network Name option in the preceding section:

✔ **Text Color:** As you can imagine from the name, this option lets you change the color of the text in the body of your network. Changing this color has a very visible effect throughout your network because most of the content on your network shows in the color you select here.

If you need to change the text color, link color, or subheader color, pay close attention to the contrast between the text and the background against which it will be sitting. Doing this is critical to ensure that the written content in your network is easy to read.

Also, depending on the audience your network serves, consider avoiding certain colors altogether. For example, in a network for people with Daltonism (red-green colorblindness), you should have neither green nor red as your text or link color.

✔ **Link Color:** This option lets you change the color of the links in your network in all places but two: the network navigation and the footer. The network navigation takes its color from the Network Name color. The color of the links in the network footer cannot be edited on this page. Their color is automatically picked to ensure that they contrast with the color you choose for the top bar and footer.

✔ **Subheader Color:** This option lets you change the color of a number of elements on the network. Among these are the titles of pages, headers of sections within a page, profile information on profile pages, and a few other items. I encourage you to be bold and try a color that stands out so you can easily spot all the places in your network that are affected by changing this color.

✔ **Subheader Background:** This option lets you change the background in such places as the headers above the list of forum topics and blog posts on the main page.

✔ **Body Background:** This option works much like the Header Background and Sides options explained earlier in this chapter, letting you change the background color for the body of the network. Now that you've met the other elements, you can easily spot the *body* of the network: It's the middle space below the header, between the sides, and above the footer.

You can also add an image to serve as the background of the body of your network. The image can be tiled, repeated vertically or horizontally, or simply sit not tiled or repeated behind your network's body of content.

If all this talk about different areas, colors, and backgrounds in your network seems hard to follow, don't kill yourself over it. It may not seem easy, but once you play with the different settings, you'll see it isn't hard.

If you aren't a savvy designer but still want to tweak your network's color settings, you can use online tools to find great-looking color palettes. One of these tools is Kuler (`http://kuler.adobe.com`), a Web site where designers submit and vote on fabulous color palettes to help inspire you.

If the options covered so far still do not let you accomplish that last little bit you are seeking to accomplish in terms of how things look, there's a chance you need to add your own CSS code. If you are up to the task, jump to Chapter

19, where I go over some of the most important elements of CSS that you need to wrap your head around in your network on Ning.

Managing Your Tabs

Most of the time, the order in which the tabs appear in the navigation bar works just fine (the thinking heads at Ning have tried to make sure the default order fits most needs). But in case you want to shift the order of the links in your network's navigation bar, here is how to do it:

1. **Click the Manage link on the navigation.**

2. **Click the Tab Manager option below the Your Network heading.**

   This takes you to the Tab Manager page, shown in Figure 8-6.

3. **Click the tab you want to move in the list on the left side of the page, drag it to the new location, and drop it.**

Click to add a new tab.

Click to delete a tab.

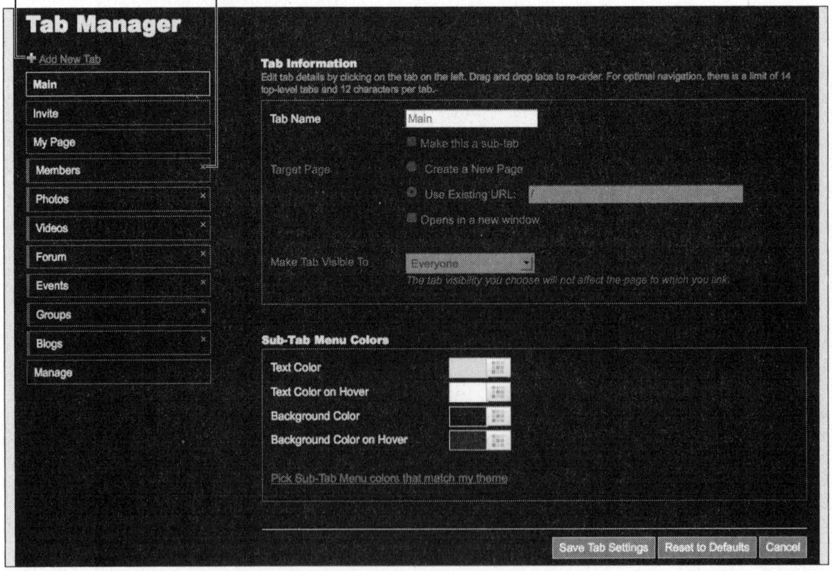

Figure 8-6: The Tab Manager page lets you rename, reorder, and add tabs to your network's navigation.

If you want to remove a tab from the list, simply click the X to the right of the tab (refer to Figure 8-6). You cannot remove the Main, Invite, My Page, and Manage tabs. Every other tab can be removed from the navigation.

On the Tab Manager page, you can also add a new tab to link to an existing or a new page on the network. Here's how:

1. **Click the Add New Tab link at the top left of the Tab Manager page.**

   This adds a new tab (coincidentally labeled New Tab) right above the Manage tab.

   To keep things sane in your navigation, Ning limits the number of top-level tabs you can add to 14. This should be plenty, but it's good to bear in mind, just in case.

2. **Fill in information for your new tab, on the right side of the page:**

   - *Tab Name:* You probably want your tab to be called something other than New Tab. Because your network's tabs cannot exceed 12 characters, you have to be creative with the names of any new tabs.

   - *Make This a Sub-Tab:* You can make the tab appear only when members position their mouse over an existing tab to create the effect of a menu opening beneath it. To do this, check the box next to Make This a Sub-tab. The new tab is indented to the right in the list of tabs.

   - *Target Page:* Each tab needs a page to connect to. If this is an existing page, select the Use Existing URL option and paste the URL into the field next to it. If you want to connect the tab to a new page, select the Create a New Page option and read Chapter 23 for details on what to do next to finish adding a new page. Regardless of the option you choose, you can open the tab in a new window by checking the box next to Opens in a New Window.

   - *Make Tab Visible To:* This drop-down list lets you choose whether you want the tab visible to Everyone (members and other visitors to your network), Members, or Administrators only.

3. **(Optional) Adjust the colors of the subtab menu.**

   Under the Sub-Tab Menu Colors heading on the Tab Manager page, you can change Text Color (the color of the link), Text Color on Hover (the color the link appears in when someone hovers his mouse on it),

Background Color (the color behind the link), and Background Color on Hover (the color behind the link when someone hovers her mouse on it).

These options function exactly the same way as the options to change colors on the Appearance page discussed in the previous section.

4. Click the Save Tab Settings button, and you're done!

If you mess something up, fear not. You have two options for starting over:

- *Click the Cancel button, and you're taken to the Manage page.* From here, you can begin again or leave the settings alone.

- *Click the Reset to Defaults button.* Any tab information you may have entered reverts to how it was before you made any changes.

In Figure 8-7, you can see the result after I added a link to the Dummies. com Web site next to the Manage tab of my network's navigation.

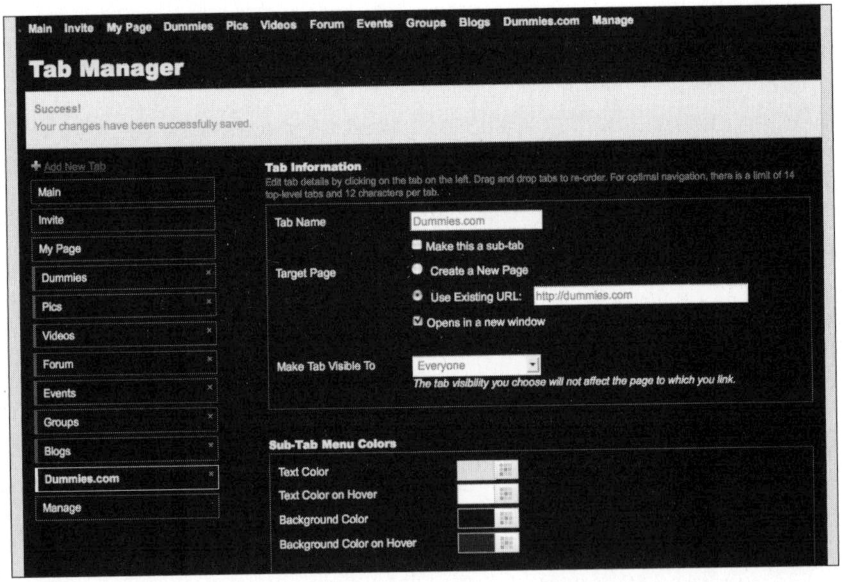

Figure 8-7:
Adding a
new tab
with the Tab
Manager is
a breeze!

When you click a tab, the Tab Information section for that tab becomes editable. You can edit the name of any tab whatsoever, and you can edit all the information about the tabs — except the Main, Invite, My Page, and Manager tabs.

This is handy if you want to rename the tabs in terms more familiar to your members. In Figure 8-7, you can see that I renamed the Members tab Dummies and the Photos tab Pics. This is reflected both on the list of tabs in

Chapter 9

Tweaking Your Network's Main Page

In This Chapter

▶ Adding and removing features

▶ Changing your main page's layout

▶ Managing features on the main page

▶ Adding items to the right column

▶ Including RSS feeds on your main page

▶ Using Text Boxes

*F*irst impressions count! If you don't believe me, why do you think you sometimes find trays with fresh cookies at open houses showing homes for sale or rent? The folks showing the home want to make a good first impression on you.

The same applies to your network. Too bad you can't offer trays with cookies for your visitors, but you can make sure their first impression is a pleasant one. Hopefully, they'll be so happy with what they see that they'll join your network, keep coming back, and tell others about it.

In this chapter, I start to deal with what you can control to make the experience for your members visually appealing, useful, and satisfying when they visit the main page of your network.

Adding and Removing Features

When you created your network, you chose some features to add. Since then, you may have played with the network and decided you should add a few more features — or remove some that don't belong in your network.

You add or remove features on the Add Features to Your Network page. To get there, click the Manage link in your navigation and then click the Features option under Your Network. As shown in Figure 9-1, this page looks like the one you step through during the creation of your network to add features to it.

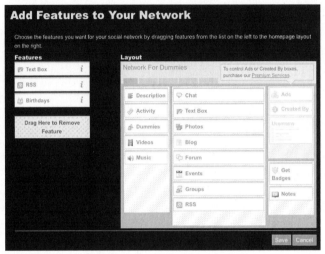

Figure 9-1:
This page lets you add, move, and remove features from your main page.

I discuss how to add features in Chapter 7. If you need to add more features to your network, you just drag them from the list on the left side of the page to your desired location on the right side of the page where the layout of the main page is shown.

If you need to remove a feature you've added, simply drag it from the layout to the gray box labeled Drag Here to Remove Feature.

Changing Your Main Page's Layout

You know how to add features: check! You know how to remove features: check! As you might expect, you can also move features around the main page. You also do this through the Add Features to Your Network page by dragging the feature and dropping it where you want it to appear on the main page — it's that easy.

You have a lot of freedom to move things around, but there are a couple of restrictions:

- ✔ **Username:** You cannot move the Username box anywhere or remove it under any circumstance. This box, safely stationed in the top-right corner of the main page, shows your name and gives you convenient access to your inbox and friends, among other things.

- ✔ **Ads:** You can move the Ads feature only if you purchase the Ning premium service that lets you run your own ads. I talk about premium services in Chapter 18. Even if you are paying for this, you can move the Ads feature only within the right column or the left column, but not into the middle column.

- ✔ **Created By:** You can move or remove the Created By feature only if you purchase the Remove Ning Promotion links premium service, as explained in Chapter 18.

If you're paying for the Control the Ads premium service and need to add an ad to your network's middle column, you can do so with a Text Box. I cover the use of Text Boxes in the final section of this chapter.

Remember the movie in which the aquarium fishes escape and find their way back into the ocean, only to find out they're floating on the sea inside plastic bags? One of them pops the question "Now what?" I'm going to take a wild guess that you may feel that way at this point.

When you start moving features around your main page's layout, you start to get an even better grasp of how much control you have over your network. The possibilities are truly endless, but that doesn't mean all possible layouts will serve your members well.

Depending on their focus, different networks can benefit from the features available in different ways. For example, some networks cannot exist without the Music Player, whereas others may rely more heavily on the Videos or the Photos features.

How you arrange features on the main page of your network directly affects the way in which your members participate, how compelled they may feel to go past the main page during their visits, and how much a visiting nonmember will want to join the network.

Therefore, *always* try to stand in the shoes of your current and potential members. Consider their interests and needs. Take into account the kind of access they have. You may find it hard to believe, but some people still depend on their phone to surf the Web. To help you a little bit, the following considerations should come in handy:

✔ **Show members prominently.** Members are the lifeblood of a network. This is so true that the Members feature is one of the few features your network automatically includes in its layout. (The other two are the network description and the Latest Activity feature.) Displaying members on your main page prominently gives people visiting your network a feel for the members in your network and even hint at the overall type of network you run: family-oriented, animal lover-centric, and so on. Most of my favorite networks include the Members feature near the top of the main page.

A very simple but powerful feature to add somewhere near Members is Birthdays, which shows your member's upcoming birthdays.

✔ **People love to chat.** Chat became available to networks on Ning by mid-2008. Since then, it's become extremely popular. The Ning chat feature lets people do just that in real time. Also, because the chat shows all members who are participating on it as being online, it can come in handy as a means of finding out who is "around" when you visit the network.

If you prefer to have a bit more control of all things chat, you can determine when to hold live chat sessions, which you announce to members. When the session is about to start, you can enable the chat (that is, make it visible to the rest of the members) by checking the box next to Chat in the Add Features to Your Network page, as shown in Figure 9-2, and clicking the Save button. When the chat session is over, you can disable it by unchecking the same box.

Because chat is a feature that involves real-time participation of members, the only way to have total control over it is to monitor it all the time. If you cannot afford time to do this but need to make sure you keep an eye on all conversations in your network, you may be better off not adding the chat feature. Be warned, though: Your members will ask for it.

✔ **Latest Activity pays off.** Your network's Latest Activity feature gives current and prospective members an idea of how active your network is. You should show this feature as close to the top of the main page as possible so it's easy for visitors to the network to see that it is "happening." If you're concerned that your network is still too small and doesn't show enough activity, move it down a bit for now, but don't take it off the main page: The more members join and participate, the more useful the Latest Activity feature becomes.

✔ **Show your pictures and videos.** You may be surprised at how quickly your members start to share photos and videos on your network. They are two of the most used features in social networks on Ning. Knowing this (and how important it is for you to get in your members' shoes), give prominence in your network to the Photos and Videos features.

✔ **Discussion topics galore.** Because of the ease of use (you don't need a photo or video camera to contribute to it), the discussion forum is another incredibly popular feature. Make some room for it in the middle column because the forum is a feature almost all members will expect to find on your network; however, you may not need to station it too close to the top. Reserve those spots for Members or more visual features like Photos and Videos.

✔ **Groups are your member's networks.** The Groups feature empowers members unlike any other feature on the Ning platform. Because your members are bound to come up with ideas you didn't even dream of, groups that become popular are great candidates to feature on the main page as a means to attract new members into the network and give existing members more reasons to come back. Check out Chapter 16 on the use of Google Analytics to learn about popular groups on your network.

✔ **Feature blog posts on the main page.** When you see your members engage in writing blog posts, you may want to feature your members' posts more prominently on your main page as a way to highlight content that is relevant to current and potential new members. Doing so can also be a means to give members recognition. Chapter 17 deals with ways to keep your members engaged and coming back to your network.

✔ **If it's appropriate, put the Music Player front and center.** Networks that focus on artists and music or offer podcasts as a means of connecting with members are ideal candidates for this feature — make the Music Player prominent on the main page. If this is not your network's focus, I don't recommend adding it.

Figure 9-2:
You can easily enable and disable chat through this checkbox.

Managing Features on the Main Page

Adding features to your network and deciding how to place them on the main page are the "What" and the "Where" elements of managing features on your network. This section discusses "How" to display your chosen features.

All features on the main page give you control of at least two things (sometimes more):

✔ How many items to show per feature

✔ How you want the items to display

To select how to display features on your main page, click the Edit button at the top right of the feature box you want to manage.

Next, I deal with the options available for each of the features discussed so far:

✔ **Members:** As shown in Figure 9-3, the Members feature box gives you three options:

- *Display:* This drop-down list lets you choose between Small Thumbnails (shown in Figure 9-3) and Large Thumbnails (shown in Figure 9-4).

- *From:* This drop-down list lets you choose among Newest, Most Popular, and Featured. The Newest option displays the most recent members in the network. The Most Popular option displays the members with the most recent activity on the network, whether comments left to them or contributions on their part. The Featured option allows you to display members that you've previously featured, as explained in Chapter 10.

- *Show:* This drop-down list lets you choose the number of rows of member thumbnails to display, ranging from 0 to 3 if the Members box is in the middle column or 0 to 5 rows if it is in the left or right column. This option gives you a level of control that is very useful when you try to tighten your main page's layout: If you need to shorten the height of the page, you can reduce the number of rows, for instance.

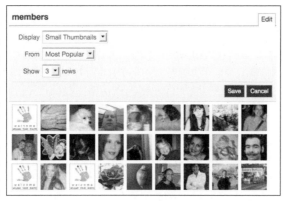

Figure 9-3: You have three options to tailor how you display members on the main page.

Figure 9-4: Large Thumbnails may be a better option for networks with fewer members.

✔ **Birthdays:** The Birthdays feature box has only a single option for you to worry about. You can choose only how many birthdays to show: 1, 3, 5, 10, or 20.

✔ **Latest Activity:** This feature box lets you choose how many and what kinds of events to display. The Show drop-down list lets you choose how many events to show: 0, 4, 8, 12, 16, or 20. Below the drop-down list, clicking the Set What Activity Gets Displayed link takes you to the Latest Activity page, where you can choose what elements should appear in the Latest Activity box. (You can also get to this page by clicking the Manage link in the navigation and then clicking Latest Activity under the Spread the Word heading.)

As shown in Figure 9-5, the Latest Activity page lets you set your display preferences and add a message to the Latest Activity stream.

- *Display Preferences:* Here, you can choose what displays in your network's Latest Activity: New Content; New Profile Comments; New Blog, Discussion and Media Comments; New Friendships; New Members; New Events; Member Updates (changes to their profile pages); and Application Activity. Select the check box next to the type of activity you want Latest Activity to display.

- *Add Message to Latest Activity:* Here, you have two options: Add Facts about the Network and Or Write Your Own Message.

  Add Facts about the Network lets you pick among a number of preformatted messages detailing facts about the network, such as the number of members, the number of photos, the most popular forum post to date, and the number of events. These messages have the heading Did You Know on the Latest Activity box, as shown in Figure 9-6.

  Or Write Your Own Message lets you create your own personalized announcements up to 140 characters in length. These messages have the heading Announcement in the Latest Activity box, as shown in Figure 9-6.

Figure 9-5: This page lets you control the information that appears in Latest Activity.

Figure 9-6: You can also add messages to your network's Latest Activity box.

✔ **Photos:** This feature box lets you choose how many photos to display; what kind of photos to display; and in some instances, from where to pull the photos to display. Click the Edit button to see your choices.

The Display drop-down list lets you choose among these options:

- *Slideshow:* 100 photos are shown automatically, cycling from one to the next until the last one. The slideshow takes up the width of the column where the Photos feature box is located, as shown in Figure 9-7.

- *Thumbnails:* When you choose the Thumbnails option (see Figure 9-8), the Show drop-down list becomes visible, letting you choose the number of rows of photo thumbnails you want to display: 0, 2, 4, 6, 8, or 10. This option may be the most convenient for you to use if you want to make sure visitors with a slower Internet connection have a positive user experience because the slideshow significantly increases the load time of your network's main page.

  The Slideshow and Thumbnails options on the Display drop-down list let you choose where the photos to display are pulled from. You can choose Recently Added, Most Popular, and Featured. But you can also choose among the photo albums you've created. This gives you a very fine level of control over the photos shown in the Photos feature box.

- *Albums:* You can select among Recently Added, Most Popular, and Featured albums via the From drop-down list. You also can choose how many rows of albums you want to display from the Show drop-down list: 0, 2, 4, 6, 8, or 10.

Figure 9-7:
The Photos Slideshow shows the most photos as big as they can be displayed.

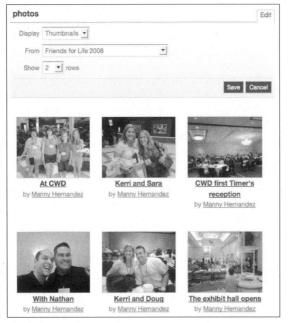

Figure 9-8:
The
Thumbnails
option
allows you
to display up
to 10 rows
of photo
thumbnails.

✔ **Videos:** The Videos feature box lets you choose the following:

- *From:* This drop-down list gives you the Featured, Recently Added, and Highest Rated options.

- *Show:* This drop-down list lets you choose to display 0 to 12 videos.

If the Videos feature box is in the left or right column, videos appear as thumbnails you can click, taking you to the video page, which does not have as much impact on page load times. However, videos in the middle column display in a video player, which translates into longer page-load times. Therefore, if you have your Videos feature in the middle column of your network, I recommend you limit the number of videos to display to no more than three or four.

✔ **Forum:** The Forum feature box gives you the most options to choose among, as shown in Figure 9-9.

The View drop-down list gives you two options: Categories and Discussions. Choosing Categories displays categories you may have created in your discussion forum for topics to be classified under. You can read more about creating and managing forum categories in Chapter 11. Additionally, choosing Categories displays only the Show drop-down list, letting you display 0, 1, 2, 3, 4, 5, 10, or up to 20 categories.

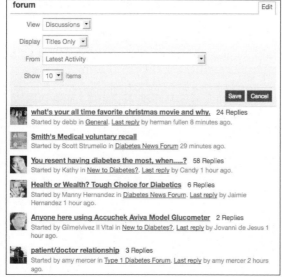

Figure 9-9:
The Forum
feature box
provides
you very
detailed
control.

Selecting Discussions displays discussion topics in the Forum feature box. Three other options become available:

- *Display:* This drop-down list gives you the option to show titles only or a detail view. The Titles Only option (shown in Figure 9-9) limits the information displayed to the title of the topic, the number of replies, the member who started the discussion, the category it belongs to (if any), and the time stamp of the last reply.

  In addition to the information shown with the Titles Only option, the Detail View option (shown in Figure 9-10) displays the first three lines of the opening post below the discussion title.

- *From:* This drop-down list lets you choose among a wide range of options: Latest Activity, Newest Discussions, Most Replies, Featured, My Discussions Only, and Discussions from a Category.

  Latest Activity displays topics with the most recent activity (new topics as well as recent replies) at the top.

  Newest Discussions shows only the most recent discussions.

  Most Replies shows the discussion topics with the most replies at the top.

  Featured showcases featured topics in the Forum feature box. (Featuring discussions is discussed in Chapter 11 — and let there be no discussion about it.)

My Discussions Only lets you display only your discussion topics, which may be useful in very special cases. (One of them would be if you have a super-sized ego.)

Discussions from a Category lets you display discussions that are added to a specific category in your forum.

- *Show:* This drop-down list lets you display 0, 1, 2, 3, 4, 5, 10, or up to 20 discussion topics.

✔ **Groups:** The Groups feature box gives you two very straightforward options:

- *From:* This drop-down list gives you the following options, Most Recent, Most Members, Latest Activity, and Featured.

Most Recent displays the groups that have been added most recently to your network.

Most Members shows the group with the most members.

Latest Activity lets you be a bit more hands-off; it dynamically displays the groups with the latest activity.

Featured lets you control which groups you want to display, picking only those groups you've featured (see Chapter 12).

- *Show:* This drop-down list lets you display 0, 1, 2, 3, 4, 5, 10, or up to 20 groups.

Figure 9-10:
The Detail
View option
lets you see
a bit more
about each
discussion.

✔ **Events:** Because of their uniqueness (they represent activities with a location, date, and time tied to them), events have a few options that are not available in other feature boxes. The three drop-down lists available when you click the Edit button in the Events feature box are

- *Display:* This drop-down list lets you pick List View, Calendar, or Detail View. List View is shown in Figure 9-11. In addition to the event name, date, and time, you see only the location for each event.

  If you choose Calendar, the colorful icon next to each event is dropped for a handy-dandy calendar showing the current month with convenient links labeled Last Month and Next Month underneath it. The Calendar view is shown in Figure 9-12.

  If you choose Detail View, the icons shown are a tad bigger and the information shown for each event includes the event organizer, the event type, and the first few lines of the event description.

- *From:* This drop-down list lets you choose between Upcoming Events and Featured Events. Upcoming Events shows all upcoming events, up to the total number that you choose to show. Featured Events gives you an extra bit of control over the events shown on the main page, letting you feature individual events, which in turn displays them in the feature box. You find out how to feature events in Chapter 12.

- *Show:* This drop-down list lets you display 0, 2, 4, 6, 8, or 10 events.

✔ **Blog Posts:** The Blog Posts feature box gives you three drop-down lists to control how and how many posts display:

- *Display:* This drop-down list works just like the Display drop-down list for the Forum feature box, giving you the option to choose between Detail View and Titles Only.

- *From:* This drop-down list lets you choose among Recently Added, Most Popular, Most Comments, Featured, and My Posts Only.

  Recently Added displays the most recent blog posts only.

  Most Popular displays the most viewed blog posts.

  Featured gives you the means to display posts you may have featured, which is a great way to highlight contributions from your members.

  My Posts Only is similar to the My Discussions Only option and is a handy tool to conveniently make announcements on the main page.

- *Show:* This drop-down list lets you display 0, 1, 2, 3, 4, 5, 10, or 20 posts.

 You can hide a certain feature from view on the main page without removing it from your network. Click the Edit button above the feature box and select 0 (the first option available) from the Show drop-down list within the panel that appears.

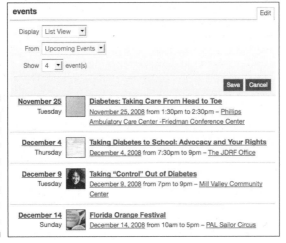

Figure 9-11:
The Events
List View
displays
just enough
information
about each
event.

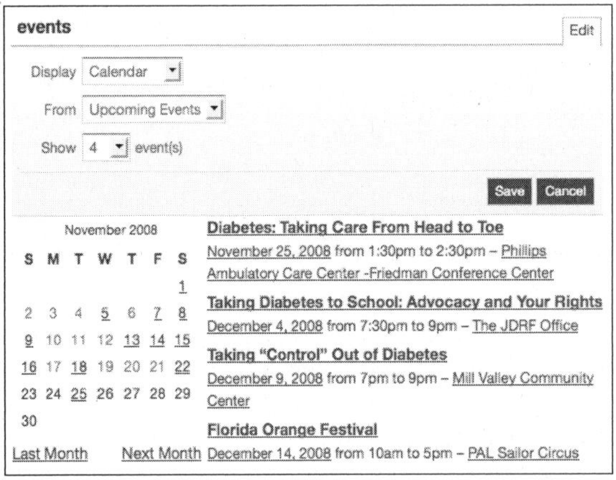

Figure 9-12:
The Events
Calendar
offers
additional
conve-
nience to
the List
View.

Adding Items to the Right Column

You can add features on your network's main page in the left column, the middle column, or the right column. Whatever you add to the left column and middle column appears only on the main page. But the right column is a different story.

Features you add to the top part of the right column appear on all pages of your network (refer to Figure 9-1, earlier in this chapter). This makes the right column a very important element of your network.

So what do you put in the right column? Glad you asked. Here are a few items that garner the most attention from appearing in the right column (and members always know where to find them):

- **Your own ads:** If you pay the premium service to run your own ads (see Chapter 18), you need to make sure to place the ads in the right column. Even if you add other ads on your main page or throughout your network, having ads in the right column of the network ensures that all pages visited by your members present an ad. If you use a service like Google AdSense, which displays different ads depending on the context of the page, you see how having the right column as the place for your ads is a no-brainer.

- **Donate buttons:** These buttons are there to help you raise money, so you should also place these in the right column to maximize their chance of getting seen (and clicked).

- **Elements tied to spreading the word about your network:** This includes the Get Badges feature and any text boxes that include links to other pages you may use to help you drive traffic to your network, such as your profile pages on Twitter, Facebook, or MySpace.

- **Links to reference pages:** If you have them, you might want to include a link to reference pages, such as a User Guide or your Terms of Use.

Including RSS Feeds on Your Main Page

Let's face it: Because someone else has done it before or someone else does a better job at it than you can afford, there may be cases where you might benefit from syndicating someone else's content. Nowadays this is done very easily by using a technology called RSS (Really Simple Syndication).

In a nutshell, RSS "pushes" changes to Web sites that include so-called RSS feeds in them. RSS feeds can come from blogs, news sites, Web sites with frequently updated content, and so on. You too can take advantage of RSS feeds in your network on Ning. Here's how:

1. **Go to your Features page by clicking the Manage link in your navigation and then clicking Features below the Your Network heading.**

2. **Drag the RSS feature from the list of features on the left to the place on the main page layout where you want it to display.**

   Do this as many times as you need, one RSS feature per RSS feed you want to add.

3. **Click the Save button.**

4. **Click the Main link in your navigation.**

5. **Locate the RSS feature box on your main page and click the Add RSS link, as shown in Figure 9-13.**

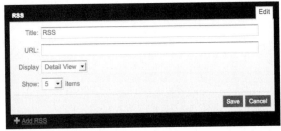

6. **Change the title from RSS to something relevant to the RSS feed that you're adding.**

   For example, I added a feed pulling all entries in Google News with the words *for dummies*. (If you perform a search for a term in Google News, the results page gives you a link to an RSS feed that you can use as explained in Step 7.) For this RSS feed, an appropriate title could be Dummies in the News.

7. **Add the URL for the RSS feed; you can obtain the URL in the Web site that offers the RSS feed.**

   Typically, you can copy the URL from your browser's navigation bar (where you type a Web address) after clicking the little orange RSS icon (shown in Figure 9-14).

8. **Choose between Detail View and Titles Only in the Display drop-down list.**

   Detail View shows the details beneath the title for each entry in the RSS feed. Take a look at the details for a few entries in the feed you are using to determine whether showing them is a good idea. If not, choose Titles Only to display only the title for each of the entries pulled by the RSS feed.

9. **Determine how many items you want to show from the feed and choose 0, 1, 2, 3, 4, 5, 10, or 20 from the Show drop-down list.**

   This decision is based strictly on the space available on your main page.

10. **Click the Save button.**

After you add an RSS feed, the items you choose to display appear in the format you select (detailed or title view), as shown in Figure 9-15. When visitors to your main page click a link, they are taken to the page that hosts the content.

Figure 9-14:
The RSS
icon directs
you to RSS
feeds you
can add
to your
network.

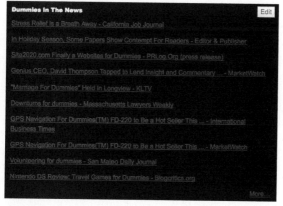

Figure 9-15:
RSS feeds
blend
into your
network's
main page,
offering visi-
tors more
content.

Although you can add as many as 10 RSS feeds to your main page, I highly recommend that you don't add more than two or three. This consideration has to do with speed: Your main page will load as fast as the slowest RSS feed. Stacking RSS feed upon RSS feed adds to your total home page load time, potentially resulting in a painfully slow home page experience.

Using Text Boxes

Ning has already thought of most of the features you need to build your social network. But they knew you'd have needs that may not be covered by the features they offer, no matter how long the list.

Text Boxes are there to cover those special needs. Think of them as empty boxes that let you add almost anything to your main page: plain text, links, bulleted or numbered lists, images, video, JavaScript code, and the list goes on and on.

When you add a Text Box (by dragging and dropping Text Box on the Features page just like you do with RSS features), the Add Text link appears. Click it or the Edit button at the top right of the Text Box. Your editable space opens, as shown in Figure 9-16.

Figure 9-16:
A Text Box lets you add almost anything not already offered by Ning.

The top line in Figure 9-16 lets you insert a title if you want to. In the text area at the bottom, you can type away and format your text; add an image; upload a file; or copy and paste HTML code from another Web site, such as YouTube. To add an image, click the second icon from the right. To upload a file, click the last icon on the right. In both cases, you can upload an item or insert an existing one.

At the bottom of the Text Box, you see the Add a Widget to This Textbox link. When you click the link, you're taken to the Widgets page, which contains examples of widgets to let you add popular news items from CNN, interesting trivia, the latest *Dilbert* comic strip, clips from *Saturday Night Live,* and so on. If these don't get your widget juices flowing, the page contains a list of widget providers to help you find what you need.

The examples on the Widgets page are all well-designed third-party Adobe Flash applications for you to embed in your Text Boxes. But beware of widgets! Some widgets can be resource hogs: Add too many of them, and you may hurt the load time for your network's home page. Other widgets may even cause your network to break or not display correctly, so try out any widgets you may want to add on a test network before you add them to your actual network.

Chapter 10

Managing Members and Profile Pages

Members can make or break your network. I don't mean break as in "crash, bring to its knees" break, but rather "I ain't coming back to this site anymore" break. Sounds like a big statement; it is. Largely, the members you welcome and feature in your network set the tone of your network. Therefore, it pays to spend time managing them.

In this chapter, I discuss the tools that you and your network's Administrators can use to manage your members: selecting who can and cannot join, featuring members after they've joined, promoting members if they can help you more, and blocking members if they're not being good citizens in your network. Additionally, you find out how to limit what your members can do with their profile pages.

Moderating Members

The first option you have to manage your members is to make your network private and set it up so that only invited people can join, as explained in Chapter 7. This may be ideal if you want to run a network for a private organization, a school, or a family where it's important to restrict access. But making a network private isn't the best option if you want as many people as possible to join.

A slightly more relaxed level of management is to moderate the members that request to join your network. This is done very easily:

1. **Click the Manage link in your network's navigation.**

2. **Select the Network Privacy option below Your Members.**

   The Network Privacy page appears.

3. **On the Network Privacy page, select the Approve New Members before They Can Join check box, as shown in Figure 10-1.**

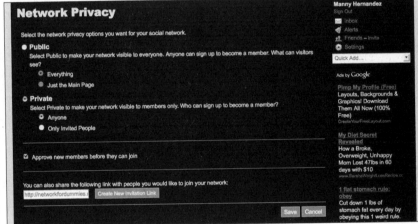

Figure 10-1: The Network Privacy page lets you moderate new members in your network.

The ability to set up your network with member moderation is independent of the network's being public or private. *Public* networks can be set up to let anyone see the main page of the network or see pages beyond the home page without being a member. *Private* networks can be set up to be invite-only or available to anyone to join; in both cases, nothing in the network is accessible to nonmembers.

New members who sign up for your network receive a message explaining that their membership is pending approval, as explained in Chapter 2.

As a Network Creator, you have the chance to review, approve, decline, or ban the membership request. You have a new member to approve when:

- ✔ **You receive an e-mail notifying you.** The e-mail contains the member's name and e-mail address, as well as a link that takes you to a page where you can view the person's profile. This page lets you accept or decline the membership request, as shown in Figure 10-2. You can handle the request by clicking the Actions drop-down list and selecting either Accept Membership or Decline Membership.

✔ **You view the number of new members awaiting approval.** The number of new members awaiting membership is shown in the Awaiting Approval box in your network's right column (refer to Figure 10-2). When you click the link with the number of new members, you're taken to the page where you can accept them or decline them.

Either way, if you approve the person's membership request, he receives a welcome e-mail.

Figure 10-2:
You can approve, decline, or ban new members from the network.

Featuring Members

People like to feel loved and recognized. Luckily, networks on Ning give you the means to show your members some love — *featuring* them.

You feature members two ways: through the Members section or through the member's profile page. Either one results in the member's photo being added at the beginning of the Featured Members bundle at the top of the Members section, as shown in Figure 10-3.

Figure 10-3:
You can feature members through the Members section.

To feature a member via the Members section:

1. **Click the Members link on the navigation.**

   The Members page appears.

2. **Find the member you want to feature.**

   Type in the member's name in the search box at the top of the page and click the Search Members button; or click successive pages (at the bottom of the Members section) showing the photos of members until you find the member you want to feature.

3. **Click the Feature link next to the member's photo.**

   This adds the member to the top of the list of Featured Members.

To feature a member via the member's profile page, as shown in Figure 10-4:

1. **Go to the member's page.**

   Click the member's photo anywhere on the network.

2. **Click the Feature link below the Admin Options header on the left side of the profile page.**

   This step adds the member to the top of the list of Featured Members.

If you choose to display your featured members on your network's main page, the members you feature in the Members section will appear in the Members box on the main page.

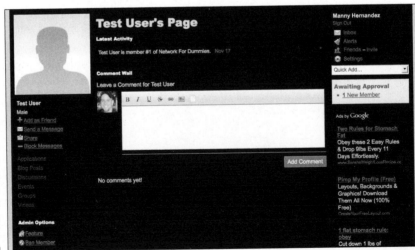

Figure 10-4:
You can also feature members through their profile page.

Managing Members

When members have been around long enough, they show their true colors. Some of them stand out particularly as candidates to become Administrators. Some of them also stand out because they don't belong in your network.

This section discusses how to manage both extremes.

Promoting members

Promoting someone to Administrator should not be taken lightly, because Administrators have lots of power in the network (power to do things and to undo them, including the removal — accidental or not — of lots of content from the network). For details on the things that Administrators can and cannot do in the network, make sure to read Chapter 13.

Promoting someone to Administrator in the network is very easy to do:

1. **Click the Manage link in your network's navigation.**

2. **Select the Members option below Your Members.**

   This step takes you to the Manage Members page, as shown in Figure 10-5.

3. **Find the member you want to promote.**

   Search for her by using the Search box next to the Search button or clicking successive pages at the bottom of the Members section until you find the member you want to promote.

4. **Select the check box next to the member's name, click the Actions drop-down list, and select the Set Role: Administrator option.**

   If you need to demote an Administrator to member level, follow the same steps, but choose the Set Role: Member option from the Actions drop-down list.

Figure 10-5:
This page allows you to promote, demote, and ban members.

Manage Members

Manny Hernandez
Sign Out

Members (6574)   Administrators (9)   Invited (6133)   Banned (208)

✦ Invite More People

Inbox (313 new)
Alerts
Friends (4 requests)
Settings

Actions... ▾   🖉 Manage Roles   manny   Search

Quick Add...

Showing 2 members matching "manny". View All Members   Advanced Search

	Name	Email	Role	Date Joined
☐	manny contreras		Member	Oct. 22, 2008
☐	Manny Hernandez		Network Creator	Mar. 5, 2007

Help TuDiabetes

Donate

Our Community Supporters

✦ Export All Member Data (.CSV)

Ads by Google

To save yourself the need to search for the Administrator, you can click the Administrators tab (next to the Members tab), which hides all members who aren't Administrators from view. (The Administrators tab is visible only to Network Creators and Administrators.)

Banning members

Promoting members, as I discuss in the preceding section, is not something you do (or need to do) every day. However, promoting a member feels good. You announce it to other members, and it's a fun event. Too bad you don't need to promote people more often! Why? Because the opposite action (banning someone) is not as much fun and, unfortunately, happens a lot more.

I'm not saying you're going to be banning members from dawn 'til dusk, but no matter how innocent your network is or how much you believe this is not going to affect it, you're going to find yourself banning members.

You may be able to avoid banning a member by reaching out to him via private messages first. You can explain to him why his actions or some content posted by him could lead to your banning him. However, this may not work. Some people clearly don't care about you or your network: They want promote their scam or spam your members promoting their product without your consent. So you'd better know the two ways to ban someone from your network:

- ✔ **Through the Members management page:** Follow the same steps you follow to promote a member. After you check the box next to the member you want to ban, click the Actions drop-down list and choose Ban from Network. You're then asked to confirm your decision; click the Ban button.

- ✔ **Through the member's profile page:** Follow the same steps you follow to feature a member, but instead of clicking the Feature link, click the Ban Member link.

Banning a member presents you with the confirmation window shown in Figure 10-6. To proceed with the ban, click the Ban button. To backpedal on the ban, click the Cancel button.

When the member is banned, the profile page is no longer visible to others, and all contributions the member made to the network (content added, comments left on other members' walls, and so on) are deleted. This means contributions do not come back even if you remove the ban on the member later. If you remove the ban on the member, the profile information originally entered reappears on the member's profile page.

If a banned member tries to sign into the network, she sees the page shown in Figure 10-7, which explains that she's been banned from the network.

The same page gives the member an opportunity to contact you. This typically results in a variation of the "Why was I banned?" message, which you can expect to hit your inbox a short while after you click the Ban button.

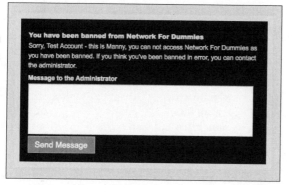

If you need to remove the ban on a member, follow these steps:

1. **Click the Manage link in your network's navigation.**

2. **Select the Members option below Your Members.**

3. **Click the Banned tab above the list of members.**

4. **Check the box next to the name of the member that you want to remove the ban from.**

5. **Click the Remove Ban button.**

Managing Profile Pages

Moving things around, changing colors, and adding applications to your profile page can be some of the most fun a member can have in a network on Ning. But hey! Maybe you have a very good reason to forbid your members from changing anything on their profile pages. The good news (for you) is that you can control what they can do on their profile pages.

By clicking the Manage link in your network's navigation and clicking the Feature Controls link, you arrive on the Feature Controls page, as shown in Figure 10-8.

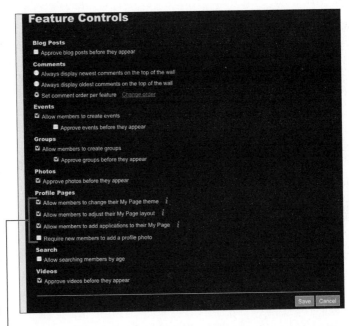

Figure 10-8:
The Feature Controls page lets you limit the use of a number of features.

Use these options to control what members can change on their pages.

At the bottom of this page, you have three options to control how much or how little your members can do on their profile page. All three are selected by default:

> ✔ **Allow members to change their My Page theme:** This option allows your members to customize the appearance of their My Page. If you deselect it, the option to change the My Page theme becomes unavailable to members.

✔ **Allow members to adjust their My Page layout:** This option lets your members move features on their My Page. If you deselect it, all the profile pages have the same layout.

✔ **Allow members to add applications to their My Page:** If deselected, this option removes all OpenSocial applications from your members' profile pages. If you select this check box, your members are able to add OpenSocial applications to their profile page. You can find out more about OpenSocial applications in Chapter 21.

There! Not the most popular options to disable — if you ask me — but you may have very good reasons to do so.

Exporting Member Data

You may want to export your member data for a number of reasons:

✔ To analyze it in Excel, so you can learn about the demographics of your network

✔ To gather members' e-mail addresses so you can send them a newsletter, assuming you've asked them whether it's okay for you to do so

✔ To have a backup of the data

Whatever your reason for doing it, follow these steps to export all the answers your members entered during their registration:

1. **Click the Manage link in your navigation.**

2. **Click the Members link below the Your Members heading.**

3. **Scroll to the bottom of the page.**

4. **Click the Export All Member Data (.CSV) link.**

5. **Click OK in the window that appears, which prompts you to confirm whether you want to start the export process.**

   The more members you have, the longer this process takes.

6. **Make sure to keep the browser window open during the export process.**

   When the export finishes, you're presented with a window confirming the success. As shown in Figure 10-9, click the link titled This Link to save the CSV document containing the member data on your local hard drive.

Figure 10-9:
Ning lets
you con-
veniently
export all
your mem-
ber data.

complete!

Your Member Data has been exported.
Click this link in order to save it to your
desktop.

OK

Chapter 11

Managing the Forum, Notes, and Chats

*Y*ou have your network up. You've made it look nice. You have members coming in the door, and you've decided what they can do (and not do). Now you have to deal with the features in more depth, creating and managing content so your network starts to take shape.

In this chapter, you read about your network's Forum, Notes, and Chat features — how to set them up and make the most of them.

Your Network's Forum

The *forum* is the area in your network where members can initiate new discussion topics or respond to existing ones. (You may have heard about this referred to elsewhere as a *discussion board.*) Unlike chat, the forum lets members in your network communicate publicly with one another in a way that doesn't require them to be online at the same time.

The forum is bound to be one of the busy areas in your network, so it's worth paying close attention to: creating categories for posts to go in, featuring discussions, moderating them, and starting new ones.

Managing the forum

Managing the forum is almost an art. I know that sounds clichéd, but it really is. Let me show you why.

Click your network's Manage link at the top, and on the Manage page that appears, click the Discussion Forum link below the Your Network heading. The Manage Forum page appears, as shown in Figure 11-1.

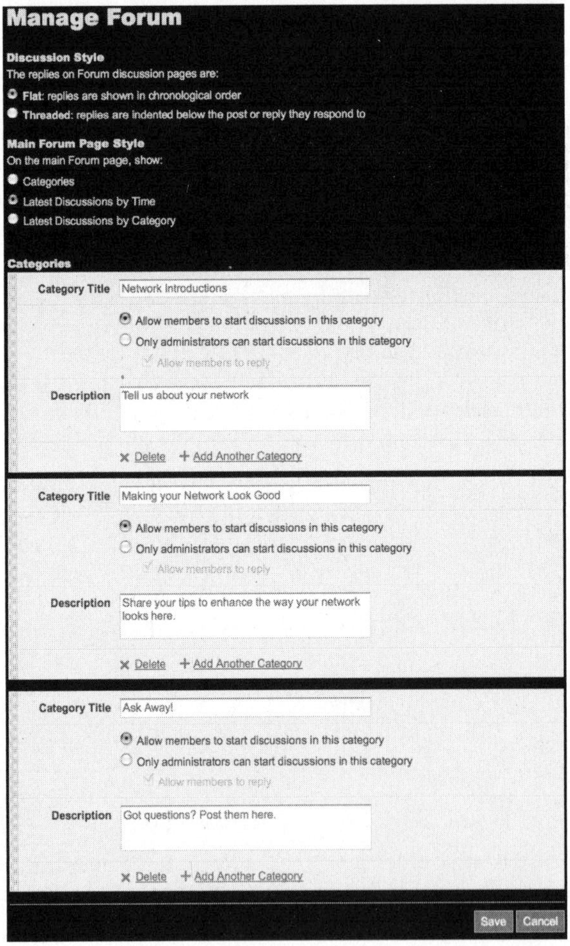

Figure 11-1:
The Manage
Forum page
lets you
control your
forum's
style and
categories.

Starting from the top, this page lets you change the following on the forum:

- ✔ **Discussion Style:** This area controls how replies in a forum topic are shown. You have two options:

  - *Flat:* This option shows all replies in a forum topic in chronological order (from oldest to most recent). This can be convenient in some cases but confusing if you want to follow "conversations" between members within a topic. Figure 11-2 shows how the flat discussion style looks.

  - *Threaded:* This option indents replies that are posted about a specific post, allowing members to more easily follow the flow of a discussion. This style is my favorite. Figure 11-3 shows how the same discussion topic looks with the threaded discussion style.

- ✔ **Main Forum Page Style:** This option lets you modify how the main page of your forum looks. You have three choices:

  - *Categories:* This option displays all the categories in your forum. This is one of the cleanest options available, although it doesn't make it easy to visualize the most recent discussion topics. Figure 11-4 shows how the main Forum page looks when you select the Categories option. From the View drop-down list, members can switch from Categories to Discussions. When you choose Discussions, you're given more options in a Sort By drop-down list. The options you can sort by are Latest Activity, Newest Discussions, and Most Popular.

  - *Latest Discussions by Time:* This option simply lists the most recent discussion topics sorted by latest activity (when the topic started or when a new reply was posted). When this option is selected, members can sort the discussion topics by Latest Activity (the default order), Newest Discussions, or Most Popular by selecting one of those alternatives from the Sort By drop-down list, as shown in Figure 11-5.

  - *Latest Discussions by Category:* This option shows all categories as a list on the left side of the main Forum page. It also groups discussion topics under their respective category, sorting them chronologically. It is a blend of sorts between the first two options (Categories and Latest Discussions by Time). You can see how it looks on the main Forum page in Figure 11-6.

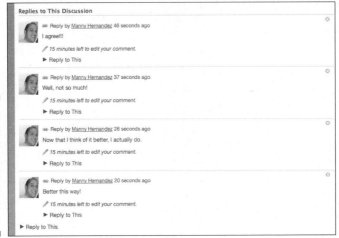

Figure 11-2:
Choosing
Flat as the
discussion
style lists
all replies
chrono-
logically.

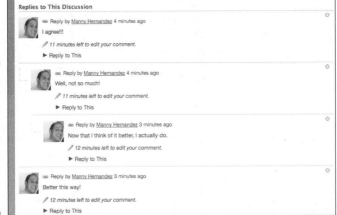

Figure 11-3:
The
Threaded
discussion
style lets
readers
follow the
topic more
easily.

Figure 11-4:
Listing
categories
provides a
cleaner look
but makes
it harder to
find recent
topics.

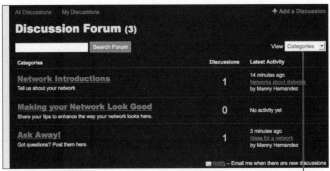

Choose an option to determine how this page looks.

Figure 11-5:
Listing
Latest
Discussions
by Time:
better to
identify
recent
topics.

Figure 11-6:
Listing
Latest
Discussions
by Category
is a nice
compromise.

✔ **Categories:** At the bottom of the Manage Forum page, you have the listing of categories in the forum. Before you create any categories, there is an empty Category Title/Description placeholder for a category, so you can start fleshing out and adding information for that category and new ones you may need. As shown in Figure 11-1, earlier in this chapter, you can enter the following information for each category (you can actually do this for multiple categories at a time):

• *Category Title:* The category is listed in the forum under this name.

• *Who can post on the category:* You have two options. You can allow members to start discussions in the category or allow only Administrators to start discussions in the category. If you select the second option, the check box below it lets you set up the category to allow members to reply (checked by default). If you don't want members to be able to reply in the category you're creating, uncheck the box. This can be useful when you want to keep a category for network announcements (one-way communications to members).

- *Description:* This text explains what kinds of discussions are appropriate in the category you are creating. The description text appears below the category title on the main Forum page as well as on the category page itself.

- *Delete or Add Another Category:* If you change your mind and don't want the category anymore, click the Delete link. If you want to add another category, click the Add Another Category link that appears directly above the location on the page where you want the new category to appear.

When you finish making any changes to the style or categories in the forum, click the Save button at the bottom to save your changes.

Managing forum discussions

A Network Creator or an Administrator has a lot of control over discussion topics on the network. As shown in Figure 11-7, the following options can be found below the Admin Options header:

- ✔ **Feature:** Clicking this link pushes the discussion topic to the top of the featured discussions list. If you set the Main Forum Page Style option to list Categories or Latest Discussions by Time, featured discussions appear at the top of the main Forum page under the Featured Discussions header. Also, featured discussions appear in the Forum feature box on the main page of the network if you set it up as explained in Chapter 9. When you click this link, it changes to read Stop Featuring, which you can click to, not surprisingly, stop featuring the discussion.

- ✔ **Close Discussion:** Clicking this option prevents any further replies from being added to the discussion. This option is also available to the member who started the discussion, not only to Administrators and to the Network Creator. When you click the link, it changes to read Re-open Discussion, which you can click to allow further replies to be posted. It's a good practice to leave one last post in the topic explaining the reason for closing the discussion.

- ✔ **Add Tags:** This option (also available to the member who started the discussion) works just like the Add Tags link for photos and videos (see Chapter 4), letting you describe with keywords what the topic is about.

- ✔ **Delete Discussion:** Clicking this link results in the removal of the entire discussion topic, deleting the initial post along with all the replies. Before removing the topic, you get a confirmation box asking whether you are sure that you want to do so. This option, along with the Feature option, is visible only to the Network Creator and to Administrators of the network.

If you want to remove a single reply in a discussion topic, not the entire discussion, click the small X on the top right of the post you want to delete, as shown Figure 11-8.

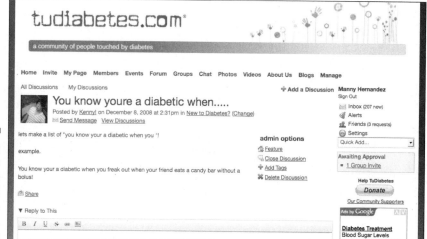

Figure 11-7:
The Admin Options give you control over discussion topics.

Figure 11-8:
Network Creators and Administrators can delete posts by clicking the X.

Click to delete this single reply.

Notes in Your Network

If you've heard of Wikipedia, the Notes feature lets you do something similar to a certain extent: It's a *wiki* (a Web page on which content can be added or edited by people who visit it). However, the big difference is that Notes can be added or edited only by the Network Creator or Administrators.

The Notes feature lets you create static pages with HTML formatting, which comes in handy for a variety of things. For example, you can create Notes for a network Help page, an About Us page, a New User Guide, articles, recipes, and much more.

This section goes into detail about the Notes feature and about how you can take advantage of it.

Adding notes

Notes is not included by default among the features that launch with your network, so before you can add any notes, you need to make sure to add Notes as a feature to your network. To add the Notes feature, click the Manage link on your network's navigation and click the Features icon below the Your Network header. Click the Notes feature in the Features list on the left and drag it where you want to include it on your network's main page, as explained in Chapter 7. One area I find it useful to add Notes to is the bottom-right corner of the main page, where it's fairly nonobtrusive.

When you add the Notes feature, Notes is a new option in your network's navigation. Click it to add a note. The page that opens is in itself a note, titled Notes Home by default, as shown in Figure 11-9.

Figure 11-9:
Clicking
Notes takes
you to
the Notes
Home page.

From the Notes Home page, you can do the following:

- ✔ To add a new note, click the Add a Note link at the top right of the page.

- ✔ To view all notes, click the All Notes link on the left side of the page or click the Click Here link next to To View All Notes.

- ✔ To feature the note you're on, click the Feature link under the Admin Options heading. Featuring a note has a similar effect to featuring a discussion topic but highlights it on the Notes page and the Notes box on the main page.

- ✔ To edit the note you're on, click the Edit Note link below Feature. When you click Edit Note, the page shown in Figure 11-10 appears.

When the note is in editing mode, you can modify its title, which appears with a yellow background, and the note's content.

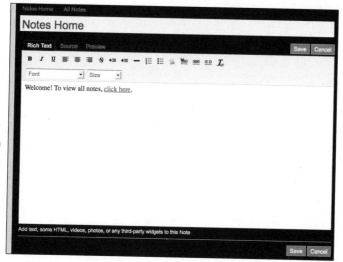

Figure 11-10:
Editing a
note lets
you modify
its title and
its content.

You can edit the content of the note in Rich Text format or in Source format and preview your changes:

🖝 **The Rich Text option** lets you edit the note in a way that resembles how the note appears to those who view it after it's saved. You have a bar above the content window, with buttons that facilitate the formatting of the note's content. You can see the bar in detail in Figure 11-11.

A couple points to keep in mind while you use the Rich Text option are

- Adding an image larger than the width of the note results in the image's resizing. If you aren't happy with the resulting size (if it's still too big), click a corner of the image and slide it to resize it to your liking — all of this without having to mess with the HTML code!

- The Rich Text formatting options take care of most of the needs you are bound to run into. But if you need to tweak things down to the pixel level, you're better served with the Source option. For example, if you want to embed video and other widgets, you would have to select the Source option.

🖝 **The Source option** allows you to control the HTML code of the content in the note. If you're familiar with HTML, help yourself. However, you're bound to run into some natural restrictions put in place by the folks at Ning, mainly for your own protection. See the Technical Stuff note about what flies and what is stripped from the code if you try to add it to a note.

Notes support plain text and basic HTML. JavaScript, CSS expressions, and the following HTML tags are not supported: `<script>`, `<frame>`, `<iframe>`, `<html>`, and `<body>`.

✔ **The Preview option** allows you do just that: preview your note before you save the changes. This option lets you see the note exactly as it will look when published, but it doesn't allow you to make any edits; you have to go back to the Rich Text option or the Source option to do that.

When you finish with any changes to a note (these details apply equally when adding or editing notes), click the Save button (either the one above the content window or the one below it). You're taken to the note's page, which reflects the changes you made.

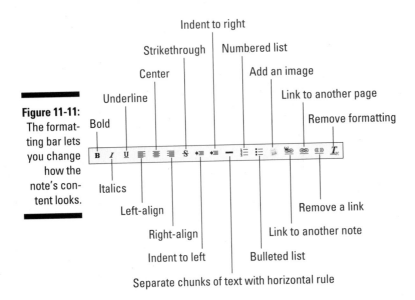

Figure 11-11: The formatting bar lets you change how the note's content looks.

Indent to right

Strikethrough   Numbered list

Center   Add an image

Underline   Link to another page

Bold   Remove formatting

Italics

Left-align   Remove a link

Right-align   Link to another note

Indent to left   Bulleted list

Separate chunks of text with horizontal rule

The many uses of notes

I hope your wheels are spinning with the many ways you can use Notes. In case you're not as excited as I am, here are some things you can do with Notes:

✔ **Help section:** You can create for your members an FAQ (frequently asked questions) section that includes the most common questions you receive and answers to them.

✔ **About Us page:** You can talk a bit more about your network, how it started, who's running it, and so on. You can even include a photo of you back when you were thinking of starting the network.

✔ **Guidelines for your network:** You can describe what content is fair play and what actions will get a member banned. Your network's Terms of Use are discussed in detail in Chapter 17.

✔ **New User Guide:** You can give tips to your members here, such as how a member gets started or how to get over the fear of saying "hi" to others in the network.

✔ **Links page:** Web sites commonly carry a list of other Web sites they recommend. This is another great use for the Notes feature.

The folks at Ning made life easier for you by making the HTML templates available for the examples mentioned in this section, along with a few more that you're welcome to copy and paste into a new note in your network. This way, you don't have to play with the formatting as much and you can focus on the content. Get the code by visiting `http://networkcreators.ning.com/notes`.

Chats in Your Network

Considering how popular chat is in networks on Ning, you'd imagine I would talk about it earlier. But the best comes to those who wait. I know that sounds corny, but I had to say it!

Chat gives your members a tool to interact with one another uniquely. Chat is a unique feature because the interaction between your members happens right away, in real time — unlike how interaction happens when they leave each other comments through the forum.

This section deals with chat in your network and the tools you have to make it a successful feature.

Adding Chat to your network

Adding Chat to your network is a fairly easy task. Like Notes, Chat is not one of the default features launched with all networks, although it won't be surprising if that changes in the future.

To add the Chat feature, click the Manage link in your navigation, click Features, and select the check box next to Chat from the Features list. Then click the Save button. A Chat bar gets added at the bottom of all pages throughout your network. Any member whose status is set to online (see Chapter 6) can chat with other online members without intervention from you or your Administrators.

Why do this? Having the ability to enable and disable Chat on the main page gives you a great level of control. This is ideal when you want to have scheduled chats (a great way to keep your members coming back): You promote the chat, create a network event for it, and invite all the members and/or use a banner on the main page. When the scheduled chat session is over, you can disable the chat window by clicking the X in the top-right corner of the chat window.

Moderating chat in your network

There are two nifty tools to help you keep things in check in a chat. Network Creators and Administrators can clear the messages from the chat server, in case you want to get rid of any inappropriate messages that may have been posted throughout a chat session. (This option is not available to members.) To do this, click the third icon that appears above the text box where you type in your messages in the Chat window. (This icon is shown in the margin.)

A second resource to help you moderate your chat is the ability to ban any member from it. In Chapter 6, you see how other members can engage in private chats and easily access each other's profile pages. Another option that Network Creators and Administrators have that members don't see when they click the icon of one of the chat participants is the one that lets you ban a member from the chat.

If someone is being too smart for her own good, you can pull your "chat stun gun" if you will and ban them from chatting for a while. Click the member's icon and the Ban Member option at the bottom lets you do just this. When you click the Ban Member link, you're presented with a message asking you to confirm whether you really want to ban this member and for how long (4 hours, 8 hours, 12 hours or 24 hours), as shown in Figure 11-12.

If you choose to ban the member, the next time she tries to type anything in the chat, she's presented with the message `You have been temporarily banned from this chat`. (A *permanent* ban from the chat can be accomplished only by banning the member from the network.) Everything else in Ning works just fine for this member, and everyone in the chat will probably be just fine too. Gotta love it, don't you think?

Figure 11-12:
You can
ban mem-
bers from
the chat
temporarily.

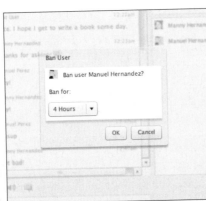

Chapter 12

Managing Multimedia, Groups, and Events

. . . .

. . . .

Multimedia, groups, and events give social networks on Ning an impor-tant part of the edge that makes them stand out.

Without photos, videos, and music, social networks would be missing elements that most people nowadays take for granted in other networks, like Facebook and MySpace. Without groups, big networks would become too much like a big city where you can easily get lost. And without events, members would not have the chance to conveniently learn about relevant activities taking place around them.

It is true that the forum, chat, and notes (covered in Chapter 11) constitute the backbone of the network. The features discussed in this chapter give you — the Network Creator — the power to make your social network as powerful and complete as it can be these days.

Multimedia Features in Your Network

Multimedia features of networks on Ning consist of photos, videos, and music. These features are among the Ning-integrated ones among which you can pick and choose during the network setup process.

If you didn't add photos, videos, or music while setting up your network, you can do so at any time by clicking the Manage link in your network's naviga-tion and then clicking the Features icon below the Your Network header.

If you want to add photos or videos to your network, click the respective feature in the Features list on the left and drag it where you want to include it on your network's main page. When you're done, click the Save button at the bottom.

If you want to add music, click View All Features to display the Music option and then follow the same steps you would follow for photos, videos, or any other feature.

After you add these features, your members can add content to the newly created Photos or Videos sections or to the Music Player on their profile pages.

Importing photos from Flickr

You and most of your members may prefer to upload photos directly to your network, as explained in Chapter 4. However, there is a chance that some of them (and even you) have an account already set up with Flickr, one of the most popular photo-sharing services on the Web. To make it easier to integrate photos from your Flickr account, your network supports importing photos from Flickr.

Before anything else, make sure you have an account on Flickr. If you don't have one, go to www.flickr.com and sign up for one. If you have a Flickr account, keep going.

To set up your network to import photos from Flickr, you need to obtain a Flickr API key. An API key is a unique code that is used to identify your network.

Make sure to get a different Flickr API key for every social network that needs to have Flickr photo importing. All of them can be set up through the same Flickr account.

To set up Flickr photo importing, here's what you do:

1. **Click the Manage link in your network's navigation, and click the Flickr Importing option under the Your Network heading.**

   The Flickr Import Setup page appears, and it walks you through the steps to set this up, as shown in Figure 12-1.

2. **Click the Apply for a New API Key link.**

   You're taken to a page on Flickr with a form.

3. **Complete the form on Flickr with your name, e-mail address, use for the key (select noncommercial use), and a description of the application, and click the Apply button.**

For the use of the key, you can write something like "To support import-ing of photos from Flickr into my social network."

After you click Apply, Flickr sends you to a new page, as shown at the top of Figure 12-2.

4. **Click the Edit Key Details link on Flickr to configure user authentica-tion for the new key.**

   You arrive at the API Key Authentication Setup page.

5. **Copy the Web address below Setup Your Key on the Flickr Import Setup page (shown on the left in Figure 12-2), paste the Web address into the Callback URL field of the API Key Authentication Setup page on Flickr, and click the Save Changes button.**

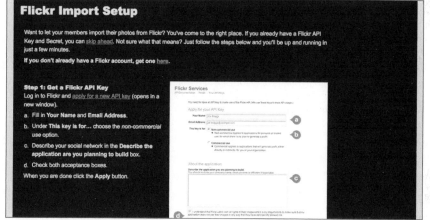

Figure 12-1:
You can set up your network to allow importing of photos from Flickr.

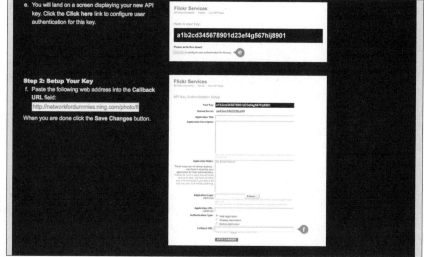

Figure 12-2:
Setting up a Flickr API key is simple: You only need to copy and paste.

The confirmation page you're taken to in Flickr contains two elements that you must copy and paste into the respectively named boxes in the Flickr Import Setup page: Your Key and Your Secret. The two boxes are shown on the left in Figure 12-3.

6. **Copy and paste your key and secret into the appropriate text boxes.**

7. **Click the Save button, and you're set.**

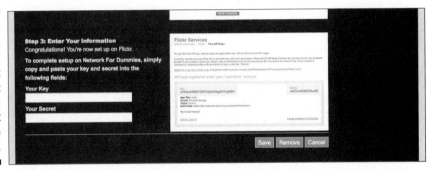

Figure 12-3: Pasting the key and the secret is the last step of the Flickr Import Setup process.

Your members can now import photos from their Flickr accounts by following the instructions explained in Chapter 4.

Adding music tracks to your network

It's easy for a member to add music to his profile page, as you see in Chapter 4. Note that only the Network Creator or Administrators can add music to the network for everyone to enjoy through the Music Player on the main page or for members to choose tracks to add to their own Music Players.

To add music to the network, click the Add Music link below the Music Player on the main page, as shown on Figure 12-4.

The page you're taken to looks exactly like the one members see when they add music themselves. Turn to Chapter 4 for details on uploading music to your network past this point.

Figure 12-4: Adding music to your network is very easy.

Managing the music in your network

You can manage the music in your network in two ways:

- ✔ **Managing the network's playlist:** Management begins by clicking the Edit Playlist link below the Music Player on the main page (refer to Figure 12-4, earlier in this chapter). The remaining steps involved are identical to how members manage the playlists on their profile pages, as described in Chapter 4.

- ✔ **Editing the settings of the Music Player:** You can edit the settings by clicking the Edit button at the top right of the Music Player on the main page. This gives you three check boxes and a drop-down list, as shown in Figure 12-5.

Figure 12-5: You can configure the Music Player on the main page in a number of ways.

When you click the Edit button in your Music Player, you get the following options:

- ✔ **Autoplay:** When you select the Autoplay check box, the music on the playlist of the Music Player starts to play automatically when someone lands on the network's main page. This can come in handy when used as part of a welcome-message podcast or an announcement of a new release in a social network for an artist, such as the Britney Spears or 50 Cent social networks. However, the Autoplay option can also be annoying in some circumstances, so use it wisely: You don't want members to stop visiting your network because a song started playing . . . while they were Web surfing at work!

- ✔ **Show Playlist:** This check box is useful if you want visitors to the main page to have an idea of what tracks they can expect after the one currently playing. If this option isn't as important to them (or to you), there's no need to select it. This option simply shows the playlist below the controls of the Music Player.

✔ **Shuffle Playlist:** Selecting this check box sets the Music Player playback mode to Shuffle mode every time someone visits the main page. The result is a playlist that jumps randomly between tracks. Again, it may or may not be important or useful to your members or you.

✔ **Play:** This drop-down list gives you the most control over the Music Player. You can choose among the following options:

- *Playlist:* This option simply displays the tracks the Network Creator or the Administrators have uploaded through the Add Music link on the main page, in the order that they were added to the network.

- *Most Recent:* This option works just like the Playlist option except for the fact that it also includes all tracks added by network members to the list of available tracks, in the order in which they were added to the network.

- *Featured:* This option includes in the Playlist only those tracks that have been featured. Tracks can be featured only by the Network Creator and the Administrators through their profile pages. While the track is playing in the personal Music Player, clicking the Feature link above the controls of the player features it.

- *Highest Rated:* This option sorts tracks with the ones that have the highest rating sitting at the top going down to the ones with the lowest rating.

- *Podcast:* This option lets you take advantage of an existing audio podcast you (or someone else) may be recording that is relevant to the topic of your network. If you choose this option, a new URL field is displayed below the Play drop-down list, where you need to enter the address for the podcast. Typically, the URL can be found on the Web site through which the podcast is made available and then copied and pasted here.

When you're done making changes to how you want your Music Player to behave, click the Save button.

Besides managing your Music Player, you can edit your network's playlist by clicking the Edit Playlist link below the Music Player. The page you're taken to looks exactly like the one that members see when they edit their own playlists, which I explain in detail in Chapter 4.

Moderating photos and videos

Moderating photos and videos is possible in your network on Ning. This may not be necessary if your members are well behaved, but you may find yourself needing to keep an eye on user-submitted media. If this is your case, you can set things up so that you (or one of your Administrators) must approve photos or videos before the rest of the members can view them.

TIP

Be prepared to do more maintenance work in your network if you choose to moderate photos. Considering the popularity of the Photos feature, you may find yourself having to view (and decide on) a large number of photos every day.

If you want to approve photos or videos before they appear on your network, click the Manage link in your network's navigation and then click the Feature Controls link below the Your Members heading. On the Feature Controls page, select the check box next to either Approve Photos before They Appear or Approve Videos before They Appear, depending on which (photos and/or videos) you want to moderate. You can see both options in Figure 12-6.

When this option is set for photos or videos, members who upload either media get a message when they're done, confirming that the items were successfully uploaded and are awaiting approval.

If any items are awaiting approval, below the Quick Add drop-down list in the top-right section the Network Creator and Administrators can see a link with the number of photos and videos awaiting approval inside a yellow box, as shown in Figure 12-7.

Also, when photos or videos are waiting to be approved, the Network Creator and the Administrators receive an e-mail with a link to approve them. Clicking the link leads to the same page where the photo or video can be approved.

Figure 12-6:
You can moderate photos and videos before they appear on the network.

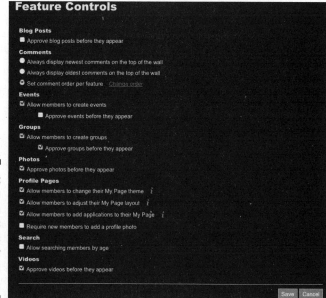

You have three ways to approve or delete photos:

- ✔ **Approve or delete all photos at once:** The Approve Photos page lets you approve or delete all photos submitted for approval by clicking the Approve All or Delete All buttons, as shown in Figure 12-8. This can be convenient from a housekeeping point of view if you have a large number of photos to approve.

- ✔ **Approve (or delete) one page of photos at a time:** You can choose to show 10, 20, or 50 photos per page, to approve or delete batches of photos at a time but not *all* photos at once. To approve all photos on the page you're viewing, click the Approve Page button. To delete them all, click the Delete Page button.

- ✔ **Approve or delete photos one by one**: To do so, click the Approve or Delete button next to each of them. This method gives you the opportunity to more closely evaluate each photo: You can click a photo and approve or delete it from the page you go to, as shown in Figure 12-9. To approve the photo, click the Approve button. To delete it, click the Delete link.

The approval process for videos is identical to the process for photos.

Figure 12-9:
Photos
added to
the network
can also be
approved
or deleted
individually.

Managing photos and videos

Once photos can be viewed by the network at large, you have three options available to manage photos and videos, as shown in Figure 12-10:

- ✔ **Feature:** Below each photo or video, the Network Creator and the Administrators can see a Feature link. Clicking it pushes the photo or video into the Featured Photos or Featured Videos list. These appear at the top of the Photos or Videos page, below the Featured Photos or Featured Videos header.

  To stop featuring a photo or a video, simply click the Stop Featuring link below it. Doing so removes the item from the list of Featured Photos or Featured Videos.

- ✔ **Add Tags:** This option works the same way as the Add Tags link for photos and videos described in Chapter 4, which is available to the member who added the photo or video. It lets you add keywords that help describe what the photo or video is about.

- ✔ **Delete Photo or Delete Video:** Clicking this link results in the removal of the video after presenting you with a confirmation box asking you if you are sure you want to remove the item. This option is visible to the member who added the photo or video, the Network Creator, and the Administrators.

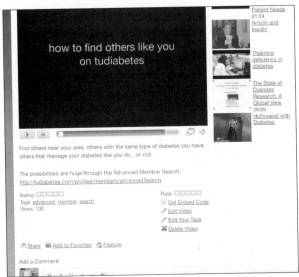

Figure 12-10:
You can feature, tag, or delete photos and videos.

Photos and videos on the main page

As discussed in Chapter 9, featured photos and featured videos appear in the Photos and Videos boxes on the network's main page, if you set the boxes up to display featured items. This isn't the only option available when you click the Edit button for the Photos or Videos box.

Photos can be displayed in three ways, and the options are available within the Display drop-down list. Your display options are

- ✔ **Slideshow:** This option displays photos taking up the whole width of the main page column where they are placed in, as shown in Figure 12-11. The slideshow can pull photos from among the Recently Added, the Most Popular, the Featured ones, Random photos, and from your own Albums. These options are available through the From drop-down list.

- ✔ **Thumbnails:** This option displays photos in a format similar to the one on the Photos page. If the photos feature is in the middle column, three thumbnails are shown per row, as shown in Figure 12-12. If it is placed in the right or left column, only one thumbnail is shown per row. The thumbnails can pull from among the Recently Added, the Most Popular, the Featured ones, and from your own Albums. Last, with this option, you can pick 0, 2, 4, 6, 8, or 10 from the Show drop-down list to choose how many rows of thumbnails you want to display.

- ✔ **Albums:** This option displays rows of three album covers, letting you choose the photo albums among those Recently Added, Most Popular, and Featured from the From drop-down list. Last, you can also select to 0, 2, 4, 6, 8, or 10 rows of albums.

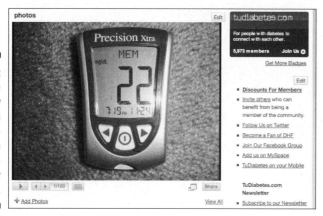

Figure 12-11:
The Slideshow option shows photos in the most attractive way possible.

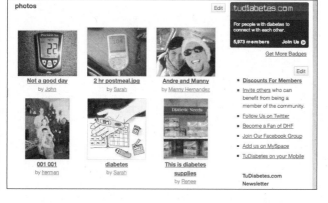

Figure 12-12:
Thumbnails give a quick way to browse through many photos at a time.

The Video box on the main page gives you only a couple of options, as shown in Figure 12-13:

- ✔ **From:** This drop-down list lets you choose which videos to display. You can select Featured, Recently Added, or Highest Rated.

- ✔ **Show:** This drop-down list lets you choose how many videos to display. If the Video box on the main page is in the left or right columns, you can display 0 to 12 videos. If the Video box is in the middle column, you can choose to display 0, 3, 6, 9, or 12 videos. This restriction is in place in order to ensure that rows of three videos are displayed.

The Photo box on the main page also gives you From and Show options. The From option lets you choose Recently Added, Most Popular, or Featured photos, along with all your photo albums. The Show option lets you pick 0, 2, 4, 6, 8, or 10 rows of photos.

Figure 12-13:
The Video
box gives
you fewer
options to
configure it.

Allowing music downloads

One of the most important controls you can have in terms of music in your
network is the ability for your members to download (or not) music added
to the Music Player. If you allow this to happen, however, nothing prevents
distribution of copyrighted music tracks among your members through your
network other than their own restraint from uploading copyrighted content
or, if they find it on your network, from downloading it.

If you spot a song that you suspect to be material posted without permission
from the copyright owner, you can (and should) delete it from your network.

Still, Ning lets you make the ultimate decision. If you trust your members to
do the right thing, you can allow Music Player tracks to be downloaded. This
may actually be perfect if you intend to use it as a means to distribute music
or podcasts that you have the rights to.

To enable Music Player tracks to be downloaded, follow the same steps to
set up photo and video moderation explained earlier in this chapter, select
the check box next to Enable Music Player Download Links (it is deselected
by default) on the Feature Controls page (refer to Figure 12-6, earlier in this
chapter) and then click the Save button.

Groups in Your Network

Groups are my favorite Ning feature. The reason I love them so much is
because they give members the power to create smaller networks within
your network. A network on Ning with multiple groups is the ultimate expression of success: It means your members have made the network theirs so
much that they want to help co-create a part of it with other like-minded
members.

The Groups feature, like the other features discussed earlier in this chapter, can be added to your network as it's created. Like other features, to add Groups to your network, click the Manage link in your network's navigation, click the Features link under Your Network, drag and drop the Groups option from the Features list into the spot where you want it to appear on the main page, and click the Save button.

Controlling groups

When you first add the Groups feature to your network, members can add groups without any restriction. You can control whether members can add groups, and if you allow group creation by members, you can also set things up so that you must approve groups before they appear on the network.

To control group creation and moderate groups, click the Manage link and click the Feature Controls link under the Your Members heading. If you want your members to be able to create groups (something I strongly recommend you do), make sure to leave the check box next to Allow Members to Create Groups (under Groups) selected, as shown in Figure 12-14.

Figure 12-14:
You can control group creation or moderate groups before they appear.

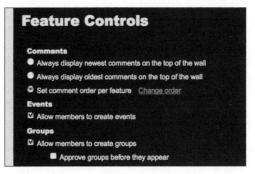

If you allow your members to create groups, you have an option that is equivalent to the one that lets you approve photos and videos before they appear on the network. If you want to have this kind of control over groups, select Approve Groups before They Appear check box and click the Save button at the bottom of the Feature Controls page.

If you set up groups to be approved before they appear, after a member goes through the steps to create a group (as explained in Chapter 6), instead of being able to immediately invite everyone and her mother to the group, she gets a message indicating that the group is waiting for approval, as shown in Figure 12-15.

In the same way as with photos and videos, when a group is waiting for approval, the Network Creators and Administrators receive an e-mail with a link to the Approve Groups page, as shown in Figure 12-16.

In this page, you can approve all pending groups (by clicking Approve All) or a page worth of outstanding groups (by clicking Approve Page). To approve groups individually, click the Approve button next to each group. You can also access the Approve Groups page by clicking the link below the Awaiting Approval header in the right column of the network.

Figure 12-15: When groups are being moderated, they need to be approved before they appear on the network.

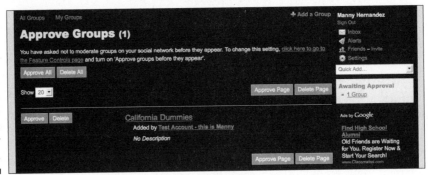

Figure 12-16: The Approve Groups page lets you approve groups in batches or individually.

Managing groups

Besides allowing members to create groups and setting up your network to approve groups before they appear on the network, you can edit groups. To edit a group, go to the group's page and click the Edit Group link below the group's Admin Options, and you're taken to the page shown in Figure 12-17.

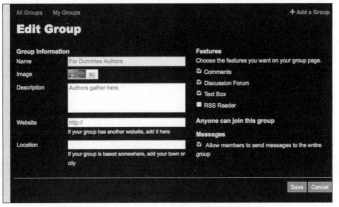

All Groups   My Groups   ➕ Add a Group

Figure 12-17:
You can
modify most
of the group
details by
clicking
the Edit
Group link.

Editing a group means you can change anything in the Group Information section (name, image, description, and so on) except for the group address (the URL for the group). You can also modify the group's features and whether members are allowed to send messages to the entire group. The only thing you cannot edit is the group's privacy settings, which are set up during the creation of the group.

Being able to edit groups may come in handy for a number of reasons. For example, sometimes members need help adjusting something in the group that they have a hard time with. Also, if you don't moderate new groups before they appear on the network, by editing the group you can adjust certain things (the group image, for example) that may be objectionable but not reason enough to remove the group altogether.

Another admin option you have available lets you remove a group. To do this, click the Delete Group on the right side of the Group page.

Think of this scenario: A member joins your network and has a field day spamming other members. He also creates a new group that you find objectionable. Banning the member will hide him from view and remove all his contributions to the network. However, the group he created doesn't disappear from the network. If you want the group to be removed, you need to delete it separately from banning the member.

Here's a great option available to the Network Creator and Administrators: You can feature groups by clicking the Feature link under Admin Options. This results in the group appearing under the Featured Groups heading on the Groups page, as shown in Figure 12-18.

You can control how many groups get displayed in the Groups box on the main page: You can display 0, 1, 2, 3, 4, 5, 6, 10, or 20 groups at a time. Besides featured groups, on the Groups box on the main page, you can show the Most Recent groups, groups with the Most Members, and groups with the Latest Activity. All these options are available through the From drop-down list, as shown in Figure 12-19.

My advice to you is to let your members get creative with groups. Give them the ability to create groups. If things get out of control, you have group approval as an option. The nice thing is you can always go back and change things on the network, but after you kill your members' creativity by locking all doors to group creation, it's harder to get them excited about starting new groups.

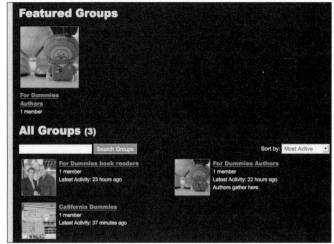

Figure 12-18:
You can also feature groups just in your network.

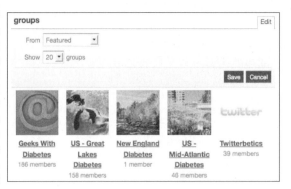

Figure 12-19:
You can select what kind of groups and how many groups to display on the main page.

Events in Your Network

Events are a fabulous way for your members to connect with one another. They can connect online (through chat sessions, for example) or offline (by meeting up with other members).

Like the other features discussed in this chapter, the Events feature needs to be added to the network before members can create events. I won't go through this again, You know the drill: Manage⇨Features⇨Events⇨drag and drop⇨Save! That's one of the things I love most about Ning: It's easy to use, and it's consistent across the network.

By default, members are allowed to create events once you add the Events feature. If, for some reason, you want to be the only one (along with your Administrators) to be able to add events, click Manage and then click Feature Controls. On the Feature Controls page, deselect the Allow Members to Create Events check box (shown in Figure 12-14, earlier in this chapter), and then click the Save button at the bottom.

Managing events

Each event has the following admin options available, as shown in Figure 12-20:

- ✔ **Feature:** You can feature the event, just like you can feature other items in your network. Clicking the Feature link displays the event at the top of the Events page, below the Featured Events heading. Also, featured events appear on the main page if you choose to display featured events in the Events box.

- ✔ **Edit Event Type:** As the Network Creator or an Administrator, you can edit the event type, which is equivalent to editing the tags or keywords associated with an event. This helps add descriptors such as *party, conference,* and *chat* to events. When you click the Edit Event Type link, a panel opens below it, where you can add or edit keywords. When you're done, click the Save button below the panel.

- ✔ **Delete Event:** If you click the Delete Event link, you get a confirmation message asking whether you're sure that you want to delete this event. If you agree to do so, the event is removed from the network altogether.

Figure 12-20:
You can
feature an
event, edit
the event
type, or
delete the
event.

Events on the main page

The Events box on the main page give you three options to manage how events get displayed, as you can see in Figure 12-21:

- **Display:** This drop-down list lets you choose among the following options:

  - *List View:* Choosing this option displays events in the Events box, as shown in Figure 12-22, including the event's icon, name, date, and time.

  - *Calendar:* Choosing this option displays a calendar in the event box with the current month. You can navigate back and forth by clicking the Last Month and Next Month links. Next to the calendar, the same information that the List View shows is included, except for the event icons. You can see what the Calendar option looks like in Figure 12-22.

  - *Detail View:* Figure 12-23 shows how the Detail View appears in the Events box on the main page. It has the same information as the List View, plus a little bit of detail from the event's description. You also see who the organizer is and larger icons.

- **From:** This drop-down list lets you choose between Upcoming Events and Featured Events.

- **Show:** This drop-down list lets you choose how many events to display: 0, 2, 4, 6, 8, or 10.

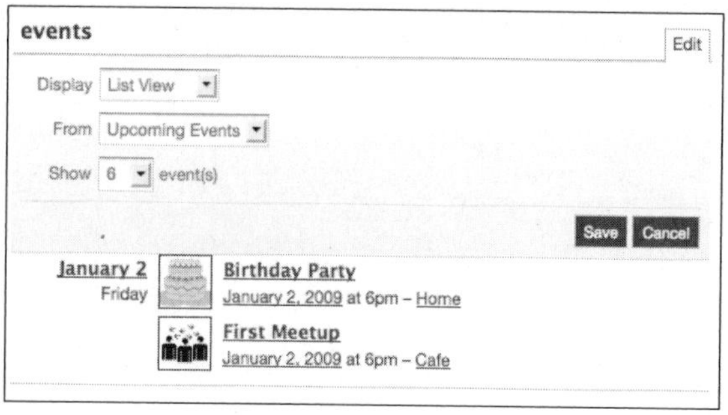

Figure 12-21:
You have
a number
of options
to display
events
on the
main page.

Figure 12-22:
The
Calendar
option
includes a
calendar
on your
main page's
Events box.

Figure 12-23:
The Detail
View gives
just a little
bit more
information
than the
List View.

Chapter 13

Enlisting Help to Manage the Network

. . . .

In This Chapter

▶ Knowing what an Administrator cannot do

▶ Understanding what an Administrator *can* do

▶ Promoting members to Administrators

▶ Managing Administrators

▶ Checking out the multiple levels of Administrators

. . . .

I sometimes remember a commercial from a few years ago. The people who were opening an online store finished setting it up and sat back to watch the orders come in. As they saw the first customers checking out, they clapped in joy, but in the next moments they couldn't hide their fear as they saw thousands of orders starting to pour in. They clearly were not ready to handle the load.

Should your network ever run into this kind of trouble (not with orders but with new members pouring in), at least you can prepare yourself by recruiting Administrators.

This chapter deals with what Administrators can and cannot do, how to promote members to Administrators, and how to manage their contributions. Last, you discover how to create multiple levels of Administrators and assign smaller and specific responsibilities to different members in the network.

Discovering What Administrators Cannot Do

Administrators can do almost everything the Network Creator can do. The key word here is *almost*. To help you visualize how far that *almost* goes, take a look at the Manage page that an Administrator gets on Figure 13-1. Now take a look at the Manage page that the Network Creator gets on Figure 13-2. You can spot some pretty obvious differences.

Figure 13-1:
Admini-
strators get
only some of
the permis-
sions that
a Network
Creator has.

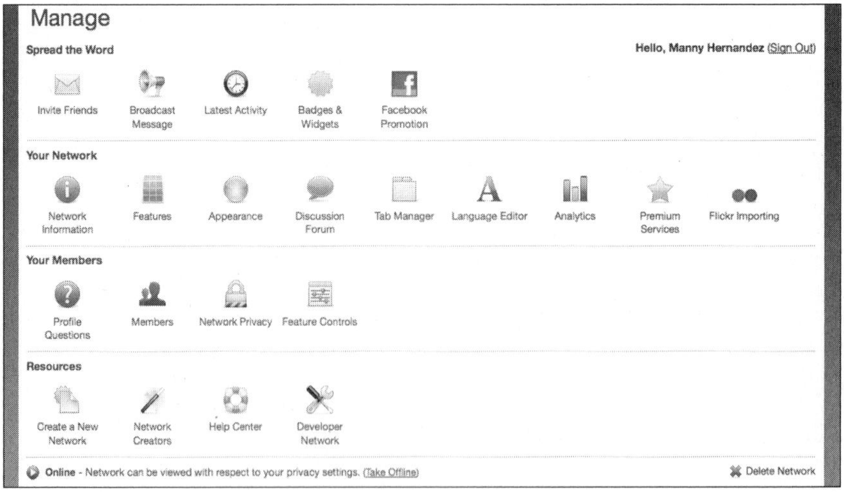

Figure 13-2:
The
Network
Creator is
the only
one with
complete
control over
the network.

To ease any concerns you may have about giving away control over matters in your network, let me tell you what Administrators cannot do before I tell you about anything else. The differences between an Administrator's Manage page and that of a Network Creator are

- ✔ **Administrators cannot change the network information.** Network information includes the name, tagline, and description of the network, along with the network keywords, language, time zone, network icon, default profile photo and *favicon* (the small icon that appears in the browser, next to your a Web site's address). Most of these options are filled during the initial setup of the network.

- ✔ **Administrators cannot modify the analytics code for the network.** How the Network Creator can add or modify this code and why this is important are discussed in great detail in Chapter 16.

- ✔ **Administrators cannot add or remove premium services.** This matter is critical because premium services are the only elements in a network on Ning that you pay for (if you use them). I discuss premium services in Chapter 18.

- ✔ **Administrators cannot modify the network privacy.** This involves switching the network to public or private and the variations on these two themes that are covered in Chapter 7.

- ✔ **Administrators cannot alter feature controls.** Feature controls include control over what can be changed on profile pages, which you can read about in Chapter 10. Feature controls also let you manage your members' events, groups, photos, videos, and music, as explained in Chapter 12.

- ✔ **Administrators cannot take the network offline.** When the network is offline, only the Network Creator can view it. The rest of the members, including the Administrators, get a screen like the one shown in Figure 13-3.

Figure 13-3:
This is the
message
everyone
besides the
Network
Creator gets
when a
network
is offline.

Ning

Q Search popular networks

Sign Up or Sign In / Popular Social Networks

This social network has been taken offline by its owner

It's likely that the owner will bring it back online shortly.

In the mean time, you can create your own social network, view popular social networks or check out the Ning Blog.

If you are the owner of this network, sign in to see your network.

✔ **Administrators cannot delete the network.** I should not have been mean, leaving this one for last. You can sleep peacefully! If you ever experience an Administrator uprising, your Administrators aren't going to be able to delete the network.

In addition to the differences in the Manage page, Administrators cannot designate additional Administrators. This gives you an extra level of control.

Finding out What an Administrator CAN Do

As your network grows, as long as you choose the right people to be Administrators, you'll be thankful for having them there, as they become your right-hand helpers.

Given the extent of the things they can do, it isn't practical for me to name them all, but some of the most important ways in which Administrators can help you are

✔ **Featuring members and their contributions:** With a large network, Administrators can help you feature members and their contributions worth highlighting. This is discussed in Chapters 11 and 12.

✔ **Moderating and banning members:** Administrators can help you maintain the network clean of trolls, spammers, and other ugly online creatures. You can read more about the moderating and banning process in Chapter 10.

✔ **Moderating discussion topics:** If things get heated in a discussion in the forum, administrators can close it or remove it altogether if needed. I include plenty of detail on how to manage things in the forum in Chapter 11.

✔ **Managing chat sessions:** Another great task for your Administrators to help you with is managing chat sessions in the network. Chat management is dealt with in Chapter 11.

✔ **Moderating new content and new groups:** If you've set up your network to approve new photos, new videos, or new groups before they appear, Administrators can help you with the moderation. I explain the process of moderating photos, videos, and groups in Chapter 12.

This list is by no means exhaustive, but it gives you some ideas of the kinds of areas where enlisting the help of Administrators can be a blessing!

Promoting Members to Administrators

In the preceding sections, I identify what Administrators can and cannot do to convince you of the value of having Administrators by your side. If I've been successful, your next task is to identify potential candidates, talk to them, and promote them to Administrators.

Potential candidates should be fairly easy to spot because they stand out: These are the members who participate regularly in the network; the people who contribute thoughtful comments in the forum; and above all, the ones who take the time to answer the questions from other members. Another way to spot them is by looking at members who have lots of friends and write on the Comment Walls of others, saying hi, welcome, and so on.

After you've identified a few of these folks, contact them and ask them whether they'd be interested in becoming Administrators. Be sure to clearly explain what you would expect from them as Administrators. If they're okay with doing it, all you have to do for them to take action is to promote them. The process to promote a member to Administrator is detailed in Chapter 10.

Managing Administrators

Promoting members to Administrators is only the beginning of your interaction with your Administrators. You have to give the people you empower with Administrator privileges the necessary training to make sure they fully understand the implications of their actions and how to do all the things you expect them to do.

In case you didn't think of it, one good thing you can do to train your Administrators is to get them a copy of this book.

Splitting up the task load

After your Administrators are trained, it's important to work as a team in the Administration tasks. Because every Administrator in the network can do the same things in the network doesn't mean they should — that's where you, as the Network Creator, step in. It doesn't matter how you split the work:

✔ If your Administrators live in different time zones, you could designate them to cover the network at different times.

✔ You could split the network into features and assign different features to different Administrators.

The important thing is that all Administrators know what they're supposed to do, so that tasks don't fall through the cracks.

Communicating with Administrators

Another important consideration when having Administrators on your network is to ensure good communication among all of them.

Because most, if not all, Administrators will *not* be sitting next to each other, I recommend that they use online tools to manage communications. Notice I don't say *e-mail,* because e-mail is one of the worst tools to ensure that organized communication takes place among a group of team members working from different locations.

A few options you may want to consider are

✔ **Adding a private group within your own network:** This would be like eating your own dog food. Members can message all members of the group (your Administrators) when something relevant needs to be communicated to the entire team.

✔ **Starting a separate network on Ning:** You can take advantage of the entire feature set that Ning makes available to you. There's no need to be constrained to the limitations that a group imposes.

✔ **Setting up a Google Group:** This is a pretty good and free solution that gives you most of the tools you and your Administrators may need to stay in touch with one another and document decisions made, members banned, and so on.

✔ **Creating a Basecamp account:** Basecamp is my favorite project communication management tool. Up to a certain number of users, it's a free solution, too. If you need to have a very large number of Administrators accessing Basecamp, there are different price plans available. You can set up a Basecamp account at www.basecamphq.com.

Whether you use smoke signals or the latest in Web-enabled technology, the key is to make sure there are clear rules on who is supposed to do what and that decisions get shared with the people in the team who may need to know about them. This clear communication not only results in informed and happy Administrators, but also reflects positively on the network and positively impacts the member experience.

Understanding the Multiple Levels of Administrators

Your members can help you manage your network without your giving them full Administrative rights to the network. Click the Manage link in your navigation and then click the Members link below the Your Members heading. On the Manage Members page that appears, click the Manage Roles link.

The Manage Roles section lets you add new roles, specific to certain tasks, so you can assign them to your members, as shown in Figure 13-4. In the figure, you can see that I've created three roles: Events Moderator, Photos Moderator, and Videos Moderator.

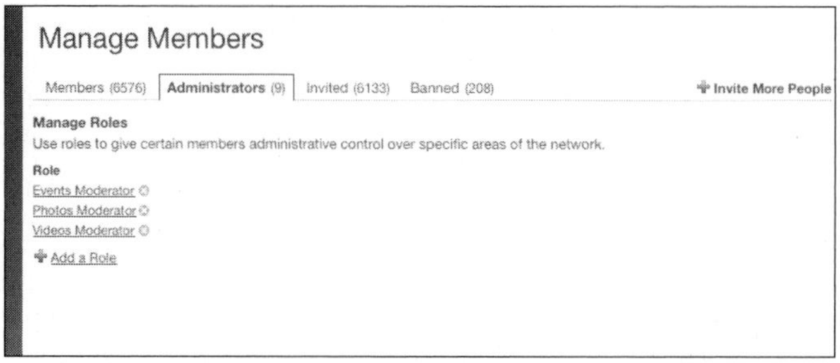

Figure 13-4:
You can give your members very specific roles so they can help you.

Manage Members

Members (6576) | **Administrators (9)** | Invited (6133) | Banned (208)   ✛ Invite More People

Manage Roles
Use roles to give certain members administrative control over specific areas of the network.

Role
Events Moderator ⊗
Photos Moderator ⊗
Videos Moderator ⊗
✛ Add a Role

If you want to remove an existing role, click the small x next to the role you want to delete. If you want to add a new role, click the Add a Role link, which takes you to the Add a Role page, as shown in Figure 13-5.

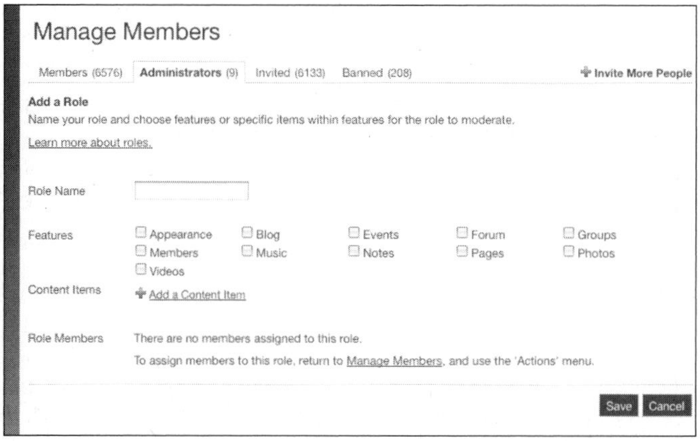

Figure 13-5:
The Add a Role page lets you define how much you want a member to be able to manage.

Manage Members

Members (6576) | **Administrators (9)** | Invited (6133) | Banned (208)   ✛ Invite More People

Add a Role
Name your role and choose features or specific items within features for the role to moderate.
Learn more about roles.

Role Name   [＿＿＿＿＿]

Features   ☐ Appearance ☐ Blog ☐ Events ☐ Forum ☐ Groups
         ☐ Members ☐ Music ☐ Notes ☐ Pages ☐ Photos
         ☐ Videos

Content Items   ✛ Add a Content Item

Role Members   There are no members assigned to this role.
           To assign members to this role, return to Manage Members, and use the 'Actions' menu.

[Save] [Cancel]

To create a new role, you need to enter the following information:

- ✔ **Role Name:** Try to give the role an intuitive name, such as Photo Moderator or Forum Moderator. This role gets displayed on the Manage Members page, in the same place where you (as the Network Creator) see Network Creator.

- ✔ **Features:** Beside each feature that can be managed in the network, you find a check box. Select the check box (or check boxes) next to the feature(s) you want the role to have administrative rights over.

- ✔ **Content Items:** If you click the Add a Content Item link, a window comes up, prompting you for the URL of a specific discussion, forum category, video, photo, note, event, page, or group for this role to administer. This option becomes very useful when you have a topic that is particularly popular, has gotten many comments, or is particularly controversial and you could use a few more eyes to keep tabs on it.

- ✔ **Role Members:** After you've assigned this role to members in your community, they're listed here.

After you've added a role, you assign it to members through the Manage Members page. To get to the Manage Members page, click the Manage link in your network's navigation and click the Manage Members option. On the Manage Members page, just click the check box next to the member you want to give the role to and pick the role you want to assign from the Actions drop-down list, and you're done!

When you're done entering the details about the role, click the Save button to add the new role to the list of roles shown when you first click the Manage Roles link on the Manage Members page. You can have as many members assigned to a role as you need, and you can create as many as 20 roles on your network.

It's important for you to realize that when you give a member permission to manage a feature, the member gets the same permissions that an Administrator would get. For example, if you create a Blog Moderator role and click the check box next to Blog while adding the role, any members you assign to that role are able to moderate blog posts before they're posted, feature blog posts, add or delete blog comments, add or edit tags on a blog post, and remove blog posts.

I hope that you're okay with relinquishing that much control. If not, and if your network starts growing a lot, you're going to have a lot of work on your hands.

Part IV
Promoting Your Network

The 5th Wave   By Rich Tennant

"You ever get the feeling this project
could just up and die at any moment?"

In this part . . .

Until you promote your network, no matter how much it rocks, it's just sitting there. You need to tell others about it so you can grow your membership.

This part is devoted to showing you how you can spread the word about your network to get more people interested in it. I also discuss the use of tools to help you learn from your members and what they do, so you can make the network experience better for them. Last, I share some tips on how to keep your members coming back . . . because, at the end of the day, isn't that what you want?

Chapter 14

Inviting Others to the Network

....

....

So your network now shines with features on your main page, looking sharp with the changes you made to a theme to give it a unique personality. You've posted a few videos and photos, started some discussion topics, posted entries on your blog, and added a handful of events and groups to get the ball rolling. Still, the main ingredient in your network is missing: members. It's time to invite members to your network!

This chapter deals with invitations: sending them out, resending them, cancelling them, and letting your members invite others to your network.

Discovering How NOT to Be a Spammer

Maybe you wouldn't think of yourself as a spammer (and most likely you aren't). But that doesn't mean you're incapable of spammy behavior . . . even by accident. So here are a few thoughts to protect you from the consequences of spamming people with invitations to your network.

 What is *spam* e-mail? At its core, spam e-mail is basically unsolicited e-mail sent in bulk. Most of the time, e-mail systems are trained to recognize the majority of spam messages: They typically get thrown into the deep dungeons of your Junk Mail folder.

Normally spam is sent with a commercial intent, but that doesn't mean it's okay for someone with noncommercial motivations to send unsolicited e-mail. To deal with spam, the United States has legislation such as the CAN-SPAM Act of 2003, which can get you in trouble for sending lots of unsolicited messages.

Because network invitations are sent via e-mail, if abused, they're just as prone to be judged as spam messages just like those that promote enlargement of body parts or 0 percent debt refinancing.

Keep in mind that when you sign up for an account on Ning and when you create a network on Ning, you agree to the Ning Terms of Service. Among other things, in the Terms of Service is a prohibition from engaging in spam as defined and covered by the CAN-SPAM Act and other laws that deal with unsolicited commercial email.

The bottom line is this: If you violate this rule, your account may be terminated, and you could get yourself into legal trouble. Not worth it, don't you think?

Now that you've been warned, consider these two tips to help you adhere to the Ning Terms of Service:

- ✔ **Avoid sending tons of invitations all at once.** Even if you're the most popular person on earth, typically this is a big red flag that spells out s-p-a-m!

- ✔ **Try to send invitations only to people you know.** At the very least, send invitations only to the people you know are interested in the topic of your network.

It's not too hard, don't you think? Well, now that you know what *not* to do, you can go to the next section and take a look at how to invite people to your network.

Inviting People to Your Network

Inviting people to join your network starts with clicking the Invite link on your navigation. When you click it, you're presented with the following options, as shown in Figure 14-1:

- ✔ **Import from Web Address Book:** When you click this option, you can pull all the e-mail addresses you have in your Yahoo! Mail, Hotmail, Gmail, or AOL Mail account to conveniently invite them. Enter your e-mail address and password and then click the Import Address Book button, as shown in Figure 14-2.

  After your address book is imported, you can choose among all your imported contacts by selecting the check boxes next to those you want to invite, as shown in Figure 14-3. If you have too many contacts, you can use the search box at the top of the page to find a specific one. When you've selected the contacts you want to invite, click the Invite button to send the invitations.

✔ **Enter Email Addresses:** Clicking this option lets you enter multiple e-mail addresses separated by commas and an optional message for them. After you've entered the addresses and the message, click the Send Invitations button, as shown in Figure 14-4.

✔ **Invite Friends:** This option is shown only if you have friends on other networks on Ning. Your list of friends shows up in a similar way to the contacts from your Web address book, letting you select or deselect check boxes next to them. You can also send an optional message to them. When you're ready to do so, click the Send Invitations button, and you can connect with your friends from other networks in the network you've created.

✔ **Import from Address Book Application:** Programs that let you store contact information, such as Microsoft Outlook and Apple Address Book, let you export your contacts in a format called CSV (comma-separated values). Your contact information is stored in a format called VCF (vCard file).

This option to invite people to your network lets you import your contacts from these kinds of programs. You can upload a `.csv` or a `.vcf` file, as shown in Figure 14-5, and subsequently invite contacts from the following page, which looks just like Figure 14-2, shown earlier in this chapter.

Figure 14-1: You have numerous ways to invite people to your network.

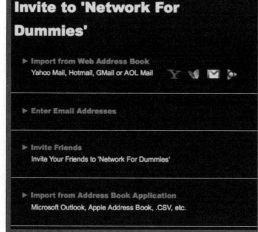

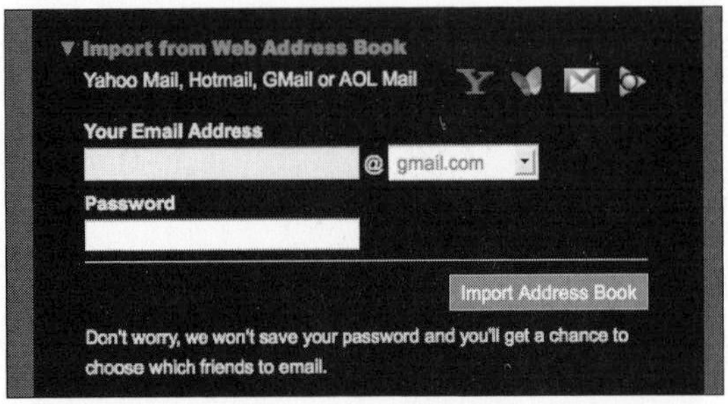

Figure 14-2:
You can conveniently invite people from your Web address books.

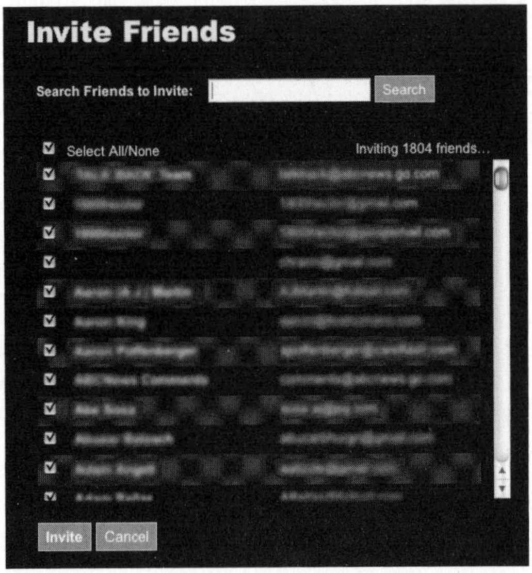

Figure 14-3:
Select the check box next to the contacts you want to invite to your network.

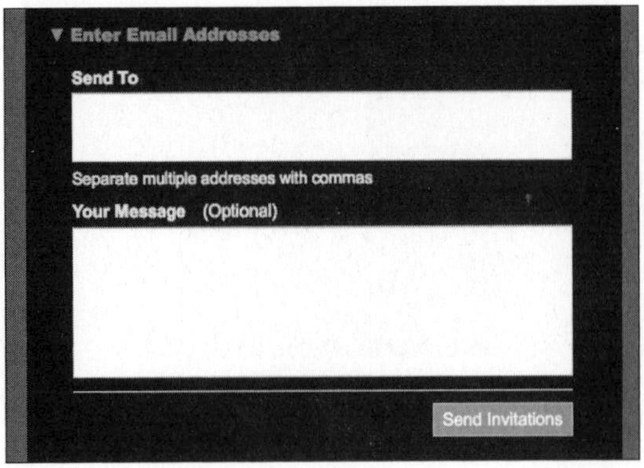

Figure 14-4:
You can also send invitations to individual e-mail addresses.

Figure 14-5:
You can
also import
contacts
to invite
from your
address-
book
application.

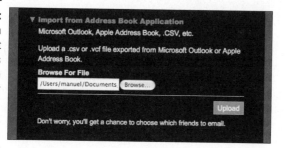

▼ **Import from Address Book Application**
Microsoft Outlook, Apple Address Book, .CSV, etc.

Upload a .csv or .vcf file exported from Microsoft Outlook or Apple
Address Book.

Browse For File
/Users/manuel/Documents [Browse...]

[Upload]

Don't worry, you'll get a chance to choose which friends to email.

Resending and Cancelling Invitations

There is a chance recipients of your invitations may have misplaced them
in their e-mail inbox. You can resend invitations to your network by clicking
the Manage link in your network's navigation and then clicking the Manage
Members option. On the Manage Members page, click the Invited tab, as
shown in Figure 14-6.

This page shows the names and e-mail addresses of people invited to your
network, as well as who invited them and the date they were invited. To
resend an invitation, select the check box next to the person you want to
invite again and select the Resend Invitation option from the Actions drop-
down list.

The Invited tab of the Manage Members page also lets you cancel invitations.
To cancel an invitation, follow the same steps mentioned above and select
the Cancel Invitation option from the Actions drop-down list.

Figure 14-6:
The Invited
tab shows
the people
who've
been invited
to your
network.

Manage Members

Dummies (5)   Administrators (2)   **Invited (3)**   ✛ Invite More People

Actions... ▼

		Name	Email	Role	Date Invited
☐		Andreina Davila	andreinadav@gmail.com	● Invited by Manny Hernandez	Feb. 4, 2009
☐		Manny TESTing	manuel@gmail.com	● Invited by Manny Hernandez	Feb. 4, 2009
☐		Mackenzie	mackenzie@ning.com	● Invited by Manny Hernandez	Dec. 10, 2008

Allowing Your Members to Send Invitations

After someone has joined your network, she can send invitations out to others: This is, after all, one of the "viral" features your network offers to help you spread the word about your network. (I talk more on this in Chapter 15, which deals with promoting your network.)

If you need to control who joins your network, you can do this by approving new members before they join. This is the ultimate level of control you can have over who can be invited to and ultimately join your network. You can turn on the optional feature to approve new members before they can join. Chapter 10 covers moderating members.

If you need to control who joins your network, you can do this by approving new members before they join. This is the ultimate level of control you can have over who can be invited to and ultimately join your network.

Chapter 15

Promoting Your Network

*I*nviting people and having your members invite other people is certainly one of the key ways that you can promote your network. There's a phrase for learning about something you may be interested in from someone you trust: It's called "word of mouth."

However, networks on Ning give you many ways in which you (and your members) can further promote your network. This chapter is dedicated to exploring these options. Also, I let you know about a few things you can do outside your network to help bring more people to it. So buckle up and get ready to let the world know about your network!

Spreading the Word with Badges and Widgets

Networks on Ning offer you badges and widgets that you can have your members embed in other sites to help you promote the network.

Badges let your members show their network pride outside the network: They show that the member belongs to your network, turning into a very valuable endorsement. *Widgets,* in turn, offer a good means of disseminating multimedia network content virally.

Getting badges and widgets

You need to make sure the Get Badges feature is available from the main page first. To do so, click the Manage link in your navigation and then click the Features link.

On the Add Features to Your Network page, if the Get Badges feature is not already included in your main page layout, drag it from the Features list on the left, drop it where you would like it to appear on the main page (see Figure 15-1), and click the Save button.

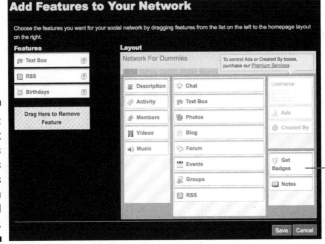

Figure 15-1: The Get Badges feature lets members obtain badges and widgets.

Drag the feature to where you want it to appear.

Your members can obtain many different types of badges and widgets by clicking the Get More Badges link on the network's main page, below the sample badge. This takes you to the Badges & Widgets page.

✔ **Member Badge:** This is a small badge with the default message "I am a member of:" followed by the network's name or logo image. (The logo is available only if you've uploaded one, following the instructions in Chapter 8.) The member adding the badge can change the message to anything else by typing it in the Custom Text text box, as shown in Figure 15-2.

✔ **Network Badge (Large):** This badge shows the profile images for 16 of your members. The images of the members shown in Figure 15-2 get updated dynamically, reflecting the network's most popular members.

✔ **Network Badge (Small):** This smaller version of the network badge shows no member images. It gives your members the opportunity to embed a more discreet badge while still helping you promote the network. You can see what it looks like in Figure 15-3.

✔ **Photo Slideshow widget:** The Photo Slideshow is a very convenient widget for members to be able to embed elsewhere. Members can customize the player in two ways, as shown in Figure 15-3:

- *Select Source:* This drop-down list gives you the option to show My Most Recent (which pulls from your most recent photos), From This Network (which pulls from everyone's photos), or My Albums (which lets you pick from the albums you've created in the network, if any).

- *Player Size:* This drop-down list lets you choose Small: 160 pixels wide; Medium: 300 pixels wide; or Large: 425 pixels wide, so you can pick the slideshow size that suits the space you have available to embed it.

✔ **Music Player widget:** The Music Player also gives members a few options to customize it, as shown in Figure 15-4:

- *Select Source:* In a similar way to how the Music Player can be customized by the Network Creator or the Administrators for the main page, this drop-down list lets members pick among Network Playlist, Most Recent, Featured, Highest Rated, and My Playlist.

- *Player Size:* This drop-down list lets you choose Small: 160 pixels wide; Medium: 300 pixels wide; or Large: 425 pixels wide, so you can tailor the embedded Music Player to the space you have available.

- *Show Playlist:* Selecting this check box displays the playlist on the embedded Music Player. Deselecting it hides the music tracks and leaves only the controls.

✔ **Video Player widget:** The last widget available to members is the Video Player. Its Select Source drop-down list offers you the following options: Most Recent, Highest Rated, and Featured for all the videos in the network; and Most Recent and Highest Rated for the videos you have submitted (grouped under My Videos).

All badges, the Music Player, and the Video Player can be added to MySpace, Facebook, and other sites. You can accomplish this by clicking the links labeled Add to MySpace, Share on Facebook, and Add to Other. Also, the HTML Embed Code text box offers you the HTML code that you can copy and paste as needed. These options are shown in Figure 15-2, earlier in this chapter. You can share the Photo Slideshow, Video Player, and Music Player on Facebook (by clicking the Share on Facebook link), or you can embed them by using the code in the HTML Embed Code text box.

Figure 15-2:
The
Member
Badge and
Network
Badge are
some of the
embeddable
items.

Figure 15-3:
Members
can embed
a smaller
version of
the network
badge and
a Photo
Slideshow.

Figure 15-4:
Members
can also
embed the
network's
Music
Player.

Customizing badges and players

Network Creators and Administrators can spice up badges and players to make them stand out even more. You can customize them in one of three ways:

- ✔ Click the Customize link below any of the badges or widgets.
- ✔ Click the Customize tab at the top of the Badges & Widgets page.
- ✔ Click the Badges & Widgets link in the Spread the Word section of the Manage page.

When you follow any of these paths, you land on a page that lets you customize the background image, color, and branding for the badges and widgets. You can see this page in Figure 15-5.

The controls for changing background image and color work just like the ones explained in Chapter 8 for modifying the header, footer, and sides. These changes affect all badges and widgets.

You can also change the network branding for badges and widgets separately. You can change the branding of the network badges in two ways:

- ✔ **Network Name:** You can modify the color of the strip behind the network name on the badge by clicking the colored icon below Network Name and proceeding as you would to change the background color.

- ✔ **Logo Image:** You can also add a logo image much like you can for your network header, as explained in Chapter 8.

Branding for widgets can also be modified. You have the following options available below the Network Branding: Widgets header (to select one of them, just click the circle next to it):

✔ **Don't Display Any Branding:** You can opt to display no branding whatsoever, which results in the display of just the content (photos, videos, or music playlists). This option may be appropriate in a handful of cases, but in general I recommend against it because it does away with a very simple opportunity to promote your network.

✔ **Network Name:** This option shows your network's name visibly on any widgets embedded in other Web sites. Although this is better than no branding at all in most cases, if you have a watermark or logo available (as in the case where you've added a logo to your network's header), you should apply it to your widgets.

✔ **Watermark or Logo Image:** If you choose this option, your widgets show the watermark or logo that you upload by following the same steps you would take to add a logo to your network's header. This is by far the best of all three options if you have a nice design available for your logo.

I know I've said this enough already, but just in case, I'll take one more opportunity to stress it: If you can afford it, make sure to get a nice design for your network's logo. As you now know, it not only helps your network's header stand out, but also helps your network's widgets shine.

Figure 15-5: You can customize your network's badges and widgets.

After you make any changes, you can see on the right side of the page how they look by selecting the right badge (Member Badge, Large Network Badge, and Small Network Badge) or widget (Video Player, Photo Slideshow, and Music Player) from the respective drop-down list and clicking the Refresh link.

When the badges and widgets are looking the way you want them, click the Save button at the bottom of the page.

Syndicating Your Network's Content

In Chapter 9, I discuss what RSS is and explain how you can add RSS feeds from other sites to your network's main page. (Your members can also add RSS feeds to their profile pages.) It turns out that your network gives you lots of ways to use RSS feeds to syndicate content you and your members contribute to the network.

If the titles of the items in your network's RSS feeds are informative and compelling enough, people visiting other Web sites that display your network's RSS feed may click the titles and end up visiting your network.

In case you're wondering what "informative and compelling" titles means, it's another way of saying search engine–friendly (or SEO-friendly, as it may be called too). Entire books are devoted to this topic, but the key concept is to make sure the titles of all content you and your Administrators create (and as much of the content created by your members) are informative, compelling, and concise:

- ✓ **Informative** means that the title gives enough information about the post or topic dealt with. "Cool idea!" is a very good example of a poor title, for instance.

- ✓ **Compelling** means that the title invites the reader to click it. A compelling title is as important for your network as it is for content syndicated outside it. "Ten ways to make your network succeed" is a good example of a compelling title.

- ✓ **Concise** means that the title is neither too long nor too short, but just long enough to give enough information to get the reader to click it.

Some of the most popular RSS feeds from your network that you can add elsewhere are

✔ **Everyone's blog posts:** If you click the Blogs link in your navigation, the page you get to contains the title and first few lines of every blog post made by members of your community. This is a great candidate for syndication because many of your members are bound to write original content on their blogs on your network.

✔ **Discussion forum posts:** Over time, as more and more topics are started and discussed, the discussion forum becomes a hub of activity, and that makes it a great source of content for other sites to carry.

✔ **Group discussions:** Every single group on your network with discussion forums on it has an RSS feed associated with it. In the case of particularly busy groups, these feeds can offer valuable content to syndicate through other Web sites.

✔ **Recent public photos and latest videos:** Depending on the level of adoption by your members, the Photos and Videos section of your network can also be great sources of material to syndicate elsewhere through the RSS feeds they offer.

To obtain the RSS feed for a particular page on your network, keep your eyes open for the famous orange RSS icon. In most cases, if a page on Ning has one or more RSS feeds associated with it, the RSS icon is found at the bottom of the page. When you spot it, click the icon and copy the URL from your browser's navigation bar.

How you can syndicate the content carried by that RSS feed on another site depends largely on the way the other site handles feeds, and that varies from site to site. I trust that you know your way around this kind of stuff for the site where you want your network's content to be showcased, so I won't go into further detail here.

Sending Messages to All Members

Just because you can do something doesn't mean that you should do it willy-nilly. A good network-related example of this is the ability for you and your

Administrators to send messages to all members. At least, don't do it too often: As a general guideline, I would say one message to all your members once a week may be close to too much.

Why do I caution you against sending too many messages to all members? Try to put yourself in their shoes. You get hundreds of e-mails per week, some relevant but too many of them trying to break through the noise to get your attention. Chances are good that you ignore a few of the messages you get, delete others, and then mark some more as junk. You read only a handful of e-mails: the ones that you care about, whose senders you trust.

Your goal as a Network Creator is to get your messages to make it into that select group of senders and stay there. If you start sending a message to all members every day, you stand an excellent chance of ending up just talking to yourself.

So how do you send messages to all members in your network? You have two ways: Send a broadcast message or share an item. I discuss both ways in the following sections.

Sending a broadcast message

To send a broadcast message, click the Manage link in your navigation and click the Broadcast Message link under the Spread the Word header. This opens a window that lets you enter a subject and the body of your message.

For now, you can create only text-based messages. Take a look at Figure 15-6, where you can see what the Broadcast Message window looks like. When you're done composing your message, all you need to do is click the Send button, and off it goes to all your members.

Figure 15-6:
The
Broadcast
functional-
ity lets you
easily com-
municate
with all
members.

Sharing items with all members

You can share any item on the network with all members. All discussion topics, blog posts, photos, videos, and other items on your network give members the option to share them with others. To share something, click the Share link below any content item. This link takes you to a page similar to the one shown in Figure 15-7.

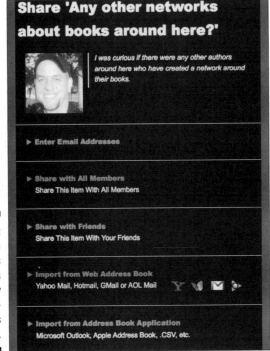

Figure 15-7:
The Share page lets members conveniently share content items with others.

If the Share page reminds you of the Invite page, that's because they look very similar. (I cover the Invite page in Chapter 14.) Members can share content items with others by manually entering their e-mail addresses, by selecting from their list of friends, by importing addresses from a Web address book, or by importing addresses from an address book application.

The Network Creator and the Administrators have one more option available: You can share items with all members in the network. When you click the Share with All Members link, you can optionally include a message or simply click the Send Message button to have all members be notified about the page you want them to visit.

Other Ways to Promote Your Network

All the methods discussed so far in this chapter are centered on your network. They take advantage of the tools that Ning gives you natively to promote your network by yourself and with the help of your members and others.

This section is dedicated to other mechanisms you can take advantage of to get the word out about your network. The following list should give you a few ideas:

- ✔ **Leave comments for others.** Your target members are out there, and they aren't too hard to find if you have the patience (and the respect) necessary. Millions of blogs, videos, and photos are posted by people that you could leave comments on, letting them know about your network.

  What's the key to having people respond positively and at least visit your network? Offer something valuable: If the blog post is asking a question, give an answer; if the photo or the video invite people to think, be thoughtful in your remarks — don't just leave a plain invitation for people to join your network.

  Also, always be respectful of the context of the place where you're leaving a comment. Leaving comments hither and thither without care will backfire and earn you a well-deserved spammer reputation.

- ✔ **Engage others through Twitter.** Twitter is one of my favorite sites. Not surprisingly, both of my networks (TuDiabetes and EsTuDiabetes) have a Twitter page, which people can follow to be periodically notified of content that has been posted in them.

  I highly recommend you look into ways to automate this process, through the use of tools like Twitterfeed, which requires you only to give it one or more RSS feeds to syndicate (something that this chapter has already dealt with for your network). You also get the chance to state how often you want each of your feeds to be published on Twitter.

- ✔ **Share through other networks.** Sites like Digg, StumbleUpon, and del.icio.us are rich repositories of content submitted by their members. Submitting pages from your network to these types of sites is another great way for other people outside your network to become aware of it. In general, it's best to do this only with pages that you feel may have particular value to others, based on analytics data (more on this in Chapter 16).

A slightly hidden feature that all pages on your network offer is the Share This Page option found in the Quick Add drop-down list below your name. When you select the Share This Page option, a window like the one shown in Figure 15-8 appears, letting you share the page on MySpace, Facebook, Twitter, StumbleUpon, del.icio.us, and Digg.

✔ **Offline is the new online.** If you sit back and think of the ways people find out about things, you'll realize that many people still pick up flyers and read bulletin boards. Keep in mind that it's important that you focus your offline efforts on people who are likely to join your network, but at the same time, don't underestimate the power of these tried-and-true methods to spread the word about your network. If your network deals with chess, for example, giving out flyers to members of local chess clubs could be a great idea.

✔ **Tell everyone.** Telling people about your network means things like including your network's URL in your e-mail signature and business cards.

✔ **Offer value.** Above everything else, focus obsessively on offering value. Members gravitate around a network they find valuable, and they become your biggest advocates if you ensure them a rich and valuable experience.

Figure 15-8:
This option lets you conveniently share every page on your network.

share this page

Share On:
MySpace   Facebook
Twitter   StumbleUpon
del.icio.us   Digg

or Send To:

Enter email addresses; separate multiple recipients with commas.

►Choose from friends

Your Message: (Optional)

Share This Page   Cancel

Chapter 16

Using Google Analytics to Learn More about Your Network

In This Chapter

▶ Discovering your network's Web analytics

▶ Setting up Google Analytics

▶ Finding out how Google Analytics can be useful

*R*emember the days before Google? There were such days . . . just like there was life before the Internet and the cell phone. It just seems difficult to imagine life without Google lately, so it's no surprise that the best way to obtain free Web analytics data comes to you courtesy of Google. It's called Google Analytics.

Google Analytics is not the only Web analytics solution available. However, not only is it free (which is a very important plus), but it also gives you most of the information you can expect from a Web analytics package with minimal work on your part, and it presents the information in a very intuitive way. This is why I keep going back to it to track Web analytics of every Web site I run.

In this chapter, I'm not going to dwell on how Google Analytics works in detail or try to turn you into an expert on Web analytics: You can find some great books on both topics, including *Web Analytics For Dummies,* by Pedro Sostre and Jennifer LeClaire (Wiley Publishing, Inc.). My goal is to get you to see the importance of setting up Google Analytics so that it can help you learn as much as you can about your network.

Understanding Your Network's Web Analytics

Web analytics sounds like a very technical and statistics-loaded term. I'm not going to lie to you: There's a bit of depth to analytics, but at the same time it's one of those things you simply cannot afford to ignore. Web analytics give you the information you need to make the best possible decisions about your network.

Some of the things you can find out through Web analytics are

- **How many visitors come to your network:** If you set up your network as public, this is the combination of your members and outside people who may just be lurking.

- **How long visits to the network last on average:** Knowing the length of typical visits is important because you need to consider the average attention span of your visitors when creating original content.

- **Where your network's visitors are coming from:** Knowing where your traffic is originating is very important. You can forge valuable alliances with your top traffic sources.

In short, Web analytics give you an x-ray of what's going on in your network. Web analytics are solid facts, which is more useful than depending on any hunch you may have or simply looking at the number of members.

With the data you gather from looking at your Web analytics, you may confirm that you're doing a great job: If so, pat yourself in the back. If you find you can improve things, you can go back and adjust things as discussed in Chapters 8 to 13, keeping in mind what aspects of your network specifically need help.

Setting Up Google Analytics

Let me show you how set up Google Analytics in your network. Here's what you need to do:

1. **If you don't already have one, set up a Google account at `www.google.com/accounts/NewAccount`.**

2. **Sign up for Google Analytics.**

   You can do this at `www.google.com/analytics` by clicking the Sign Up button.

The next page you're taken to prompts you for details about your network, as you can see in Figure 16-1:

- *Website's URL:* In this field, enter your network address without the `http://` portion.

- *Account Name:* This name is visible only to you, but it's useful to enter a meaningful name in case you start tracking analytics for multiple networks in the future.

- *Time Zone Country or Territory:* This is your country.

- *Time Zone:* Easy enough: your time zone.

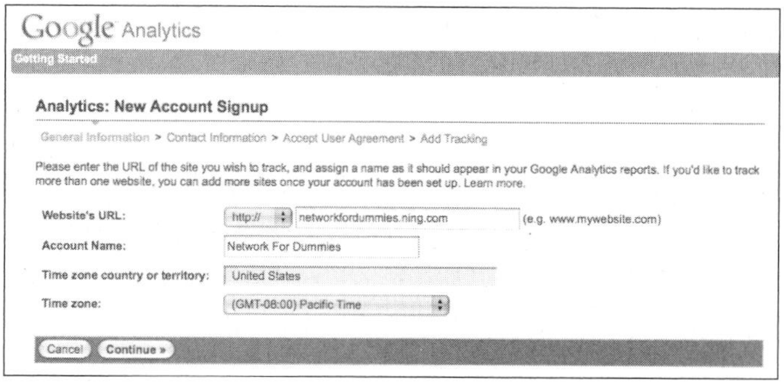

Figure 16-1:
The General
Information
page is the
first step
to sign up
for Google
Analytics.

3. **Click the Continue button.**

   You're taken to a page where you are prompted for your contact information: last and first name, phone number, and country or territory.

4. **Fill out your contact information and click the Continue button.**

   You land on the Google Analytics Terms of Service page (one of those pages you've seen a million times). If you want to use Google Analytics, you have no option but to agree to Google's terms and conditions.

5. **Click the Create New Account button, and you're almost there.**

   The page you're taken to includes the tracking code, as shown in Figure 16-2. Select all the code inside the tracking code window and copy it. (To copy, right-click with your mouse and select the Copy option.)

6. **Go to your network and click the Manage link in the top navigation.**

7. **Click the Analytics option under the Your Network header.**

8. **Paste the code in the box shown on the Analytics page, as shown in Figure 16-3, and click the Save button.**

As you can see, it's easy to start tracking your network's traffic data using Google Analytics: You only need to know how to copy and paste a little bit of code.

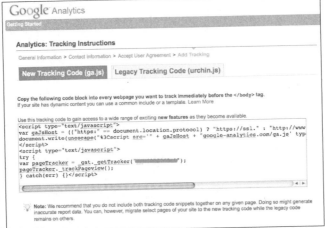

Figure 16-2:
The tracking code needs to be pasted in your network's Analytics page.

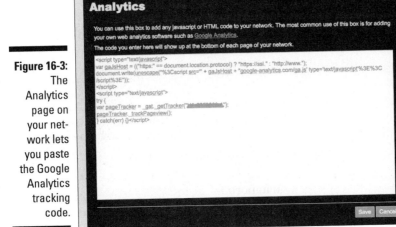

Figure 16-3:
The Analytics page on your network lets you paste the Google Analytics tracking code.

Give Google Analytics a few minutes and then go back to www.google.com/analytics to start learning from your network's visitors so you can see what works and what you need to change.

Putting Google Analytics to Good Use

Whenever you sign in to Google Analytics, you're presented with the dashboard, a page that contains the most important pieces of Web analytics information summarized visually, as shown in Figure 16-4.

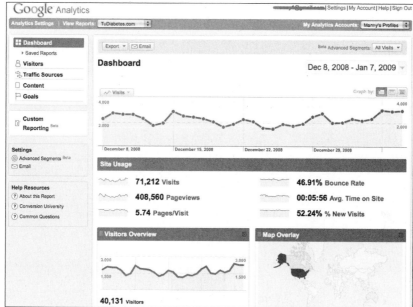

Figure 16-4:
The Google
Analytics
dashboard
offers the
critical
information
at a glance.

Among the elements shown on the dashboard are the following figures in the Site Usage section:

- **Visits:** This figure gives you an idea of how many times your network was visited during the period for which you are looking at the data.

- **Pageviews:** This figure indicates how many pages were viewed in that period.

  The Pageviews figure is an important metric if you run your own ads (which is a premium service discussed in Chapter 18): The more page views your network has, the more your members are presented with the ads you run. The Pageviews figure is one of the things advertisers typically ask when they're determining whether to advertise on your Web site.

- **Pages/Visit:** This figure is the ratio of the preceding two numbers. (Think of it as "Pages per Visit" rather than "Pages/Visit.")

- **Bounce Rate:** This is a percentage of the visits in which the visitor leaves after viewing a single page on the Web site.

- **Avg. Time on Site:** This number can be useful for you to have an estimate of your visitors' attention span. Obviously, the higher this number, the better.

If you divide the average time on site by the pages per visit, you get an idea of how long a visitor spends per page. This data can help you estimate how long a person is typically willing to spend on any given video or discussion topic posted on the network.

✔ **% New Visits:** This percentage indicates what percentage of the visits are arriving on the site for the first time in the period reported.

Knowing your visitors

Next in the list of pages you can explore in Google Analytics is the Visitors Overview page. To get to this page, click the Visitors link in the left navigation bar. Figure 16-5 gives you a feel for the kind of information that the Visitors Overview page offers.

I've said this already, but let me say it once more: If your network is set up as public, your visitors are not only your members. Your network also gets visited by folks who may come to it, get what they want, and never come back; lurkers who frequent the network but keep postponing signing up; and even so-called *crawlers,* automated scripts that go around Web sites, on search engine missions from Google, Yahoo!, and several other sites.

Don't stop with the Visitors Overview page — the entire Visitors section is packed with information about your network's visitors. This includes how many of your visitors are new to your network versus how many of them are coming back for more; what language, operating system, and browser they use; and even how many times have they visited your network. All these options are available through the links under the Visitors link in the left navigation bar.

There is a fascinating page in the Visitors section titled Benchmarking. (To get to this page, click the Benchmarking link in the left navigation bar.) Before you can see it, you need to opt in for it. It's well worth your while! To enable the benchmarking service, choose the option to share your Analytics data "Anonymously with Google and the benchmarking service" from the Edit Account and Data Sharing Settings page. You can get to this page from the page you get to after logging in to Google Analytics.

On the Benchmarking page you're presented with very useful benchmarking information comparing your network with all sites of similar size that have use Google Analytics and have opted in as well. You can see how well or not so well your network is doing in comparison with comparable sites.

Still, one of my favorite pages in the Visitors section is the Map Overlay, shown in Figure 16-6. To get to it, click the Map Overlay link in the left navigation bar. Simply put, this page summarizes the geographical origin of your visitors on a world map. You can drill down by clicking each country and state, down to the city level, giving you precious information if you need to do geographical segmentation of your visitors.

Figure 16-5: The Visitors Overview page reveals valuable information about your visitors.

Figure 16-6: The Map Overlay page shows where in the world your visitors come from.

Finding out what sites visitors are coming from

Knowing what country, state, and city your visitors come from is useful. However, knowing what Web site they were on before they came to your network is perhaps just as useful to know.

In the left navigation bar, click the Traffic Sources link to get to the Traffic Sources Overview page, shown in Figure 16-7. This page breaks down visits into the following categories:

- ✔ **Direct Traffic:** People who type the URL to your network directly in their browser or click a link that someone sent them via e-mail

- ✔ **Referring Sites:** People who visited your network from another site, where they found a link to it

- ✔ **Search Engines:** People who visited your network from a search engine

Additionally, besides showing the top traffic sources in visits and percent of the total visits, you can view the keywords that visitors typed in a search engine, ultimately leading to your network — click the Keywords link in the left navigation bar. You *need to* look at the keyword data on a regular basis (once a week is a good frequency) because it gives you priceless insight into how your visitors ask questions that your network can answer: This is the most inexpensive way of conducting market research!

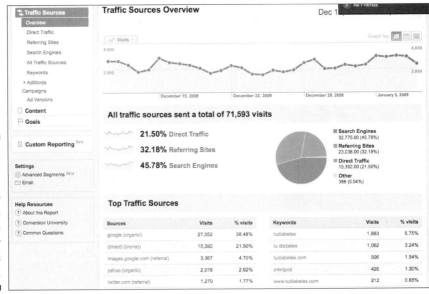

Figure 16-7: The Traffic Sources Overview page shows what Web sites your visitors come from.

Popular content on your network

The Content section in Google Analytics helps you discover what contents your visitors are checking out most often on your network. If you click the Content link in the left navigation bar and then click the Top Content link, you get to the Top Content page. This page sorts all the pages in the network by page views, as shown in Figure 16-8. You can also sort the top content by other criteria, such as Time on Page and % Exit. (The % Exit is the percentage of page views that were followed by the visitor leaving the network after viewing the page.)

Figure 16-8: You can learn a lot about your visitors' interests from the Top Content page.

Among the things you can find out through the Top Content page are

✔ **Who is the most popular member on the network?** Actually, what you find out is who's getting the most visits to his or her profile page. This is someone who perhaps should be featured and may be willing to help you spread the word about your network. You can find out who this member is by doing a search for the word *profile* in the search box at the bottom of the Top Content page.

✔ **Which forum topics and blog posts are being read and replied to the most?** By looking at the number of replies to a topic or a post on your network, you can learn only about the people who actively participated in the discussion; you need the analytics data to know how many people are actually reading. You can learn about the top forum topics or blog posts by searching for *forum* or *blog* in the search box on the Top Content page.

✔ **What groups may be worth featuring the most?** Sorting groups by Most Active in the Groups page gives you an initial reference of the groups worth featuring, but the data on Google Analytics helps you further refine this information. Searching for *group* on the Top Content page displays a list of the most popular group pages in your network.

The list could go on, but you get the idea: The Content section in Google Analytics gives you data that you can put to great use.

Tracking new members signing up

Google Analytics lets you track something it calls goals. A *goal* can be anything that involves a confirmation page: a completed purchase, a successfully submitted item (or a failed submission), or a completed registration. Except for the case of the purchase, all the other examples of goals apply to networks on Ning, so you can see how setting up goals in Google Analytics can be useful.

When a visitor completes a goal, it's referred to in Google Analytics as a *conversion* (the visitor converted to a member, for example). Figure 16-9 shows the Goals Overview page for a goal I created to track new member sign-ups. To get to your Goals Overview page, click the Goals link in the left navigation bar.

It's beyond the scope of this book to go through the steps to set up goals in Google Analytics, but you can read the details on how to do it on this Google Help page:

```
www.google.com/support/googleanalytics/bin/answer.
        py?answer=55515&topic=11089
```

Figure 16-9: You can use goals to track new members in your network.

To set up a goal to track new member sign-up, click the Edit link to the right of the profile for which you want to set up a goal. This link takes you to the Profile Settings page for that profile. On this page, click the Edit link for one of the unused (Off) goals and use the following settings to populate the Goal Settings, as shown in Figure 16-10:

- ✔ **Active Goal:** Set this option to On to make sure your goal is being tracked.

- ✔ **Match Type:** This option on the Google Analytics goal setting page needs to be set to Regular Expression Match.

- ✔ **Goal URL:** This option needs to be set to newProfile — this is necessary because every new member who signs up lands on a page that has a URL that has newProfile at the end.

- ✔ **Goal Name:** You can enter anything you want in this field. The name you give the goal is reflected throughout the Goals section, so it makes sense to give it a meaningful name such as **Member Sign Up**.

- ✔ **Case Sensitive:** You can leave this check box deselected.

- ✔ **Goal Value:** This is the value that completing the goal has to you. Unless you need to track this information, you can leave it as 0.0.

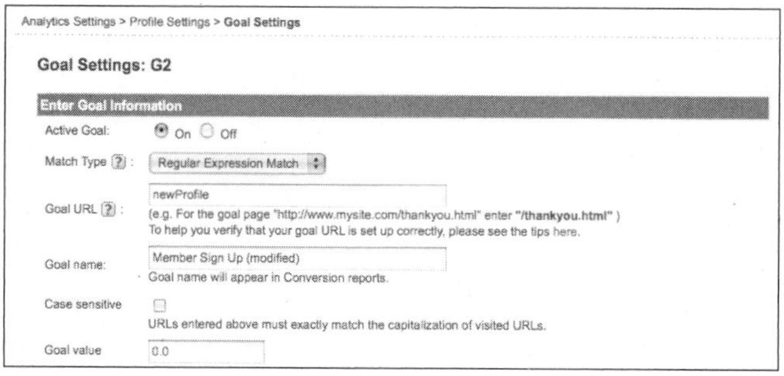

Figure 16-10: You need these settings to track new members in your network.

Analytics Settings > Profile Settings > **Goal Settings**

Goal Settings: G2

Enter Goal Information

Active Goal: ⦿ On ○ Off

Match Type ❓ : Regular Expression Match ▾

Goal URL ❓ : newProfile
(e.g. For the goal page "http://www.mysite.com/thankyou.html" enter "/thankyou.html")
To help you verify that your goal URL is set up correctly, please see the tips here.

Goal name: Member Sign Up (modified)
· Goal name will appear in Conversion reports.

Case sensitive ☐
URLs entered above must exactly match the capitalization of visited URLs.

Goal value: 0.0

Chapter 17

Keeping Your Network's Members Coming Back

Setting up your network on Ning is the beginning of the road for a Network Creator. You choose the features and the look that you want for your network. You invite people to join it, and you promote it. Thousands of people become members, and you now face a reality: If you want to keep people coming back, you have to keep working on your network as you would have to work with any other Web page.

To keep your network on Ning interesting and attractive to members, you can do a number of things. After the network is set up, you have to foster a sense of community in the network. As a result of building your community and your promotional efforts, your network will grow, and you have to prepare for this growth. To be ready for your network's growth, you need to develop and enforce clear Terms of Use that will help you deal with challenges from members who bully other members or abuse your community, posting numerous unsolicited comments and sending promotional messages in bulk.

Building Your Community

The concept of communities on the Internet is nothing new. Usenet, considered to be the initial Internet community, dates back to the early '80s, and the WELL (now at www.well.com) has been around since 1985. Because your network on Ning is not conceptually very different from other online communities, you can learn numerous lessons from past communities and then apply them to your own network.

Gathering information from your network and its data

One of the key ways that you build a community is by making it meaningful to the people who participate in it. To see why this is so important, consider a group you may have been part of in the past, whether it was the Eagle Scouts, a Jane Austen study group, or a garage band. When you have a group in mind, ask yourself, "Why did I choose to be a part of this particular group?" Chances are you participated in the group because there was something about it that you found appealing. Perhaps it was that you were getting something out of it, or the leader of the group particularly inspired you , or you simply loved to be with the people in the group. Ultimately, there was something you cared about deeply that kept you going back to the group.

Besides the Network Creator (you), networks on Ning also have Administrators (see Chapter 13) who help manage the network. Both need to always bear in mind what matters to your members most. The easiest way to find out what members care about the most is to read what they write about on the forum and other areas of the network. If members came to your network to ask about a topic they're interested in, by keeping an eye on the conversations taking place in the network, you can discover a lot about their interests.

In the case of members who prefer to read posts and watch the photos and videos posted by others, you can find out what they care about by looking at the analytics data for your network. Things such as the most visited pages or the most visited sections on the network can show you a lot about what the interests of your members. For more information on analytics, see Chapter 16.

Welcoming all new members

Saying hello to all the people who join the network is a fairly manageable task that you can easily take on your own, as long as the network is small. If you don't have the time to write a personalized message to each new member, at least make your message as personal as possible by having a skeleton message and then adding something that's relevant to that person.

If your network is set up to allow anybody to join without prior approval, having the discipline to welcome new members can also help you screen them. In a network on Ning, each new member has to answer any required registration questions that the Network Creator added while setting up the network. By taking a look at the answers provided by new members, you can spot spammers or other folks who do not meet the requirements to be a part of your network while you are welcoming those who are part of your target audience.

If you've set up your network to approve new members before they join, saying hi to them after you approve their membership makes them feel even more welcome.

As your membership grows, make sure new members continue to be welcomed, even if you, as the Network Creator, don't do it. You can ask other members to help welcome new people (something they don't need to be Administrators for), reminding them how it felt to be welcomed by you (or someone else) when they first joined. You might be surprised by how eager your members will be to help!

If by now you still wonder how important welcoming new members really is, just consider how different it feels to arrive in a party and not having anyone greet you, compared to having someone (ideally, a few people) showing you around and introducing you to things you can do while you're visiting.

Alongside welcoming newly arrived members, consider having a Welcome Center on your network where you can give some general instructions about the network. You can create a Welcome Center through the use of the Notes feature (which I cover in Chapter 11), which lets you create static content pages.

Also, consider customizing your network's welcome e-mail message that all new members receive upon signing up. This can be done using the Language Editor, a great tool that lets you modify all the messaging around the network to fit your specific needs. I explain how to change the welcome e-mail message in Chapter 20.

Providing great, fresh content

Web sites that don't offer fresh and relevant content don't do much in the way of making visitors want to come back. Social networks on Ning are no different in this respect. If someone comes to your network and finds the same content over and over, there's a good chance that the member will stop coming back altogether. Why come back to read the same things?

Here are a few things you can do to keep your content fresh:

> ✔ **Keep your ear to the ground for new trends happening in your network's niche.** Knowing the trends can help you create content (podcasts, blog posts, and so on) that your members will learn to expect, rewarding you with their loyalty. For example, to help keep TuDiabetes. com fresh, I follow a number of diabetes blogs and forums; I read health news Web sites; and I regularly monitor YouTube, Digg, and a few other sites for diabetes-related content.

Subscribing to Google Alerts is a great way to be on top of the latest news and posts having to do with a particular topic. Just visit www.google.com/alerts, enter the search terms you want to be informed about, and type your e-mail address, and you're set.

✔ **Be consistent and predictable.** Imagine how difficult it would be to follow your favorite TV show if it aired randomly. By looking at the Visitor Trending and Visitor Loyalty data in Google Analytics (explained in Chapter 16), you can determine how often you *should* be refreshing your network's content. As a general rule, do your best to refresh content no less than once a week.

✔ **Offer exclusive content.** Here, the law of supply and demand can be seen in action: If you offer great content that can be found *only* in your network, members (and other people outside your network) are more likely to visit the site to check it out.

Initially, there's a good chance you'll either have to come up with most of the exclusive content yourself or hire someone to do it for you. Exclusive content can include things like interviews with interesting people (in or outside the network) and discussing the results of a poll conducted in the network.

✔ **Have a celebrity in your network's niche join your network and contribute to it.** Though this isn't necessarily easy to accomplish, it's an ideal way to generate exclusive content in terms of outside appeal. Assume that your network is the largest online community of coffee lovers. It may not be outrageous to try to e-mail a celebrity in this space and get this person interested in your site.

When I say "celebrity," I don't necessarily mean someone like the founder of Starbucks, but perhaps the author of a famous coffee blog. As famous as the celebrity you contact may be, it's possible that he'll jump at the chance of getting more exposure for the blog he writes. After all, you both operate within a relatively narrow niche: coffee. At the very least, having him as a member and interviewing him for your network will be a great way to validate the work you do and keep other members interested.

Recognizing and rewarding your members

Over time, as your network grows in membership, you will also find yourself with a growing source of great exclusive content. Your members will start and engage in interesting discussion topics or share catchy videos that could very well be interesting to thousands more people.

Your members will generate content in the network as a result of their everyday interactions with others. It helps if you offer recognition and reward them for outstanding contributions. To help you spot gems in your network that are worth rewarding, keep an eye on your network's activity along with your analytics data. (I discuss analytics in Chapter 16.) You can easily monitor the network activity by using the Latest Activity feature that shows all posts, new members, and all the activity in the network that you choose to display as part of the network setup process.

To uncover other valuable discussions, posts, videos, and other pieces of content worth highlighting, keep an eye on your network's traffic data: You should check out the most popular pages among your network's visitors at least once a week.

Most people like getting recognition or being rewarded for their contributions. This concept can be applied to your network as well. Offering recognition and rewards are two of the best things you can do to make your members to feel good about actively participating in your network.

To recognize great content, you can feature specific blog posts, photos, and videos on the main page of your network. You can also feature members who stand out in your network. You can feature a member in two ways: Click the Feature link by the member icon on the Members page or click the Feature link below the Admin Options on the page of the member you want to feature, as shown in Figure 17-1.

Figure 17-1:
The Feature link under the Admin options lets you feature a member.

If recognition alone isn't enough, consider contests and giveaways as an option. Some networks successfully offer a prize to the member who brings along the most new members in a certain period of time. Others choose to focus contests around content creation, asking members to submit entries to be eligible for a prize. If you're short on ideas for contests, ask your members. Regardless of the type of contest you choose to hold, here are a few tips to help you:

- ✔ **Make sure to have clear judging criteria for how the winners will be selected.** You can have contests where you and a few others choose the winners or contests where you ask the community to participate in the decision. For the community to act as the judge, you can advantage of the ability to rate photos and videos.

- ✔ **When it comes to the prizes, you don't need to spend an arm and a leg to make your contest work.** Of course, giving away tickets to a popular concert or an all-expenses-paid vacation for two will attract the attention of many. But you'll find that almost any prize, no matter how small (such as a $10 gift certificate to an online store), can make a contest fun and rewarding for members.

More important than the dollar value of your prizes is choosing something that's relevant to the goals of your network. Still, if you're keen on giving out cool prizes and you're on a tight budget, here are a few ideas to get you started:

- ✔ **Contact sponsors.** You may be able to find sponsors who will fund one or more of your giveaways. It will make them look good, and you may be able to afford bigger and better prizes.

- ✔ **Talk to your members.** You may be able to find sponsors for prizes among your own members. That's another reason for you, as a Network Creator, to introduce yourself to new members when they join.

- ✔ **Keep it simple.** A $25 gift certificate to a relevant store can go a long way! For example, if you run a network for animal lovers, the gift certificate could be to a pet supply store.

Avoiding spam

Members will value the efforts you put into keeping the network spam-free. There's an overall prevalence of spam and other undesirable elements in the online experience these days, so it's important to keep the atmosphere of your network clear of those elements.

Later in this chapter, I cover the topic of handling spam in your network in more depth. For now, don't think that spam applies only to obscure-sounding folks inviting people to help them rescue money from Nigeria.

If you're overly communicative, you may end up being considered a spammer by your members too. If your members aren't expecting to receive frequent communications from the network, and they start seeing numerous messages, they may choose to turn off notifications from the network or, worse, flag messages from the network as spam and leave the network altogether.

Network Creators and Administrators have at their disposal the ability to broadcast messages to all members of the network. Use this feature with respect for your members' expectations. As a general rule, try to avoid sending more than one broadcast message per week.

Offering discounts and other benefits help

When you're promoting a product or service, in the eye of the person you're talking to, it's all about the benefits, not the features. The features you offer to your members in your network can be translated in terms of the benefits they provide to the members, such as the ability to express themselves (through blogs, the forum, photos, and videos) and the ability to connect with other people.

Consider other benefits you can offer your members, such as the ability to get discounts to services and/or products that they value. For example, you can establish partnerships with vendors that give you a discount code for your members to get a 5 percent or $5 discount as they're checking out after purchasing something. If you run a sports network, a discount to an online sporting goods store could be valuable to your members.

Sending out a newsletter

Although you'll be competing for your member's fragmented attention (people receive lots of e-mails and browse through dozens of Web sites every day), if the content your network offers is relevant, you stand a good chance of getting members to come back with a well-written newsletter. This is a good way for you to recapture members who don't visit the network often, letting them know about interesting topics or fun videos they may have missed since the last time they signed in.

Because you can't send long messages or messages containing HTML through your network, you'll be better off using an off-the-shelf solution to offer a good-looking newsletter. I've personally used Constant Contact (www.constantcontact.com) with very good results, but if you do a Google search for *e-mail marketing*, you can find a number of options that may work just as well.

Managing Your Network's Growth

If your network grows, you'll most likely be happy. Still, it may grow to a point where it may not be something you can manage by yourself. So if you suddenly realize that you're biting off more than you can chew, consider asking for the help you need to better manage your network. Managing your network as it grows is important because it directly relates to how your members feel about your network and how likely they are to come back to it after they visit it the first time and sign up for it.

If your network conveys a sense of chaos and feels like the Wild West, where there are no rules or rules are not enforced, members will eventually leave and never come back, even if you do everything I recommend to help build your community.

Communicating with your members

Communicating with the members of your network is an important and continual task throughout the life of your network. But even as the community grows, it becomes even more important to continue connecting with your members.

To communicate with the members of your network, your network gives you a number of channels that you can use to cater to different communication styles. The important thing with any of these approaches is to not over-communicate.

Here are a few ways for you to communicate with your members:

- **Community announcements:** You can write a post on your member blog or start a topic in the forum announcing information about the community. You can then set aside a visible section on the main page of your network to link to your post. As explained in Chapter 9, you can do this with a Text Box, which lets you enter any kind of text or HTML, including banner images, as shown in Figure 17-2.
- **Weekly podcasts:** Whether you do it in audio or video format, a weekly podcast will help you connect with your members in a very personal way. Letting your members see your face or hear your voice will take the communication to a level that text-based communication simply cannot accomplish. You can share podcasts in the network by uploading them as videos or taking advantage of the Music Player and uploading them as audio, as explained in Chapter 4.

Figure 17-2:
You can
include
banners in
Text Boxes
on the main
page.

✔ **Broadcast messages:** Discussed in Chapter 15, these messages are sent to all the members in the network and can serve to direct attention toward the community announcements and the podcasts when one of these has been posted. However, you should not abuse this feature, because you might start losing members who find excessive communications from your network annoying or overwhelming.

A Status Blog is a useful concept inspired by the Ning Status Blog (http://status.ning.com). The idea is to have a blog outside your network to share information about upcoming or current maintenance downtime windows, so that members may be informed of the reasons why the network is unavailable. The blog is set up using an external service such as Tumblr, Blogger, or WordPress to communicate with the members while the network cannot be accessed. You can also use the blog to share certain milestones, such as number of members and traffic metrics.

Getting your members to help

You don't have to do all of the management yourself — you can let your members get in on some of the tasks, too!

Are you familiar with the concept of *neighborhood watch,* in which citizens in a neighborhood help keep an eye on things and report suspicious behavior? You should encourage your members at large to do the same, using the Report an Issue link at the bottom of your network. These reports are sent to the Network Creator and all Administrators.

Reporting suspicious behavior is one of the many ways in which members can help manage the network. Other ways for members to help are to welcome new members posting comments on their Comment Walls and to stay active, starting discussion topics or keeping discussions flowing by replying to existing topics.

Members can also help a lot by simply being constructive with their comments. Life in the network can turn sour with only a few people injecting poison and negativity into discussions, so keeping things constructive in the face of different opinions being expressed is very important. Read the section titled "Enforcing Your Terms of Use," later in this chapter, for details on how to handle members gone astray.

Ultimately, members who act as role models in the community, welcoming others, and participating actively and constructively in discussions can be invited to become Administrators.

Getting help from Administrators

In Chapter 13, I discuss all the ways in which you can enlist help from Administrators. Administrators can do almost everything the Network Creator can do, including featuring members, moderating and banning members, and moderating content on the network. Some of the most important things Administrators cannot do are

- Administrators cannot delete the network.
- Administrators cannot designate additional Administrators.
- Administrators cannot add or remove premium services: You won't find yourself unexpectedly having to pay for things like running your own ads on your network or find that your domain name mapping stopped working due to the action of an Administrator.

Knowing what Administrators cannot do may give you the peace of mind you need to relinquish some of the control you give away when you promote someone to become an Administrator. The reality is that Administrators become your right hand as your network grows.

Even if monitoring your network is the only thing you do all day long, eventually things can begin to happen faster than you can react to them. When things start moving too fast for you, having extra pairs of eyes looking at activity in the network and being able to act on issues if needed is very useful.

You can count on Administrators to help you steer discussions that get off track and keep your network free of spammers.

Creating Terms of Use for Your Network

To help Administrators and to set clear guidelines of what is and what isn't acceptable behavior by members, you need to create Terms of Use for your network.

The Terms of Use you create for your network should not amend or supersede Ning's Terms of Service (http://about.ning.com/tos.php). This is something you agree to when you register with, use, or browse the Ning platform.

I am not a lawyer. I am merely a guy who has run a social network before and wants to save you a headache or two. If you want legal advice about this or any other matter pertaining to your social network, it's going to cost you more than a copy of *Ning For Dummies*.

Although the vast majority of your members will act reasonably while participating in your network, you will likely run into cases of members who will join your network with the goal of advertising or something more obscure. To deal with these cases, you need to define what's acceptable behavior and what's not in your network. You also need to clearly explain the consequences of not following the guidelines.

The Terms of Use will be a reflection of the values that you set for your network. These terms are pillars that normally don't change, and you can count on them to define the spirit and the environment that will drive your network. It's important that you think through the values you want your network to uphold as much as you can, so you can rely on them as you're creating or updating the Terms of Use. Examples of values you may have in your network are respect, diversity, and openness.

After you've established the values that will define your network, try to address the following areas in your Terms of Use:

- ✔ **Ownership of copyright and content ownership:** You need to clarify for your members how copyright violations will be handled. Make sure to familiarize yourself with the basics of copyright and the Digital Millennium Copyright Act (DMCA), and offer a clear way for people to report alleged infringement in compliance with the DMCA.

- ✔ **Handling of advertising and promotion:** Depending on the type of network you run, it may or may not be okay to allow members to actively promote products or services. However, even if your network allows it, you should establish what constitutes acceptable ways for members to talk about external Web sites. Be certain that you draw a clear line between what is acceptable promotion and spam.

✔ **Offensive content:** If you run an adult social network, your terms may differ from the ones of a family-oriented network. Regardless of the niche for your network, make sure to define what constitutes offensive material.

✔ **Harassment of other members:** It is never acceptable to insult or harass other members, so be sure to include terms to explain what will happen in these cases.

✔ **Trolls and inflammatory topics:** People who post topics with the intention of stirring up controversy and getting other members to react emotionally are known as *trolls* and should be dealt with as well.

✔ **Privacy Policy:** This can be an altogether separate document. It details elements such as the information your network collects from your members. The Privacy Policy should also cover how the network uses member data. As with the Terms of Use, your network's Privacy Policy cannot amend or supersede Ning's Privacy Policy (`http://about.ning.com/privacy.php`).

✔ **Termination:** It is a good idea to explain clearly what actions by a member can lead to a warning as opposed to what can get a member banned.

If you intend to run your network as part of a business, you may want to consider running your Terms of Use and Privacy Policy by an attorney to make sure you're dotting your *i*'s and crossing your *t*'s properly.

Enforcing Your Terms of Use

After you create the Terms of Use comes the real test: applying them to your network as part of your everyday operation. While your network is small, this should typically be an easy task that you may not have to spend too much time on. But as your network grows, you'll find that you need to enforce them. This may be as easy as stepping into a discussion that's turning sour or removing a video that's inappropriate for your network, or it may be as drastic as banning a member.

Enforcing the rules can be complicated, and situations aren't always black or white: There can be shades of gray. When you put your Terms of Use out there in the real world, you'll encounter cases that you hadn't thought of before. For example, your Terms of Use may indicate that members cannot promote other services or Web sites: A posted link would be in violation of these guidelines if it were posted in isolation. But how do you treat links that are part of a running discussion topic where they're relevant to the context?

How you deal with links to other Web sites depends on the policy you choose to adopt, but as you establish and update your stance on matters like this, consider that spammers are getting more and more sophisticated these days. What appears as an innocent contribution to a topic may be spam in disguise.

When you're enforcing the Terms of Use, you have to take into consideration not only the context of the place where a contribution is being made, but also the context of the member posting it. Is the poster a person who regularly contributes on topic and without any preference for citing a Web site beyond another one? Is it the first post the person makes on the Web site? Depending on the answer to these questions, your action may differ.

When you're learning the ropes, it helps to learn from the pros. One of the most popular blogs on the Web is Boing Boing (www.boingboing.net). Teresa Nielsen Hayden is one of the blog's moderators, and she wrote a fantastic piece on Boing Boing's Moderation Policy that I highly recommend you read. It can be found at

```
http://boingboing.net/2008/03/27/boing-boings-moderat.html
```

One thing is for sure: Your Terms of Use will be a dynamic document you will find yourself revising over time. As a result of the things you learn over time by observing the behavior of your members, decide how you're going to deal with new situations and update the Terms of Use accordingly so that the next time you face the same case, you have a frame of reference to fall back on.

Informing members about the Terms of Use

Thinking through your Terms of Use, writing them, and updating them as you go are only part of the job. You need to make sure you inform new members about them. There are a number of ways in which you can do this:

✔ **Edit your welcome message.** Along with allowing you to edit and customize almost every word in your network, your network's Language Editor lets you change the message that gets e-mailed to all new members as soon as they join your network (see Figure 17-3). In this message, you should include a link to the Terms of Use so that new members may bear in mind what constitutes acceptable behavior in the network.

When new members sign up for your network, they have to agree to abide by Ning's Terms of Use and Privacy Policy. In the same way, you can use it to edit your network's welcome message, you can use the Language Editor to include language in the sign-up screen requiring new members to agree to abide by your network's Terms of Use and Privacy Policy.

In the Language Editor, click the Edit link corresponding to your network's language and perform a search for *By signing up, you agree,* which is part of the language included in the sign-up screen next to the links to Ning's Terms of Use and Privacy Policy (see Figure 17-4). You can include links to your own Terms of Use and Privacy Policy in the custom text box.

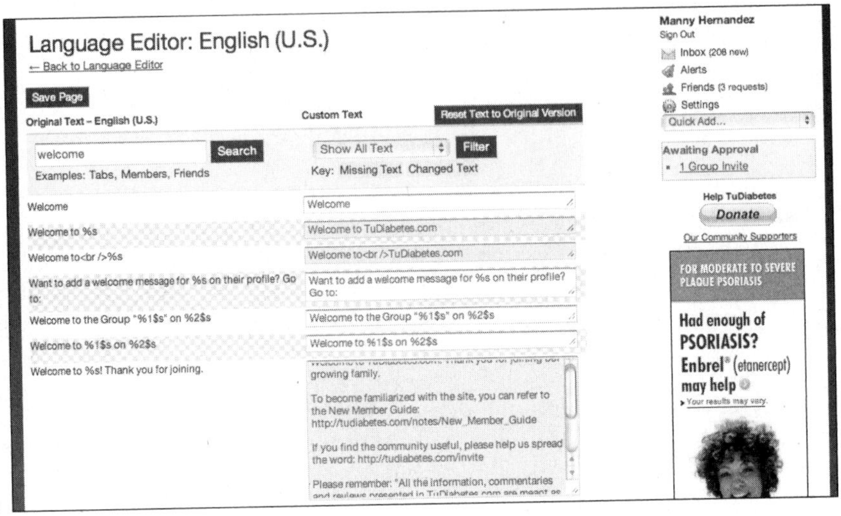

Figure 17-3: The Language Editor lets you edit your welcome message.

✔ **Implement a "Network 101" box:** You can include a Text Box (which allows you to enter plain text as well as HTML and images) in the right column of your network, where it is visible throughout the entire network to link to your Terms of Use, Privacy Policy, and other references, such as a Welcome Center.

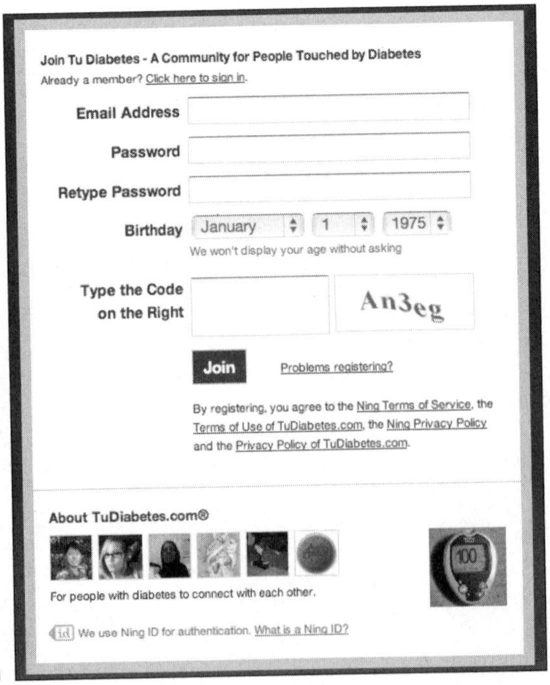

Figure 17-4: The Language Editor lets you modify the language on the Sign Up page.

Minimizing spammers in your network

Part of fostering a sense of community in your network is allowing your network's members to communicate with each other. In this section, I provide some methods that can help you lessen the occurrence of unwanted spamming in your network.

Moderating new members

One way to minimize (though not completely eliminate) issues with spammers and other undesirable folks is to moderate new members. If you've set up your network to moderate new members, either the Network Creator or an Administrator needs to approve someone's membership before he or she can get inside the network. This moderation gives you a stage during which you can evaluate new members prior to their joining the network, as opposed to letting members join the network without any evaluation on your part.

Depending on the volume of new members you get on a daily basis, moderating new members may or may not be something you can accommodate — it obviously takes additional time and effort. However, it may be a great way to keep spammers at bay. The main downside of this approach obviously is that it won't help you catch *stealth spammers,* people who appear to be legitimate members at first and eventually come out from under their cover to do what they came to do in the first place.

Adding required profile questions

When you're setting up your network, you can add *profile questions* to it: questions for members to answer so as to help build their profile pages. *Required profile questions* are questions a new member *must* answer before being allowed to finish the sign-up process into your network.

Though required profile questions aren't necessarily a deterrent for spammers, they can help you gather valuable information to help you identify potential spammers. Sometimes you'll see people entering garbage text (something like *qweqgcdsbcasd*) as a way to meet the requirement of answering a particular question. That is not a good sign and definitely should raise a red flag. A slight variation of this case is when a new member exhibits very little effort while answering profile questions — again, not necessarily a spammer but cause for a red flag to be raised.

Adding an open-ended question to which only a legitimate new member would have an answer can also help you spot people you may not want in your network. For example, in the case of a network for people with diabetes, such a question could be "What was your most recent A1C?" If you don't know the answer to this question, you won't necessarily be banned. If you have diabetes, however, it is very unlikely that you will not know how to answer this question.

Dealing with banned members

The reaction of a banned member can be quite unpredictable. It can fluctuate from utter silence all the way to complete outrage. In the case of a silent banned member, that is one less headache for you and your Administrators.

In the case of an outraged banned member, your reply to any communications from him or her needs to be as measured as possible. Here are some thoughts for you to consider if you're in this position:

- ✔ **If a banned member writes and asks you about the reason for the decision, provide concrete examples.** In as much detail as you find necessary, explain the reason for the ban and cite the section of the Terms of Use that was violated.

- ✔ **Expect a reply from the person.** If he or she took the time to write the first time, there's a very good chance a reply from you will be followed by a reply back, and this reply may be stronger than the first communication.

- ✔ **Not having read the Terms of Use cannot be an excuse for unacceptable behavior in the social network.** Be firm in your decision. At the same time, keep doors open and consider the context that the person presents you with. Under certain circumstances, you may want to consider letting a member back in the network. These cases typically involve an apology and a promise on his or her part to not repeat the behavior that led to getting banned.

- ✔ **Always keep your cool and think before replying.** The person who got banned was banned for a good reason. If his or her approach to getting unbanned involves insulting one of the Administrators, you can safely imagine what this person's behavior would be if he or she were let back in the network.

- ✔ **Everything has a limit, and you aren't obligated to reply indefinitely to a thread of replies from a banned member.** Decide when you will stop any further communication, inform the person at that point, and be firm about not continuing the conversation past that point.

Part V
Advanced Tips and Tricks

The 5th Wave   By Rich Tennant

"We take network security here very seriously."

In this part . . .

*I*f you have a knack for handling technical challenges, this is the part that you'll love! Why? Because using the information you find in this part gives your network an edge. I write about ways to further customize the look and feel of your network. I discuss how to get your network to read exactly the way you want it to. And I show you how you can expand your network's features through the use of OpenSocial applications.

Chapter 18

Purchasing Premium Services

● ●

● ●

*E*ver since I found out about it, I thought the platform offered by Ning was fantastic for a free service. Think about it: You can create and run a social network (your own flavor of Facebook or MySpace) focused on any topic you want, without having to worry about all that goes on behind the scenes to make it happen.

But you might need a little more than the basic package: You may need to control your own ads, use your own domain name, remove Ning's promotion links, or get more storage and bandwidth. If this is your case, Ning has four premium services that you can pay for on a monthly basis to take care of these needs.

In this chapter, I cover the premium services, explaining what each of them allows you to accomplish.

Purchase Premium Services

Purchasing premium services in your network is a straightforward process. Just follow these steps:

1. **Click the Manage link in your navigation and follow the Premium Services link under the Your Network header.**

   You're taken to the Add Premium Services to *Your Network Name* page, shown in Figure 18-1.

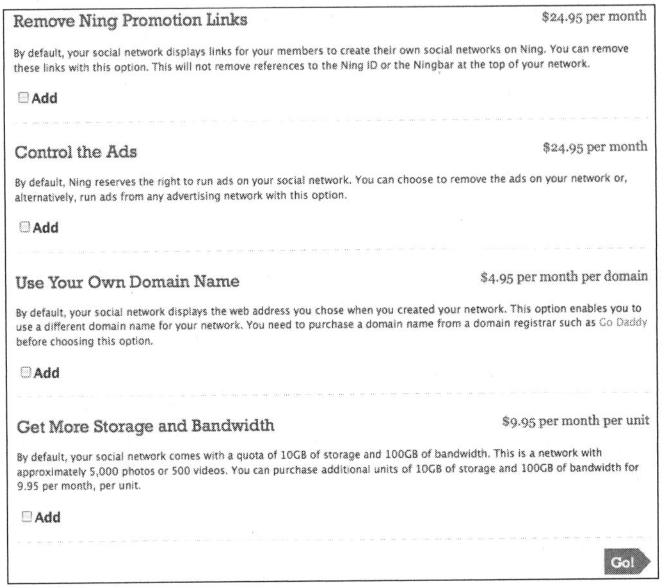

Remove Ning Promotion Links $24.95 per month

By default, your social network displays links for your members to create their own social networks on Ning. You can remove these links with this option. This will not remove references to the Ning ID or the Ningbar at the top of your network.

☐ Add

Control the Ads $24.95 per month

By default, Ning reserves the right to run ads on your social network. You can choose to remove the ads on your network or, alternatively, run ads from any advertising network with this option.

☐ Add

Use Your Own Domain Name $4.95 per month per domain

By default, your social network displays the web address you chose when you created your network. This option enables you to use a different domain name for your network. You need to purchase a domain name from a domain registrar such as Go Daddy before choosing this option.

☐ Add

Get More Storage and Bandwidth $9.95 per month per unit

By default, your social network comes with a quota of 10GB of storage and 100GB of bandwidth. This is a network with approximately 5,000 photos or 500 videos. You can purchase additional units of 10GB of storage and 100GB of bandwidth for 9.95 per month, per unit.

☐ Add

Go!

Figure 18-1:
This page lets you easily add premium services to your network.

2. **Select the Add check boxes next to the service(s) of your choice and click the Go button at the bottom of the page.**

   There are four premium services you can add to your network, (discussed in detail in the following sections of this chapter):

   - *Remove Ning Promotion Links:* $24.95 per month
   - *Control the Ads:* $24.95 per month
   - *Use Your Own Domain Name:* $4.95 per month per domain
   - *Get More Storage and Bandwidth:* $9.95 per month per unit

   If you previously purchased other premium services, you can skip to Step 4; otherwise, proceed to Step 3.

3. **Fill out your credit card information and review your services.**

   To keep your finances straight, keep in mind that each Ning account can be associated with only one credit card. So, for example, if you have two networks that need to be run using two different credit cards, you need two different Ning accounts to run the networks under the separate credit cards.

   Also, to make accounting departments happy, when you purchase premium services, the credit card you enter is charged, and a receipt is e-mailed to you. From that point on, your credit card is charged every 30 days (unless you cancel your premium services), after which you get an e-mail with a receipt.

4. **Click the Go button.**

5. **Enter your password for confirmation purposes.**

To cancel a premium service, follow the same steps you would take to add a new premium service. Instead of selecting the Add check boxes, you need to click View Your Premium Services. This link is shown in Figure 18-2.

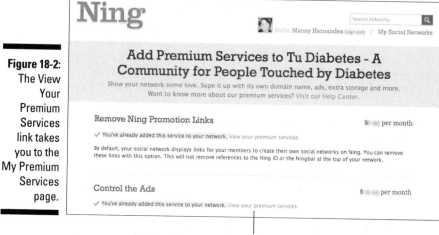

Figure 18-2:
The View Your Premium Services link takes you to the My Premium Services page.

Click to view, cancel, or edit your premium services.

On the page you're taken to, you can do the following: Cancel any premium service by clicking the respective Cancel link; view or edit your credit card information; or edit the ads on your network if you're paying for this premium service, as shown in Figure 18-3.

Tu Diabetes - A Community for People Touched by Diabetes

Service Name	Price	Next Billing Date	Actions
Remove Ning Promotion Links	($ /month)	February 4, 2009	✕ Cancel
Use Your Own Domain Name *domain: tudiabetes.com*	($ /month)	February 4, 2009	✕ Cancel
Control the Ads	($ /month)	February 4, 2009	✐ Edit ✕ Cancel

✦ Add a new service

🗔 View or edit my credit card information

Figure 18-3:
You can cancel premium services at any time.

Control the Ads

By default, your network displays AdSense ads in the right column. If someone clicks an ad, any revenue generated goes to Ning. If you don't plan on having ads become a revenue stream on your network and you don't mind having ads on your network, you don't need to do anything.

If you want to obtain revenue from running ads on your network or you prefer not to have any ads at all, you need to purchase the Control the Ads premium service.

When you select the Add check box below the Control the Ads section of the Premium Services page, a panel opens, as shown in Figure 18-4.

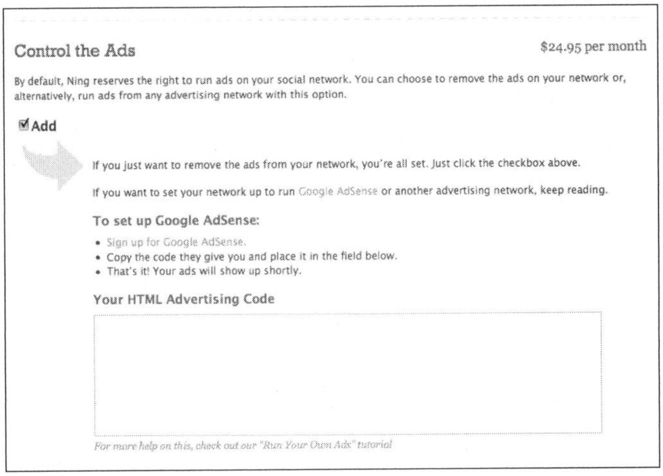

Figure 18-4:
The Control
the Ads
premium
service lets
you remove
Ning's
AdSense
ads and
optionally
run your
own ads.

Control the Ads $24.95 per month

By default, Ning reserves the right to run ads on your social network. You can choose to remove the ads on your network or, alternatively, run ads from any advertising network with this option.

☑ Add

If you just want to remove the ads from your network, you're all set. Just click the checkbox above.

If you want to set your network up to run Google AdSense or another advertising network, keep reading.

To set up Google AdSense:
- Sign up for Google AdSense.
- Copy the code they give you and place it in the field below.
- That's it! Your ads will show up shortly.

Your HTML Advertising Code

For more help on this, check out our "Run Your Own Ads" tutorial

After you pay for the premium service, Ning's AdSense ads get removed from the network. If you want to run your own AdSense ads (or ads from any advertising network), paste the HTML code from your advertising network into the box in the Control the Ads section and click the Go button at the bottom of the page.

When you pay to control the ads on your network, you are not limited to adding the code from your advertising network. Through your Features page, you can also move the Ads box anywhere you want on the main page, and you can paste HTML advertising code in Text Boxes on your main page or elsewhere in your network.

Although you can technically add the HTML code for a banner ad to a Text Box on your main page, you should *not* do it unless you pay for the Control the Ads premium service. It's against Ning's Terms of Service to run ads on your network without paying for the premium service to control the ads. When you consider how inexpensive this premium service is, putting a banner ad in a Text Box is simply not worth the hassle and wasting all your hard work.

Use Your Own Domain Name

Use Your Own Domain Name is my favorite premium service. If there's something that gives personality to a site, it's the domain name. Although the `.ning.com` appendage at the end of all networks on Ning could be considered a minor thing, using your own domain name looks more professional.

Also, by now, many of the best network URLs have already been taken, so you may find yourself stuck with a network URL you aren't particularly fond of. So that's two reasons to use your own domain name.

When you select the Add check box below the Use Your Own Domain section of the Premium Services page, a panel opens, as shown in Figure 18-5.

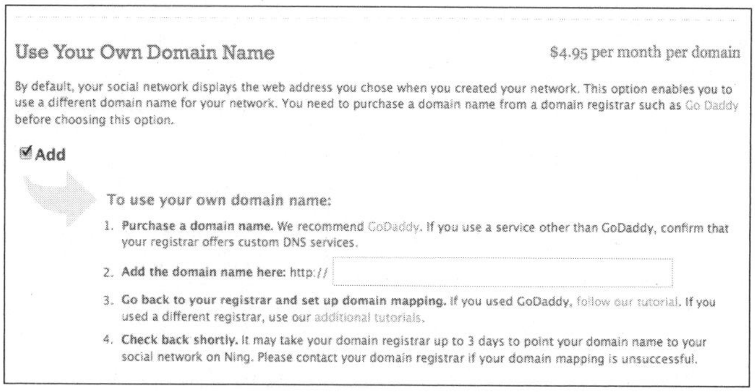

Figure 18-5:
Using your
own domain
gives your
network
a more
professional
appearance.

> **Use Your Own Domain Name** $4.95 per month per domain
>
> By default, your social network displays the web address you chose when you created your network. This option enables you to use a different domain name for your network. You need to purchase a domain name from a domain registrar such as Go Daddy before choosing this option.
>
> ☑ **Add**
>
> To use your own domain name:
>
> 1. **Purchase a domain name.** We recommend GoDaddy. If you use a service other than GoDaddy, confirm that your registrar offers custom DNS services.
>
> 2. **Add the domain name here:** http://
>
> 3. **Go back to your registrar and set up domain mapping.** If you used GoDaddy, follow our tutorial. If you used a different registrar, use our additional tutorials.
>
> 4. **Check back shortly.** It may take your domain registrar up to 3 days to point your domain name to your social network on Ning. Please contact your domain registrar if your domain mapping is unsuccessful.

Unfortunately, setting up this premium service typically entails a bit more legwork than the other ones. But it's not rocket science: It simply requires a bit more attention to detail. Here are the steps to follow to get your own domain name mapped to your network on Ning:

1. **Purchase a domain name if you haven't done it yet.**

   Ning recommends you use GoDaddy, Network Solutions, Yahoo!, Register, DomainMaze, or 1&1 as domain name registrars.

2. **When you have your domain, enter it in the URL text box shown in Figure 18-5.**

   This step notifies Ning of the domain you want to map to your network.

3. **Go to your registrar's Web site and set up domain name mapping.**

   This is where things can get hairy, but Ning has made it easier by offering tutorials for each of the registrars I mention in Step 1. You can read these tutorials here: `http://tinyurl.com/ningfordummiesdomain`.

4. **Wait up to three days for all the domain name magic to happen.**

   If you don't see your network coming up when you type in your domain name after three days, contact your registrar.

If you set up everything properly, when people type your domain name, they see your network on Ning. Your network is still available through its `.ning.com` URL unless you implement the hack to have it redirect to your domain automatically (which I explain in Chapter 23).

Remove Ning Promotion Links

The Remove Ning Promotion Links premium service is the easiest one of all to understand and set up. Networks on Ning by default carry these Ning promotion links:

- ✔ At the top left of the network is a Create Your Own Social Network button.

- ✔ In the footer is a line that reads "Created by Manny Hernandez on Ning." (Well, most networks don't say Manny Hernandez.)

- ✔ In the right column, as shown in Figure 18-6, you find an About box containing a link to Ning.com and a Create Your Own Social Network! link.

Figure 18-6:
The About box is one of the places affected by this premium service.

When you buy this premium service, the top-left button goes away, the reference to Ning on the footer disappears, and the About box can be moved or removed from the right column.

Paying for this premium service does not remove the links on the right side of the network footer, pointing to Ning's Privacy Policy and Terms of Service with your network's theme. Also, it doesn't remove mentions of Ning in the Privacy Policy and Terms of Service or mentions of Ning ID in the Sign In and Sign Up pages.

Unlike the case with the other premium services, when you select the Add check box below the Remove Ning Promotion Links, nothing happens. You just click the Go button and continue with the rest of the setup process as explained earlier in order to do away with the promotional links.

Get More Storage and Bandwidth

Get More Storage and Bandwidth is the premium service I would worry about the least if I were you, at least for now. It's meant for networks that have lots of photos and video content or networks that have been around for a while.

By default, your social network lets you store 10GB of content and use up to 100GB of bandwidth. According to Ning, this is roughly equivalent to a network with approximately 5,000 photos or 500 videos.

If your network is the next online multimedia success story, you may be one of those Network Creators who need to purchase additional storage and bandwidth. If this is your case, Ning notifies you as you're approaching your quota.

You can buy additional units of 10GB of storage and 100GB of bandwidth at $9.95 per unit. When you select the Add check box below the Get More Storage and Bandwidth section of the Premium Services page, a panel opens, as shown in Figure 18-7.

Figure 18-7:
You can purchase more storage and bandwidth if you need to.

> Get More Storage and Bandwidth $9.95 per month per unit
>
> By default, your social network comes with a quota of 10GB of storage and 100GB of bandwidth. This is a network with approximately 5,000 photos or 500 videos. You can purchase additional units of 10GB of storage and 100GB of bandwidth for 9.95 per month, per unit.
>
> ☑ Add
>
> How many units would you like to purchase?
>
> _____ unit(s)
>
> *1 unit = 10 GB of storage and 100 GB of bandwidth*
>
> Go!

Enter the number of units you need, click the Go button, and complete the rest of the process to have your storage and bandwidth needs taken care of.

Chapter 19

Breaking the CSS Code

Cascading style sheets (CSS) is a topic that can take a whole book. As a matter of fact, it *does* take many books: Doing a search for CSS on Amazon.com returns more than 40,000 titles! This is so much the case that trying to talk in a few pages about CSS is nearly impossible.

This chapter isn't meant to be a tutorial on CSS. You really need to go elsewhere for more info — such as *HTML, XHTML & CSS For Dummies,* 6th Edition, by Ed Tittel and Jeff Noble (Wiley) — for an in-depth look at this topic.

In this chapter, I discuss CSS just enough to help you understand the basic concepts underlying it and how it applies to your network. I give you some examples of changes you can do to your network's CSS. I also share a few references to books, Web-based resources, and networks on Ning for you to look into for information and inspiration.

Discovering the Basics of CSS

Back in the early days of the Internet, Web site content and presentation (the way the Web site looked) were so intrinsically connected that redesigning a Web site was a task that few people looked forward to. One day, someone thought that the content of a Web site and its look could be separated, so that the changes to how the content looks could be made relatively easily. Enter cascading style sheets (CSS).

With CSS, you can define things like font size, font family, font color, background color, and so on, completely separated from the content to which it is applied.

If you want to get a quick idea of what CSS does to a Web site, visit CSS Zen Garden (`http://csszengarden.com`) and try some of the different CSS themes the site offers. Figures 19-1 and 19-2 show two sample themes for you to get a feel. You can basically view the same information with different looks. This is not to say that changing the way a Web site is easy, but it's far easier today than it used to be in the mid- and late '90s.

Figure 19-1:
Orchid Beauty version of CSS Zen Garden by Kevin Addison.

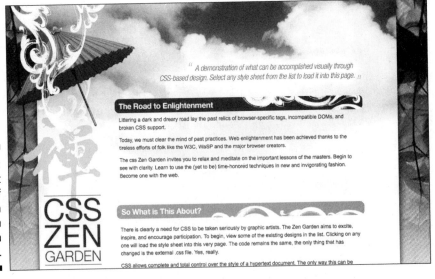

Figure 19-2:
Kyoto Forest version of CSS Zen Garden by John Politowski.

A good example of how your network takes advantage of CSS is accessing it through a mobile phone. If you add /m at the end of your network's URL, you network is presented using a CSS that's designed with iPhone users in mind. You can see a version of http://tudiabetes.com/m in Figure 19-3.

Figure 19-3:
The iPhone
version
of your
network on
Ning gives
you the
basics you
need.

Grasping the very basics of CSS

In the examples later in this chapter, you encounter a number of things that may look like a foreign language to you, so in the interest of not turning this book into a book about CSS, I limit explanations about CSS to what you need to know to understand what the examples mean.

Here's an example of a CSS style discussed later on:

```
.xg_widget_profiles_members_index .count
{
display: none;
}
```

In plain English, it translates into something like this: "When you see the class .count that is a child of .xg_widget_profiles_members_index, do not display it."

What are *classes?* To differentiate them, classes in a style sheet are always preceded by a dot, as with .count. Classes make it possible for you to define multiple formats for a single HTML tag on the same Web page.

What is a *child?* It's an element in CSS that is contained within another element, called (you guessed) its parent. This parent-child relationship is denoted by a space between the two classes, as shown in the preceding piece of code, where there's a space between index and .count.

In another example, you see the following code:

```
#xn_bar
{
float:none;
margin-left:auto;
margin-right:auto;
width:955px;
}
```

I want to draw your attention to the # sign in front of #xn_bar. This is an example of an ID, the complement to a class. IDs in a style signify elements that are referenced only once in the document. In the case of the example, this ID refers to the thin strip with the search box at the top of your network that sits at the very top of every page on your network, an element that appears only once in the entire page.

The best advice I can give you

There's nothing like "seeing" CSS in action and playing with it to start getting a good feel for it. If I can get you to remember one and only one thing after you're done reading this chapter, let it be this:

PLEASE, download and install a copy of Firebug.

You can get Firebug at http://getfirebug.com. To run Firebug, you need to run Firefox as your browser because Firebug is a Firefox plug-in.

Firebug lets you inspect a Web site's CSS by simply placing your cursor over the element you want to learn about. You can then make edits to the CSS in a nonpermanent way that lets you see how those changes would appear.

After you set up Firebug, the only things standing between you and CSS mastery are time and patience.

Making Changes to CSS on Your Network

In the following sections, I go over a few examples of things you can do in your network through CSS changes. Before I get to the things you can do, let me spend a few lines going over the ones you can't.

What you can't do with CSS

You can accomplish a lot of things, but remember, CSS is strictly focused on displaying existing information. In the case of your network, CSS can help you manage the display and positioning of elements that your network already contains.

However, CSS can't insert HTML elements that your network doesn't already contain. This is not to say that you can't accomplish some of those fantastic ideas you already have, such having a horizontal header above your navigation or an Adobe Flash header crowning your network. To find out how to do some things that involve inserting elements that your network doesn't natively carry, check out Chapter 23.

Besides not letting you insert elements that don't already exist on your network, here are a few other things you currently can't accomplish with CSS:

- ✔ **Changes to Flash content:** Your network's badges, photo slideshow, Video Player, and Music Player are all Flash applications. You can either show them or hide them, but you cannot modify them through any use of CSS.

- ✔ **Changes to content elements on profile pages:** On a member's profile page, the headers and boxes for all content elements (all blog posts, forum posts, photos, videos, and so on) posted by the member are controlled by the same class. As a result, you can't selectively hide or modify one without also affecting all the other ones. This may change in the future, but currently it is something you can't accomplish.

- ✔ **Changes to member details on profile pages:** On a member's profile page, the details below the member photo are in the same boat as the content elements just mentioned. For example, you can't hide a member's gender and display her location, or vice versa, because all the member details are controlled by the same class. If you modify the class, all the member details are affected by it.

Making changes from the Advanced Appearance tab

In Chapter 7, I show you how to play with the theme of your network so you can design it to your liking. To make any CSS change on your network, you have to go to the same place:

1. **Click the Manage link on your network's navigation.**

2. **Click the Appearance option below the Your Network header.**

3. **On the Appearance page, click the Advanced tab, as shown in Figure 19-4.**

4. **Paste into the text box available any CSS code that you want to include.**

5. **Scroll down to the bottom of the page and click the Save button.**

   The CSS styles you added should be reflected in the network at this point.

It's a good idea to get your CSS code all clean and ready to go before entering it in the Advanced tab of the Appearance page. CSS changes are one of the reasons why it's a good idea to run a test network to try out your changes before you apply them to your live network.

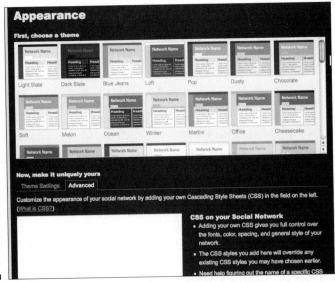

Figure 19-4: The Advanced tab in the Appearance section lets you make CSS changes.

As for tools to work on your CSS, there are plenty of nice HTML and CSS editors out there. A Google search for *CSS editor* reveals a lot of them. As long as you aren't too sloppy, all you need is a basic text editor, such as Notepad (for Windows) or TextEdit (for Mac OS), to copy your code from.

Looking at examples of CSS changes

In the following sections, I give you four examples of CSS changes to get you an idea of the kinds of things you can accomplish using CSS in your network.

New CSS classes are regularly added to the code that powers networks on Ning. Also, some CSS classes are retired occasionally.

Therefore, even though you can remove newly added styles, it's always a good idea to verify the following CSS examples before implementing them on your network, to avoid any surprises. You can do this verification on a test network, where you aren't going to annoy members on your live network.

In all the examples in this chapter, I have modified existing styles. You can create your own styles to use them in text boxes and notes if you want. To do this, you need to first define the new class in the Advanced tab of the Appearance section. You can then call the class in the HTML where you want to use it elsewhere on the network.

Hiding the number of members

This CSS style hides the number of members on the Members page. This is something some network creators like to do while their networks are still relatively small.

```
.xg_widget_profiles_members_index .count
{
display: none;
}
```

Fixing the background image

If you've uploaded a background image through the Appearance page (as explained in Chapter 8), you can use this CSS style to lock the background image of the network in place when you scroll down. You can see an example of an implementation at http://thisis50.com.

```
body
{
background-attachment: fixed;
}
```

Aligning the bar with the Ning button with the other edges

This CSS style is purely aesthetic, but it gives your network a nicer look (well, I kinda like it myself, at least). Figure 19-5 shows you what happens to the area where the Ning button is located before and after applying the new style.

Figure 19-5:
Using a new
CSS style to
make your
network
look nicer.

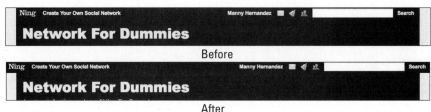

Before

After

```
#xn_bar
{
float:none;
margin-left:auto;
margin-right:auto;
width:955px;
}
```

Changing fonts on your profile page

This CSS style, which I've applied on my TuDiabetes.com profile page (it works the same way, except for showing up only on my page and being modified by clicking the Theme link below my profile photo), makes the font of headers of the modules in my page a bit bigger and changes them to use the Courier font. (I have a thing for this font lately.)

```
.xg_module_head h2
{
font-size:1.4em;
font-family:courier;
}
```

You can see the change in action in Figure 19-6, where the headers for My Events, Blood Glucose Units Converter, and Comment Wall (1,311 comments) now show the new font size and font family.

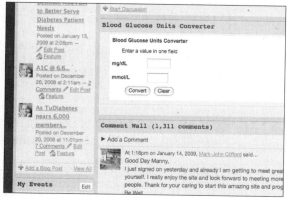

Figure 19-6:
Changes
to fonts
can have
a dramatic
impact
on your
network's
pages.

Finding Additional CSS Resources

CSS, as you can see, is a vast territory. So it helps having a few good extra references to fall back on:

- **CSS No Crap Primer:** This funny named Web site comes up at the top when you Google *CSS 101,* and for a good reason. It *really* makes understanding CSS as easy as it can get, so I recommend you start here: `http://wendypeck.com/css101.html.`

- **W3Schools.com:** The Learn CSS tutorial is the second easiest way into CSS you can find around (the first one being the CSS No Crap Primer). It goes into more detail than the primer, giving many more examples: `www.w3schools.com.`

- **Eric Meyer:** As the author of a large number of CSS titles, Eric Meyer has turned into a bit of a legend in Web design circles. The CSS section on his site (`http://meyerweb.com/eric/css`) is fairly comprehensive and has turned into a must-use reference.

- **World Wide Web consortium:** The W3C site (`www.w3.org`) is the top destination for CSS references. The W3C Learning CSS section (`www.w3.org/Style/CSS/learning`) is very useful, as is the complete CSS specification (`www.w3.org/TR/CSS21`). However, the W3C Web site isn't the best place to go to get started with CSS.

These networks are nice examples of what can be done on a network on Ning with CSS changes:

- `http://my.fidgetstick.com`: The change to a two-column layout on this network was done with CSS. The main page looks like a million dollars, as you can see in Figure 19-7.

Figure 19-7:
The main page of the Fidgetstick network has some impressive CSS work.

✔ www.finance30.com: The folks who designed this site kept the three columns, but through some CSS magic, they swapped the left column and the middle one. They also did some very cool stuff by adding a box with plenty of space in the footer in order to house the network's About section, a toolbox, and quick links.

✔ www.veloist.com and http://printjunkie.net: Both of these networks are good examples of subtle changes that go a long way. Adding feather-thin borders or separators to the different features on the main page and tweaking with fonts are two things the designers did very well.

Chapter 20

Using the Language Editor

Do you remember a song that went "You say *potato*, I say *potato*"? The first *potato* was pronounced with an American accent and the second one with a British accent. If you don't remember it, don't feel bad: That probably means you're not too old!

At the time this book is being written, Ning lets you offer your network in more than 20 languages, so you can say *potato* in more languages than you can imagine.

This chapter deals with the Language Editor, the tool that makes all this possible. The Language Editor also lets you modify specific words and some other cool things across your network.

Meeting the Language Editor and Choosing a Different Language

The Language Editor is one of the most powerful tools at your disposal for customizing your network to the max, and it's one of my personal favorites!

Chapter 19 tells how you can make your network *look* the way you want it. The Language Editor helps you make your network interface (menus, buttons, headers, legends, and so on) *read* exactly the way you want it to.

Having your network's language meet your needs may mean one of two things:

- ✔ You may need the network to be offered in a language other than the default U.S. English, so you can cater to your target member audience.

- ✔ Your network may be in English, but you may need to change certain words to match your needs or wants.

Whatever the case, the Language Editor is the tool you need, and it can even help you accomplish a few stylistic changes that go beyond textual modification. I go over a few examples of each case later in this chapter. In the following steps, I show you the simplest thing you can do with the Language Editor: Choose a different language.

1. **Click the Manage link in your navigation and click the Language Editor icon below the Your Network heading.**

   You land on the Language Editor page, which presents you first with the option to edit the language on your network, as shown in Figure 20-1.

   The Language Editor page shows you what language your network is currently using next to the words *The active language for your network is,* followed by the Change Active Language link.

2. **Click the Change Active Language link**

   You're taken to the Network Information page, where you can change the network's language to one of the languages offered by Ning. The variety of languages goes as far as offering two variations of English (U.S. and British), two variations of Spanish (Argentina and Spain), almost every other major language in Europe, and a number of Asian languages.

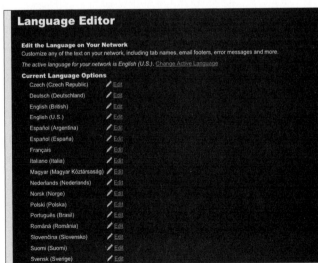

Figure 20-1:
Changing your network's active language affects all text in your network.

3. **Choose the language you want to use from the Language drop-down list, as shown in Figure 20-2.**

4. **Click the Save button at the bottom.**

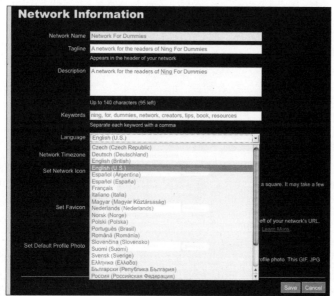

Figure 20-2:
Your net-
work can be
presented
in more
than 20
languages
offered by
Ning.

Customizing Your Network with the Language Editor

Although it's extremely useful to be able to change the language of your entire network, the true power of the Language Editor shows when you use it to tweak little things here and there throughout the network.

In Chapter 8, I rename the Members link in the network navigation as Dummies (because my test network is called Network For Dummies), as shown in Figure 20-3. I promised in that chapter that I would show you how to change the name of many other things in the network in Chapter 20 — you're finally here!

Figure 20-3:
The
Language
Editor lets
you rename
text ele-
ments in the
network.

To change Members to Dummies elsewhere in the network, you need to use the Language Editor. Follow these steps to see how you would go about making such a change:

1. **On the Language Editor page, click the Edit link next to the active language for your network — in my network, that would be English (U.S.).**

   You're taken to the page where you edit your active language, as shown in Figure 20-4.

2. **Type** Members **in the Original Text box and click the Search button.**

   As you can imagine, you get a large list of results because the word *Members* appears in many places in the network.

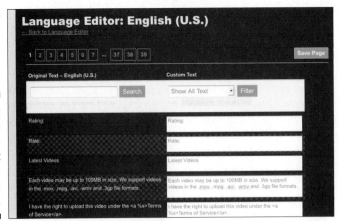

Figure 20-4:
This is the
page where
all the text
customiza-
tion magic
happens.

3. **Scan the Original Text column for instances of the word** Members **(all by itself) and type** Dummies **in the Custom Text box in the column right next to each.**

   If you wanted to be exhaustive, you would substitute the words *member* and *members* for *dummy* and *dummies* in every single result you get on this page and click one of the Save Page buttons. (There's a Save Page button at the top of the page and one at the bottom.)

   For simplicity's sake, scan for all instances of *Members* and *All Members* and substitute *Dummies* and *All Dummies* in the boxes to the right of each instance, in the Custom Text column on the right.

4. **When you're done changing every instance, click either Save Page button.**

   If you take a look at the Members . . . errr, Dummies page, the instances of the word *Members* that used to be there have been replaced with the word *Dummies* (see Figure 20-5).

5. **Repeat this process to change as many words, phrases, and text details across the network as you need.**

Figure 20-5:
All
Members
is now *All*
Dummies
after the
Language
Editor
change.

Changing your welcome e-mail message

Every time new members join, an e-mail message is sent to them, which essentially thanks them for joining and provides them with a link to your network. You can edit this welcome e-mail message through the Language Editor to include additional information and links or to make it a bit more personal.

To edit the welcome e-mail message, follow these steps:

1. **On the Language Editor page corresponding to your network's language, type the text** Welcome to %s! Thank you for joining. **in the Original Text search box.**

   In case you're wondering, the %s part gets replaced by the network name when the message is sent.

2. **Make all the changes you want to your welcome e-mail message and then click the Save Page button.**

   From that point on, all new members will receive the updated version of the message upon joining the network.

Although you can include HTML code in any custom text you enter through the Language Editor, whether the HTML gets properly rendered depends on where the text you're modifying gets displayed.

For example, because network messages don't support HTML, any HTML code you include in your modified welcome e-mail message doesn't get rendered as such.

If you want to include a link in any network e-mail messages, such as confirmations of actions such as joining the network or joining a group, simply type in the URL without any HTML code surrounding it.

Changing your network's footer

The network footer is one area on your network where you can make great use of the Language Editor. You can find an excellent example of this at www. firefighternation.com, one of the networks I recommend in Chapter 2.

Dave Iannone, Network Creator for Firefighter Nation, has customized his network's footer to include additional information such as his company's name linked back to his company's Web site, his network's partners, and a disclaimer about his network's intended use, as you can see in Figure 20-6.

Figure 20-6:
The Language Editor lets you modify your network's footer.

© 2009   Created by FFN Web Chief, a Go Forward Media, LLC Property - Dave's Blog   Partners: JEMS Connect - FireRescue - JEMS
· Contact Us: Report an Issue, Inquire About Advertising & Partnerships
This site is intended for use by current and former fire, rescue & EMS professionals. Non emergency service personnel may be subject to review and removal.
Using this site inappropriately to spam/advertise or solicit members in any way will result in account termination.

Badges | Contact Firefighter Nation | Privacy | Terms of Service

Lots of text elements in the Language Editor, like the ones I am about to explain to you, contain items called *variables* that Ning automatically translates into something else. This is a way to maintain items automatically updated across the network in case you change your network's name, your own member profile name, or any other elements that Ning handles dynamically for you.

Several text elements (shown in Figure 20-7) make up your network's footer:

✔ **© 2009 Created by Manny Hernandez on Ning:** As I'm sure you figured out already, in your network, this part of the footer obviously show your name instead of mine. When you search for this text element, you can find it by doing a partial search; for instance, searching for *Created by* brings this element up among the results. In the Custom Text column, the corresponding entry goes something like © %1$s   Created by %2$s on Ning, which warrants a bit of explaining:

- %1$s — This is a variable that gets translated into the current year in this particular case. In other lines of text in the Language Editor, it means other things. Unless you want to get rid of the current year information in the footer, you don't have to do anything to it.

-   — This item is the equivalent in HTML to nonbreaking space, which is a way of physically spacing to pieces of text on the page without introducing a line break.

- %2$s — In this line of text, this variable is replaced by whatever name you go by in the network you created. If you want, you can replace it with the name of your company or organization along with a link to your Web site, as Dave did on FireFighter Nation. Just like in the case of %1$s, this variable means other things in other lines of text.

✔ **Badges:** This link points to your network's Badges & Widgets page. If you feel the term *badges* is not well understood by your members, you give this link a different name.

Figure 20-7:
You can modify the text that appears on your network's footer.

© 2009 Created by Manny Hernandez on Ning. Create your own social network   Badges   Report an Issue   Privacy   Terms of Service

✔ **Report an Issue:** You can turn this text into the more inviting Contact Us or Feedback.

✔ **Privacy:** This link points to Ning's Privacy Policy.

✔ **Terms of Service:** This link points to Ning's Terms of Service. If you have your own Terms of Service, one good use of the Language Editor could be to change this text to "Terms of Service (Ning)."

Translating Your Network to an Unsupported Language

Although there are 24 languages supported by Ning at the time of this writing, with so many languages in the world, you may need to translate your network to a new language. The Language Editor is the place for you to do this.

To create a new translation, follow these steps:

1. **Click the Create a New Translation for Your Network link close to the bottom of the Language Editor page, as shown in Figure 20-8.**

   You're taken to the Create a New Translation page, as shown in Figure 20-9.

2. **Give the new language a name in the Language Name text box.**

3. **Choose an existing language as a starting point to base your new language on from the Based On drop-down list.**

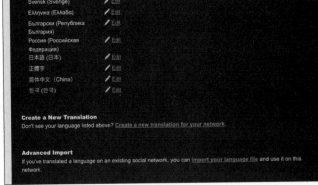

Figure 20-8:
Ning lets you create your own translation for your network.

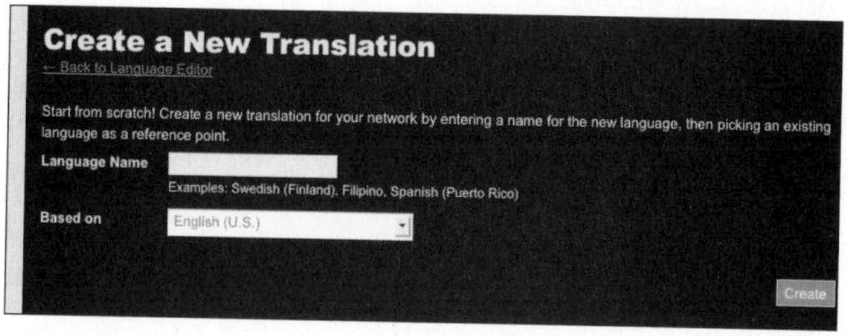

Figure 20-9:
To create a new translation, you have to base it on an existing language.

Create a New Translation
← Back to Language Editor

Start from scratch! Create a new translation for your network by entering a name for the new language, then picking an existing language as a reference point.

Language Name

Examples: Swedish (Finland), Filipino, Spanish (Puerto Rico)

Based on   English (U.S.)

Create

4. **Click the Create button.**

   The page you're taken to next looks almost exactly like the one shown in Figure 20-4, earlier in this chapter, but showing at the top is the name you've given the new translation. Instead of having the Custom Text column fields prefilled with language, the fields are empty, giving you the chance to customize every single language item in the entire network.

5. **In the Custom Text column, fill in the fields with translated text.**

6. **When you're done, click the Save Page button.**

   This can be quite an undertaking, but if the language you need for your network is not available, it may be your only option. Still, before you create a new translation, I recommend you contact Ning through the Help Center at `http://help.ning.com` and ask whether Ning has plans to offer the language you need in the near future.

7. **When you're done creating the new translation, simply follow the steps discussed earlier (in the "Meeting the Language Editor and Choosing a Different Language" section) to choose a different language from the Language drop-down list.**

Importing a Language from one Network into Another

If you've taken the road of translating a language for a network you created and you're creating a new network that you want to use the same language on, you can also do it through the Language Editor.

To obtain the language file from your previous network, follow these steps:

1. **Click the Import Your Language File link at the bottom of the Language Editor page.**

   This step takes you to the Advanced Import page, shown in Figure 20-10.

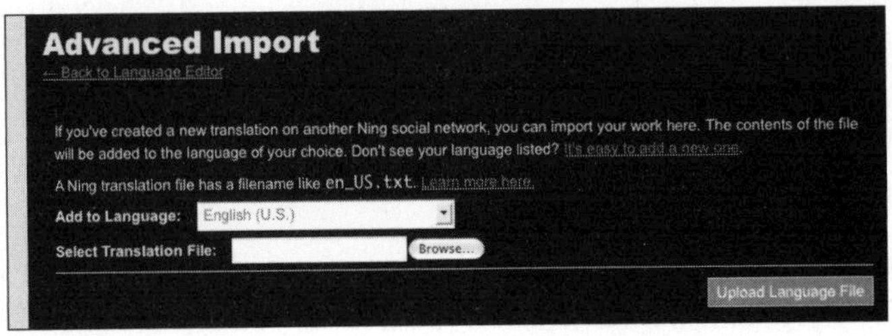

Figure 20-10:
The
Advanced
Import
page lets
you import
a previous
translation.

Advanced Import
← Back to Language Editor

If you've created a new translation on another Ning social network, you can import your work here. The contents of the file will be added to the language of your choice. Don't see your language listed? It's easy to add a new one.

A Ning translation file has a filename like en_US.txt. Learn more here.

Add to Language: English (U.S.)

Select Translation File: [   ] Browse...

Upload Language File

2. **Go to `http://<YOUR_NETWORK_NAME>.ning.com/lib/scripts/translations.php`.**

   For example, in the case of my network, I would go to `http://net workfordummies.ning.com/lib/scripts/translations.php`.

   You're taken to the Translations page, which contains links to all the translations found on your network, as shown in Figure 20-11.

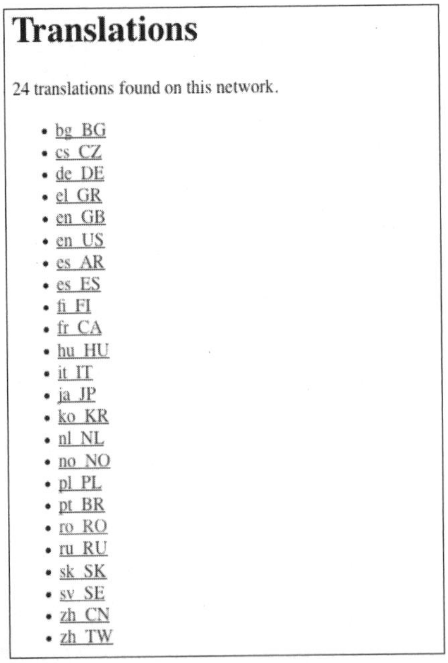

Translations

24 translations found on this network.

- bg_BG
- cs_CZ
- de_DE
- el_GR
- en_GB
- en_US
- es_AR
- es_ES
- fi_FI
- fr_CA
- hu_HU
- it_IT
- ja_JP
- ko_KR
- nl_NL
- no_NO
- pl_PL
- pt_BR
- ro_RO
- ru_RU
- sk_SK
- sv_SE
- zh_CN
- zh_TW

Figure 20-11:
The
Translations
page lets
you down-
load your
translation
files.

3. **Click the link corresponding to the translation file you need.**

   You're prompted to choose an application to open it with. A text editor such as Notepad for Windows or TextEdit for the Mac should do the trick.

4. **Open the translation file to verify it's the one you're looking for and, if so, save it on your local hard drive.**

5. **When you have your translation file, go to the Advanced Import page and choose the language you want the contents of the file to be added to from the Add to Language drop-down list.**

6. **Select the translation file by clicking the Browse button.**

7. **When you're done, click Upload Language File.**

   When the upload is done, all the blood, sweat, and tears you put into your translation file will be a part of the language you chose to add the file to in the new network.

Chapter 21

OpenSocial Applications in Your Network

*O*penSocial saw the light of day in November 2007. Google, along with a large number of partners (including most of the main social networking sites except for Facebook), developed an interface for social network applications. That interface enables third-party applications to access member data and perform network actions that are generally accessible only to a service's core features. One of my favorite examples of a social network application is Reading List by Amazon. Thanks to it, you can share the books you want to read, the ones you're reading, and those you've read and recommend with your connections on LinkedIn, a popular business-centric social network.

OpenSocial makes features from social networks such as Hi5.com, MySpace, orkut, Friendster, and all networks on Ning available to anyone who implements an OpenSocial application. For example, you could chat with friends from multiple networks in your network on Ning, or you could have your status from a social network update your status throughout multiple networks.

If this sounds complicated, the following pages should help you understand why having Ning support OpenSocial is so important for your network. In this chapter, I discuss the basics of OpenSocial, along with the steps you need to follow to create, add, or remove OpenSocial applications. I share some of the most popular OpenSocial apps and deal briefly with the future of OpenSocial on Ning.

Opening Up with OpenSocial

The concept underlying OpenSocial is fascinating. The OpenSocial API acknowledges the fact that people on the Web participate in multiple Web sites and social networks. Thus, applications that support OpenSocial can run on multiple Web sites.

Likewise, through the applications that support it, OpenSocial can make information such as friends in a network; status; preferences in music, film, and reading; and so on available from one site to another or allow the aggregation of information in unique and convenient ways.

Being able to visualize and connect with your friends through Google or Yahoo! Maps within any OpenSocial-compatible social network; sharing files with others in your network (or outside it); and having your status on one social network drive the status in your profile page in other networks are three examples of things that OpenSocial makes possible.

For OpenSocial developers, the advantages are clear: Having to develop a single application that works for multiple Web sites represents an important time and money saver.

Lucky for all Network Creators, networks on Ning are compatible with OpenSocial. I can only imagine what the future will be like as more applications are developed to increase the functionality available to networks on Ning.

Adding and Editing Profile Apps

At the end of this chapter, I deal briefly with Ning Apps, which only Network Creators and Administrators can add to the network. However, members can add applications to their profiles very easily and then edit those apps. I show you how in the following sections.

Adding applications

Adding Profile Apps to your profile page is truly a piece of cake:

1. **Visit your profile page and click the Add Applications link below your profile photo.**

   This step takes you to the Application Directory, the list of all applications, shown in Figure 21-1.

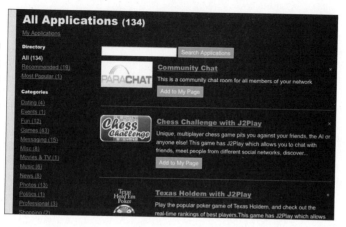

Figure 21-1:
The
Application
Directory
lets you
browse all
applications
and add any
to your pro-
file page.

2. **On this page, you can do the following things:**

   - View the Recommended applications by clicking the Recommended link on the left.

   - Look at the Most Popular applications by clicking the Most Popular link.

   - Explore all applications by category, clicking the different categories listed below the Categories heading.

   - Search for a particular term to see whether there's an existing application that meets your needs.

3. **When you find an application you want to add, click the Add to My Page button below it to add it to your profile page.**

4. **When the prompt appears (see Figure 21-2), confirm whether you want to add the application.**

   This may seem unnecessary to you, but it's an important step because it lets you read the application's Terms of Use and cancel your request by clicking the Cancel button if you don't agree with them.

Figure 21-2:
This window
prompts you
to confirm
whether
you agree to
the applica-
tion's Terms
of Use.

5. If you agree with the Terms of Use, click the Add Application button to complete the process and add it to your profile page.

The new application you've added appears at the top of your profile page.

In Figure 21-3, you can see how my profile page looks after I added the Friend Map application.

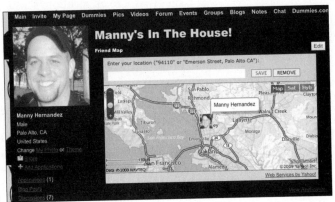

Figure 21-3:
New applications are added at the top of your profile page.

Below each application on another member's profile page, there are two links, as shown in Figure 21-4:

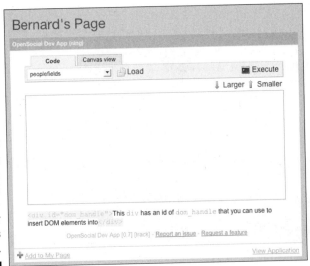

Figure 21-4:
You can easily add an application another member has on his page.

✔ **Add to My Page:** Clicking this link is equivalent to clicking the Add to My Page button in the Application Directory. This link is great to help you add an application you want on your own profile page after seeing it in action on someone else's profile page.

✔ **View Application:** Clicking this link takes you to a page where you can find out more about the application and add it to your page. Also, this page contains a Report Abuse link. Clicking this link lets you report a bug, fraud, spam, or other issues with the application. This report sends an OpenSocial Abuse Report to the Network Creator and Administrators.

If you click View Application for an application you've added, the page you arrive on also has a Remove Application link.

Editing your applications

All the applications you add to your profile page have an Edit button at the top right. If you want to make changes to your application, here's what you do:

1. **Click the Edit button in the application you want to adjust.**

   A panel opens, giving you a few options to control the display of information related to the application and your page, as shown in Figure 21-5. You find two check boxes:

   • Allow this application to add updates in the Latest Activity module on My Page

   • Allow this application to send me and my friends alerts

Figure 21-5:
The Edit panel for an application gives you control over the application.

2. **Select or deselect the check boxes, depending on what you want the application to be able to do.**

3. **If you want to remove the box where the application appears in your profile page, click the Remove Box link.**

   The application continues to be accessible through the My Applications page. You can get to the My Applications page by clicking the Applications link below your profile photo.

4. **To remove the application from your profile page and your Applications altogether, click the Remove Application link.**

Manny's Favorite Profile Apps

Ning offers hundreds of Profile Apps: You can find apps to suit all preferences. Here, I present a few applications that I find particularly useful, hoping they can help you extend the value you offer through your network. You can find any of them by searching for the application name in the Application Directory.

- ✔ **Box.net:** Enables safe file uploading and file sharing with others in your network. This opens incredible avenues for collaboration.

- ✔ **Friend Map:** Lets you view all your network friends on a Yahoo! map, zoom in and out, and navigate throughout the entire map.

- ✔ **PollDaddy:** Allows members to create polls on their profile pages and share them with others in the network.

- ✔ **RSS:** Combines and displays up to five RSS feeds. This app helps overcome the limitation of a single RSS feed per profile page.

- ✔ **ShopIt:** Lets members buy and sell products and services from their profile page and conveniently share product information.

- ✔ **Text Box:** Gives you one extra text box to include in your profile page, in case a single text box is not enough.

- ✔ **Unype Virtual World:** Lets you chat with members from Facebook, MySpace, Bebo, Hi5, Ning, and Orkut on a world map.

- ✔ **Ustream.tv:** Lets you broadcast video live from your profile page. You need only a webcam to take advantage of it.

It's a good idea to pay a visit to the Application Directory periodically to see what new applications may have been added recently, which are the most popular and typically the highest rated. New applications are created all the time, which brings me to the next section of this chapter, dealing with the creation of Profile Apps.

Creating Profile Apps

Creating Profile Apps is not for everybody. If you're a Network Creator, nobody expects you to be able to create new OpenSocial apps unless you have a background in Web software development with a solid JavaScript and HTML foundation.

Because OpenSocial development requires more advanced knowledge than can be included in this chapter, I don't discuss technical details about OpenSocial application creation here. I recommend you follow the advice in this section in order to arm yourself with the tools you need to develop your own applications.

If you have what it takes, you should start by join the Ning Developer Network at `http://developer.ning.com`, shown in Figure 21-6. This network has thousands of members constantly discussing OpenSocial application development.

Also, in the Ning Developer Network you can find all the documentation you need in order to create your application. If you click the big Create Your Application button on the main page of the network or select the Submit an Application option under Profile Apps in the network navigation, you're taken to the Submissions page.

Figure 21-6: The Ning Developer Network is an excellent resource for developers.

When you're not signed into the network, the Submissions page lets you access the OpenSocial Documentation by clicking the Learn More! link at the bottom of the page. At all times, you can also access the documentation within the OpenSocial option in the Resources menu of the network navigation.

When you're done creating your OpenSocial application, you need to submit it for approval. You need to be signed into the network in order to submit an application for review.

Go to the Submissions page, as explained earlier. The Submissions page you're taken to appears, as shown in Figure 21-7. Any previously approved applications you've submitted appear at the top of the page, such as the Blood Glucose Units Converter application, developed by Bernard Farrell, as you can see in Figure 21-7.

Below any previous applications, there's a text box where you can enter the URL to your OpenSocial application file. Paste the address where the application is found into the New Application text box and click the Add button.

The application gets submitted for consideration, and if it gets approved, you get notified via e-mail when it's added to the Application Directory. If anything about the application needs to be changed, you also get notified about what needs to be corrected. After you've made the necessary changes, you can resubmit the application by following the same steps.

Figure 21-7:
The Submissions page lets you submit an application for review.

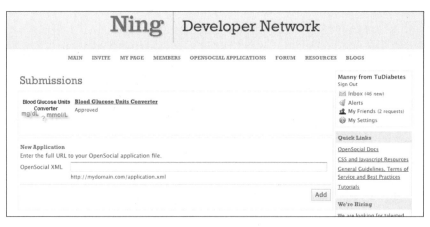

Networkwide Ning Apps

By the time you read this, Ning Apps should be available. These are network-wide OpenSocial applications that give Network Creators the ability to add new features and functionality to their networks.

Any Ning App you add to your network becomes seamlessly added to your main page and also has its own tab, just like any other feature on your network. The only difference is that Ning Apps may have been developed by Ning, or they may have been developed by third-party developers.

To find out more about Ning Apps, make sure to review the Ning resources in the appendix.

Part VI
The Part of Tens

The 5th Wave   By Rich Tennant

"You should check that box so they can't profile your listening and viewing habits. I didn't do it and I'm still getting spam about hearing loss, anger management and psychological counseling."

In this part . . .

*I*f you're thinking of making money from your network, this part is for you. I discuss ten ways to help you monetize your network.

If Part V didn't give you enough advanced tips and tricks and you feel the need for more technical challenges, I offer some hacks to make your network stand out from the crowd, as well as ten tools to help you run a network on Ning.

The last chapter in this part offers a list of ten ideas for networks on Ning (just in case you're having trouble picking one for yourself).

Chapter 22

Ten Ways to Monetize Your Network

· ·

C hances are good that you want to run your network to simply help connect other like-minded people without any thought of making money off
it, and that's perfectly fine. However, it's also fine if you want to make money
off your network. In this chapter, I discuss ten potential ways to monetize
your network on Ning.

Running Ads through an Ad Network

Though it's not free, the easiest way to monetize your network is to run ads
on your network. One of the most popular ways to run ads is to sign up for an
ad network such as Google AdSense. The advantage of doing this is simple:
The ad network analyzes the content in the pages of your network and
inserts the most appropriate ads into each page, depending on the page's
content. All you need to do is sign up, obtain the code, and plug it in your
network, as I explain in Chapter 18.

Google AdSense may be the most popular advertising network, but it is certainly not the only one. Doing a cursory search on Google (how ironic!) for
ad network returns more options than you will ever have time to explore.
If you're lucky, you may find an ad network specifically suited to your network's niche. Specialized ad networks are known for getting higher returns
than generic ones like AdSense.

Whatever you do, before you add any code you obtain from your ad network,
you must sign up for the Control the Ads premium service, as discussed in
Chapter 18.

Selling Your Own Ads

When you run ads from an advertising network, the network retains a portion of the money advertisers pay. If you want to get an even higher return for your ads, you can sell your own ads.

I would not recommend this option unless you can afford to manage direct relationships with advertisers, giving them the kind of time and attention they expect for their money.

This option also does not typically work well for networks with fewer than 2,000 members or fewer than 300,000 page views. (You can find out about your page views by using Google Analytics, as explained in Chapter 16.) At lower membership and traffic levels, you may be able to sell ads to small advertisers, but larger advertisers may not see an incentive to carry an ad on what they see as a small Web site. So until you network has grown signifi-cantly, ads from an advertising network may be your best bet.

For you to be able to sell your own ads, you need to purchase the Control the Ads premium service (see Chapter 18).

Using Ads as Fixed Background Images

In Chapter 19, I give an example of using CSS to make your network's background image fixed so that it doesn't move when visitors scroll down on the page.

A good use of this CSS example is to offer advertisers the background image as a space where they can place their ad. The downside of this option is that users can't click it, so you can't direct click-through traffic elsewhere with this approach.

You can think of this option as something similar to a billboard on the street: It can be used to promote a product or service that can be purchased offline or over the phone.

Working with Affiliate Programs

Affiliate or referral programs are older than the Web. The concept is simple: For each sale or lead you refer to another vendor or site, you get paid a commission. Some vendors have their own affiliate programs (for example,

Amazon.com has Amazon Advantage). Others sign up as part of affiliate networks like LinkShare and Commission Junction. These networks represent thousands of vendors under multiple categories.

After you sign up with an affiliate program, you're required to include a code of some kind (not unlike the case of advertising networks) in your network. The main difference with ad networks is that ad networks pay a little bit for every click on ads that you carry in your network. Affiliate programs may pay more money, but you see the money only if people click the ad *and* purchase a product or service in connection with it. Otherwise, you don't get any payoff from the click.

If you include any kind of ads on your network as part of an affiliate program you're part of, you need to purchase the Control the Ads premium service (see Chapter 18).

Charging a Network Membership Fee

As you know by now, it costs nothing to create or become a member of a network on Ning. However, you can charge a membership fee for people to sign up to your network if you want. You can do this by setting up your network so you can moderate new members, as explained in Chapter 10. Before you approve new members, you can send them the details about the membership fee, directing them to a site through which you collect fees, such as PayPal or Google Checkout.

Think before you charge for being a member of your network. Consider why would someone pay to join: Are you offering something really unique? Perhaps members in your network can mingle with others whom they would otherwise never be able to hang out with, and that alone is worth the price tag. Just make sure you're offering something worth paying for before you charge for a membership fee. Otherwise, you risk not getting people signing up to your network.

Charging Group Membership Fees

An alternative version of the network membership fee option is to charge group membership fees. One or more groups on your network may offer special benefits that members would be willing to pay for. Using this method, you can have tiered membership on your network where all members have access to most of the network and those who want access to other premium benefits can pay to join the group(s) where these benefits are available.

Until Ning offers a tiered membership option, you can implement this by setting up a group with moderated membership, as explained in Chapter 6. Before you approve new members, you can charge them the group membership fee by taking similar steps to the ones explained in the previous subsection for the network membership fee alternative.

Asking for Donations

Although donations may be an option to monetize networks that may be better suited for networks that are not for profit, don't underestimate the potential for generating revenue this way. If you do a good job with your network, your members may be willing to make a small donation to support your efforts.

To recognize donors that help your network, you can list them on a Notes page, which you can set up as explained in Chapter 11.

To facilitate the collection of donations, you can add a nice-looking PayPal Donate button like the one shown in Figure 22-1. You can add the button to a Text Box on your main page, as explained in Chapter 9.

Figure 22-1: PayPal Donate buttons make collection of donations very easy.

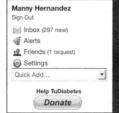

Selling Merchandise

Selling merchandise that sports your network's logo is not only a good way to monetize your network, but also a great way to promote it because people who buy merchandise normally wear it (in the case of T-shirts, hats, and bags) and carry it around and use it (as with mugs, buttons, and other forms of swag).

One of the most convenient ways to sell network merchandise is to sign up for services such as CafePress (www.cafepress.com) or Zazzle (www.zazzle.com). They let you design your own items, set up an online store, and promote the store through your network by using code you can include in a Text Box. For every item that sells in your online store, the service pays you a commission. The service takes care of manufacturing and shipping of the orders.

You can also design and order your own merchandise to sell it yourself, so you can potentially make a bigger profit. The downsides of this are obvious: You need to keep an inventory, which costs you money, and you have to take care of the fulfillment of the orders, which also costs money and takes time away from your running the network. However, this may be a good option for you if you can afford it.

Applying for Grants

Grants can come from government sources as well as private foundations. Though many grants are directed to nonprofit organizations, not all of them are: Some grants are intended for small businesses.

As more and more attention is being paid to social media as a viable channel to create social change these days, you may find that you qualify for grants to help develop your social network on Ning.

Performing a search for *grants* or *small business grants* in a search engine returns a very large number of results that you need to sort through to find the options that are suited to your unique situation.

Future Options through OpenSocial

In Chapter 21, I discuss OpenSocial applications, including a brief mention of OpenSocial network applications. One of the applications I mention is ShopIt, an application that lets you and your members buy and sell products and services through your network.

New ways to monetize your social network on Ning may become available in the near term thanks to the rollout of OpenSocial network apps, letting you monetize your network in new and creative ways.

Chapter 23

Almost Ten Ways to Make Your Network Rock

. . . .

*T*hroughout this book, I show you how to join, participate in, create, customize, manage, and promote a network on Ning. This chapter gives you a few more tools to help make your network rock!

A few of the tips discussed next require that you install *tracking code hacks,* which are pieces of code (typically JavaScript) that must be included alongside any tracking code you may have added to your network's Analytics page, as explained in Chapter 16.

I denote where you must install the hacks with the words **tracking code hacks** in bold. (I don't want you to miss it!) For your convenience, here are the steps you must follow to install tracking code hacks:

1. **Click the Manage link in your network's navigation.**
2. **Click the Analytics option under the Your Network heading.**
3. **Add the code included in this chapter (corresponding to the hack you want to apply) into your tracking code box.**

    Make sure you do not overwrite any existing code you find in the box (unless that is what you want to do).
4. **Click the Save button.**

Redirecting Your Network to Your Own Domain

As discussed in Chapter 18, when you purchase and configure the Use Your Own Domain premium service, it ensures that visitors who enter your domain name are taken to your network. However, your network continues to be reachable through its `.ning.com` address. To make sure any visits to your network are directed to your own domain, follow the steps in this section.

Make sure to do this only after you can access your network at `yourdomain.com`. If you take these steps before you can access your network at `your domain.com`, your social network may become inaccessible.

1. **Sign in to the network as the Network Creator.**

2. **Visit `http://YOURNETWORKNAME.ning.com/admin/index/edit DomainRedirection`.**

   For example, in the case of TuDiabetes, I would go to `http://tu diabetes.ning.com/admin/index/editDomainRedirection`.

   You're taken to the Domain Redirection page, as shown in Figure 23-1.

3. **From the Redirect To drop-down list, select the domain you want your network's visitors to be redirected to automatically.**

4. **Click the Save button.**

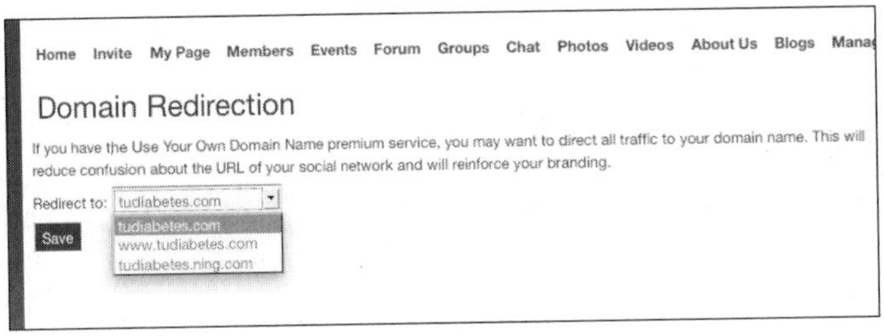

Figure 23-1:
The Domain Redirection page lets you send all visits to your network to your own domain.

Home Invite My Page Members Events Forum Groups Chat Photos Videos About Us Blogs Mana

Domain Redirection

If you have the Use Your Own Domain Name premium service, you may want to direct all traffic to your domain name. This will reduce confusion about the URL of your social network and will reinforce your branding.

Redirect to: tudiabetes.com

tudiabetes.com
www.tudiabetes.com
tudiabetes.ning.com

Save

Adding a New Page

Occasionally, you may need to add JavaScript code or an iFrame to a static page on your network, or you may want to enable comments at the bottom of a static page. You can't accomplish either of these things through the use of Notes. Here's where Pages come in handy, something you can add to your network using the Tab Manager, which I explain in Chapter 8.

The ability to create and edit pages is a *beta feature,* meaning that you may still run into a bug here or there. But for the most part, they do what they're intended for. So if you need to create a new page, follow these steps:

1. **Go through the steps to add a new tab, as explained in the last section of Chapter 8.**

2. **In the Tab Information section, select the Create New Page option and click the Save Tab Settings button.**

   This step adds the new page to your navigation based on where you placed the tab.

3. **Click the tab in your navigation to go to the newly created page.**

4. **On the new page, click the Edit link to edit the page.**

5. **Type or paste any content or code you may have at hand into the page's text box.**

6. **Click the Update Page button when you're done.**

Having a Flash Header

If you want to replace the image in your network header with an Adobe Flash (SWF) animation, you can do it with this **tracking code hack.** The Flash movie file needs to be 959 pixels wide by 179 pixels high.

1. **Write a blog post and upload the SWF file to it using the Upload File button.**

2. **When the post is live, right-click the SWF file and copy the link to it.**

   The URL begins with `http://api.ning.com/files`.

3. **You no longer need the blog post, so you can delete it.**

4. **In the following code, substitute the http://API_LINK URL for the URL you just copied:**

```
<script type="text/javascript"><!--
/**
 * Tracking Code Hack: Replace the Header of the
        network with a swf
**/

var headerSwfUrl    = "http://API_LINK";
var headerSwfWidth  = 959;
var headerSwfHeight = 179;
var newHeaderHtml   = '<embed src="'+headerSwfUrl+'"
        width="'+headerSwfWidth+'"
        height="'+headerSwfHeight+'"
        type="application/x-shockwave-flash"
        pluginspage="http://www.macromedia.com/go/
        getflashplayer <http://www.macromedia.com/go/
        getflashplayer> "> </embed>';
```

```
var headerElement    = document.getElementById('xg_
        masthead');

//replace the old header with the new one
headerElement.innerHTML = newHeaderHtml;

//change the id as a simple way to remove all css
        attached to it
headerElement.id     = 'newheader';

//-->
</script>
```

 5. **Copy the entire code with the new URL you just substituted into the tracking code box, as explained in the beginning of the chapter.**

 6. **Click the Save button to finish.**

Adding a Horizontal Banner to Your Network

If you pay for the Control the Ads premium service, you may want to run a horizontal banner that extends across the top of your network. The following two **tracking code hacks** let you insert a banner (or any other content, for that matter) below the thin strip with the search box at the top of your network or below the network navigation, as shown in Figure 23-2.

Figure 23-2:
You can add a banner or any other content below the colored strip at the top or below the navigation.

Below the strip with the search box

Copy the following code into the tracking code box, substituting **HEADLINER_HTML** with the HTML and CSS that you'd like to display below the thin strip with the search box at the very top of your network.

```
<script language="JavaScript">
//insert under the colored strip at the top, below the
        navigation only if it exists
var ningBar = document.getElementById('xn_bar');
if(ningBar) {
    var headlinerAd = document.createElement('div');
    headlinerAd.id='headliner_ad';
    headlinerAd.innerHTML = 'HEADLINER_HTML';
    ningBar.parentNode.insertBefore(headlinerAd,ningBar.
        nextSibling);
}
</script>
```

Below the network navigation

Copy the following code into the tracking code box, replacing **HEADLINER_HTML** with the HTML and CSS that you'd like to display below the navigation:

```
<script language="JavaScript">
var insertionPoint = document.getElementById('xg_head');
//if the exceptin ID exists we abort
var exceptionElement = document.getElementById('signin_
        email');
if((exceptionElement == null) && insertionPoint) {
    var bannerAdHtml = 'HEADLINER_HTML';
    insertionPoint.innerHTML += bannerAdHtml;
}
</script>
```

A cool use of this tracking hack is to post Urgent Announcements in a way similar to CNN Breaking News.

Opening RSS Links in a New Window

By default, any links in an RSS box on your network's main page open on the same window you are on. As a result, anyone clicking them effectively leaves your network's main page.

This **tracking code hack** lets you change this, so all links in all RSS boxes on the main page of your network open in a new window. Simply insert this code into your network's tracking code box:

```
<script language="JavaScript">
x$(document).ready(function() {
  x$('.module_feed').find("a").attr("target", "_blank" );
});
</script>
```

Speeding Up Load Time of Static Files

If you have images, scripts, and other static files, you can speed up their load time significantly by storing them in your network's `xn_resources` folder. Anything stored in this folder is optimized for faster download. To take advantage of the `xn_resources` folder, follow these steps:

1. **Connect to your network's file system using WebDav, as explained on this page:**

   `http://tinyurl.com/ningfordummieswebdav`

2. **Click the `xn_resources` folder and create a new folder.**

   For example, if you want to save static images, you can create one called `images`.

3. **Drag and drop all files you want to optimize for faster download into the new folder.**

4. **Anywhere the newly uploaded files appear, change the link that points to them.**

   The new URL where you can download these files can be found at `http://static.ning.com/yournetwork/newfolder/filename`. For example, an image file named `logo.jpg` uploaded to a new `images` folder in the `xn_resources` folder for TuDiabetes would be available at

   `http://static.ning.com/tudiabetes/images/logo.jpg`

Adding a Favicon

Favicons are those cute little icons that appear on your browser's address bar when you visit some Web sites. They also appear in your bookmarks if you bookmark the Web site.

By default, your social network's network icon will be applied as its favicon (only smaller). However, you can also add a different favicon to your social network by following these easy steps:

1. **Create a favicon for your network.**

   You can either do it yourself (it's a 16x16 image saved in the ICO format) or, more conveniently, do a Google search for *create a favicon* and use any of the resources listed in the results to help you create it.

2. **Click the Manage link in your navigation and click the Network Information link under the Your Network heading.**

3. **In the Set Favicon section of the Network Information page, click the Browse button to find the recently created `.ico` file in your computer.**

   The Network Information page is shown in Figure 23-3.

4. **Click the Save button.**

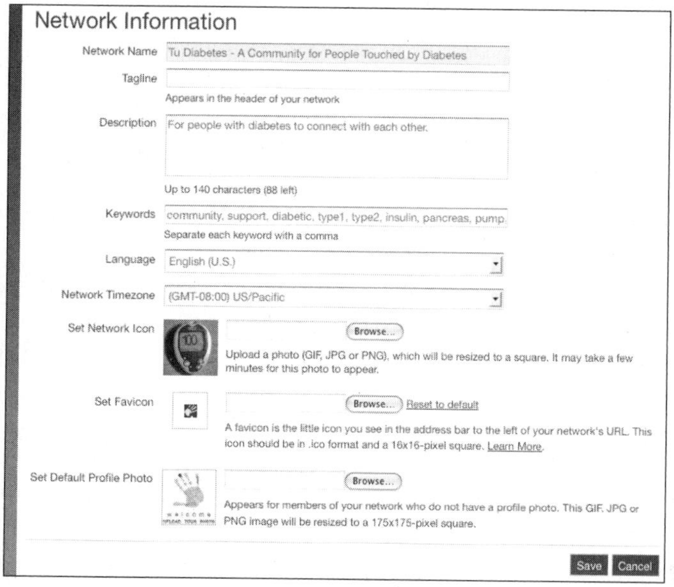

Figure 23-3:
The Network Information page lets you add a favicon and many more things.

Changing Your Default Profile Photo

The default profile photo gets displayed when a new member hasn't uploaded his or her own profile photo. You can choose what this photo looks like, further customizing your network. Follow these steps to change your default profile photo:

1. **Go to the Network Information page (to get there, see Step 2 in the preceding section).**

2. **In the Set Profile Photo section of the Network Information page, click the Browse button.**

3. **In the window that appears, find on your computer the profile photo you want to use as a default and click the Open button.**

4. **Click the Save button.**

Preventing Members from Modifying Their Profile Pages

I am all for letting members do with their profile pages as they please. However, you may have some good reasons to disable their ability to pimp out their pages. If this is the case, the following steps can help you accomplish just that:

1. **Click the Manage link in your navigation and click the Feature Controls link under the Your Members heading.**

2. **Deselect the check box next to Allow Members to Change Their My Page Theme if you want to prevent them from changing the way the look and feel of their profile pages.**

3. **Deselect the check box next to Allow members to adjust their My Page layout if you want to prevent them from moving feature boxes around their profile pages.**

4. **Click the Save button.**

Chapter 24

Ten Handy Tools to Help You Run Your Network

. . . .

*E*very industry and trade has a recommended brand or a power tool that everyone in the know takes advantage of. Being a member or running a network on Ning is no exception to this.

This chapter gives you nine programs or plug-ins and a hardware item that make your life as a member or a Network Creator easier, starting from the most basic ones to the most sophisticated.

Firefox

www.firefox.com

I have to hand it to Microsoft: Internet Explorer has improved dramatically in the past few years. However, my heart has a very special place for Firefox. This is not an emotional decision: Firefox is a very stable, fast, and safe browser, and there are some very powerful extensions developed for Firefox that are simply not available for Internet Explorer. Firebug (mentioned later on) is one such extension.

Flash Player

www.adobe.com/products/flashplayer

There's a good chance that you don't need to worry about installing Flash Player because most of the world's Internet user have it on their computers. However, Flash is not only a nice-to-have application, but also a necessity when you run a network on Ning. Network features such as the video player require Flash to even appear on your screen.

Java

`http://java.com/getjava`

Just like you need to have Flash Player to run some features on your network, to use the bulk uploading option for photos, videos, and music explained in Chapter 4, you need to make sure you install Sun's Java Runtime Engine.

A Text Editor

Though any text editor can do the job, Notepad and TextEditor natively come loaded with Windows and Mac OS, respectively. They come in handy when working with your network's CSS, Language Editor or adding any code to a Text Box in your network, to make editing tasks more comfortable to perform.

Firebug

`http://getfirebug.com`

In Chapter 19, I discuss CSS for your network on Ning. Firebug is a fascinating Firefox extension that allows you to inspect a Web site's CSS by placing your cursor over the element you want to find out about and make edits to the CSS in a non-permanent way that lets you see how those changes would appear.

A Video Converter

Windows: `www.videora.com`

Mac: `www.macupdate.com/info.php/id/19769/isquint`

As explained in Chapter 4, you may find yourself needing to convert your videos to a format supported by Ning. Two applications that are well suited for this task are iSquint for Mac and Videora for PC.

An Audio Converter

www.apple.com/itunes

The same way a video converter comes in handy for videos, an audio converter is helpful for audio files because your network's Music Player supports only MP3 files. One of the best programs you can get to help you convert audio files (and much more) is iTunes, which is available for both Mac and Windows platforms.

A Tool for Screenshots

Windows: www.wikihow.com/Take-a-Screenshot-in-Microsoft-Windows

Mac: http://skitch.com

When members communicate with you or you communicate with them or with Ning to get help with an issue, having screenshots makes the process easier.

To take screenshots in a Windows computer, you can follow the steps on the www.wikihow.com page. A great solution to obtain (and comment on) screenshots for the Mac is Skitch.

A Digital Video Editor

Mac: www.apple.com/ilife

Linux: www.kinodv.org

If you run a network on Ning, you might as well dust off that webcam because video gives you an excellent means to offer unique content and connect with your members. To make your videos look good, get a digital video editor.

Most Windows computers have Movie Maker natively installed. You can download a free copy from here:

```
www.download.com/Windows-Movie-Maker-Windows-Vista-/
          3000-13631_4-10729231.html
```

For Apple computers, you can get iMovie, which is part of the Apple iLife suite. Linux users can count on Kino Video Editor.

Dual Monitors

This last tool is not a program or a plug-in but a hardware accessory. If you haven't tried working with two monitors, you don't know what you're missing. Well beyond the "cool" factor, using two monitors expands the space available for you to spread windows on, ultimately increasing your productivity.

Chapter 25

Ten Ideas for a Network on Ning

· ·

*Y*ou've gotten to the end of the book. In case you still don't have an idea of what you can start a network about, in this last chapter I give you ten ideas for starting your own network on Ning.

To Reconnect with Classmates

Everyone has classmates, whether they be from high school, college, grad school, or even grade school. Ning gives you a great place for you to run a magnificent social network where you can catch up on stories about your long-lost friends from school and their whereabouts.

To Share with Other Fans

Whether you're a die-hard rocker or love the latest pop idol, whether you love classic literature or modern books, whether you love football or baseball, you surely are a fan of *something*. Guess what? You're not alone, and if someone hasn't done it, you can start a social network to connect with all those other fans out there.

To Rally People around a Campaign

If you're running for office or you support a candidate in an election, a network on Ning provides you with a great vehicle to coordinate volunteers and drive fundraising efforts.

To Connect with Other Patients

This is how I became involved with Ning. TuDiabetes.com and EsTuDiabetes. com connects people touched by diabetes. You can connect patients with all kinds of chronic conditions and ailments.

To Communicate with Your Students

If you teach a class in school, you and your students can benefit from being a part of social network. Communication in the network can reinforce and improve the classroom experience.

Find out more about these kinds of networks at

```
www.classroom.com
```

To Raise Awareness about a Cause

Whether you are fighting global warming or defending human rights, you can connect with others like you through a network on Ning, letting you spread the roots of your cause like wildfire.

A good example of this kind of network is

```
http://alternativeenergy.com
```

To Network with Other Professionals

People today are super busy with career and family. It's difficult to find time to meet and connect with professionals who are in your line of work. Enter Ning. Many professionals are able to network with others who work in the same line of business through a network on Ning. What could be more convenient?

Firefighters communicate on

```
www.firefighternation.com
```

To Offer a Space for Online Learning

You can combine the features offered by a network on Ning with other outside resources to offer a very complete online learning experience.

For example, this network helps Brazilians learn English online:

```
http://verdeamarelo.ning.com
```

To Help Conference Attendees Network

The bigger the conference, the more overwhelming it feels. But it doesn't have to be that way: Conference attendees can successfully connect and share tips about the event outside the venue and after hours through a network on Ning. People who have attended SXSW and MacWorld know it.

```
http://sxsw.ning.com/
```

```
http://macworldexpo.ning.com/
```

To Discuss Your Favorite Movies

Maybe you're an all out movie buff. Or you care about the classics. Or instead, you prefer foreign or independent movies. Whatever your preference, you can set up a network on Ning for it.

A great example of a movie review network is

```
http://my.spill.com
```

Appendix

Ning Resources

• •

*I*n spite of how awesome you may think this book is (something that I wholeheartedly agree with), as any other book dealing with Web matters, it's bound to become obsolete at some point.

To help you stay on top of the latest and greatest that Ning has to offer in an ongoing basis, I recommend you check out the following resources regularly. If you use some kind of RSS reader, all of them offer RSS feeds so you can keep tabs on them.

Each of the sites I discuss here has its own reason for being. I highly recommend you check them out regularly to reap the benefits each of them has to offer.

Ning Blog

http://blog.ning.com

The Ning Blog is updated up to three to four times per day. Many blog posts feature networks on Ning. The Ning folks highlight the elements they find appealing about each network they feature, so you may learn from the best examples around. Considering the number of networks that cross their paths on a daily basis, getting featured on the Ning Blog is quite a feat!

Besides featuring outstanding networks on Ning, the Ning Blog offers the following:

✔ Regular posts that explain **new features or feature updates** in great detail. This is done well before features are rolled out; as feature releases approach, so you may know when to expect them; and once features have been made available to the networks.

✔ **Valuable tricks** to show you how to make the most of the platform.

✔ Space for Ning to make **company announcements.**

Ning Help

`http://help.ning.com`

If you have problems or questions about your network, don't call Ghostbusters! (Okay, that was a bad joke. . . .) Go to the Ning Help Center.

The Ning Help Center is a well-thought-out resource to help you get the answers to your questions about your network. It offers access to information in multiple ways:

- ✔ **Search:** You can find answers by entering keyword(s) in a search box. The results you get all contain the keyword(s) you entered.
- ✔ **Browse:** You can browse categories by diving into topical areas and reading the titles of all the questions that pertain to the same kind of issue.
- ✔ **Drill down:** You can go into issues that pertain to Network Creators, Administrators, network members, or visitors.
- ✔ **Contact Ning:** If you still can't find an answer to your question, you can fill out the Contact Us form. The folks at Ning are amazingly fast at replying to inquiries.

So now that you know: Who you gonna call? Er . . . visit . . . well, you know!

Network Creators Network

`http://networkcreators.ning.com`

The Network Creators network is an ideal network on Ning for Network Creators to join. The folks at Ning are "eating their own dog food," which speaks volumes about their commitment to the product they offer.

The network isn't set up as typical network in a couple of respects:

- ✔ The forum contains a very long archive of topics from a period during which it was one of the mechanisms that Network Creators employed to reports issues or ask questions. All the content in the forum is still there and searchable, so you can find lots of answers to your questions in it too.
- ✔ Photos are not enabled, and videos are only one way. They haven't made the photos feature available: There is no need for it on this kind of network. The videos feature is enabled, but it has been renamed Screencasts and is set up to moderate videos submitted. Ultimately, folks use it to post screencasts detailing new feature releases.

Besides these two particulars, this is a great network that every Network Creator should sign up for. Here are some of the benefits it offers:

- **Tutorials:** The Notes section is structured as a container for several great tutorials that you should not miss.

- **Groups:** More than a hundred different groups gather Network Creators around common interests. There are groups for designers, groups about Web analytics, groups in Spanish, and — the biggest and best group of all — Ning For Dummies! Yep, I'm not kidding.

- **Members:** As networks on Ning grow, so does this network. At last count, it had more than 22,000 members, but by the time you read this book, it will likely be much bigger. The members are all folks who are on the same boat as you, so it makes sense to connect with and learn from them.

- **Preview:** One of the coolest things in the network is the Preview section. In it, Ning shares info ahead of feature releases: You get full-size screen shots and detailed accounts of how new features or feature updates are going to look like, so you know what to expect and won't be caught by surprise.

It's very valuable. It's free. There is absolutely no reason why you should postpone signing up for the Network Creators network.

Ning Developer Network

http://developer.ning.com

This is another network on Ning. I discuss it in Chapter 21 as part of the discussion about OpenSocial.

This is another network that every Network Creator should consider joining, though it's not necessarily for everyone. You don't *have* to be a developer to join, but it helps since a lot of the discussion revolves around specific developer-related topics.

The discussion forum is structured around the following categories:

- OpenSocial Development and Application Support
- Announcements
- HTML, CSS, and Design Help
- PHP, API, and Documentation
- "How To" / Hacks

> ✔ General Discussion
>
> ✔ Development Services Needed
>
> ✔ Development Services Offered

The notes page on the network has been used beautifully to offer numerous resources for developers and network creators alike.

The Developer Network contains the documentation for OpenSocial development, the Application Directory, and the mechanism to submit new applications.

Ning Status Blog

`http://status.ning.com`

The last element in the list of Ning resources is the Ning Status Blog. At first inspection, this blog may appear to be one of those blogs that people start and eventually stop contributing to. Don't let this appearance deceive you.

After you've launched your network, the Ning Status Blog gives you perhaps the most critical pieces of information about the systems that make it possible for your network to be up and running.

This blog is communicates with Network Creators, Administrators, and curious members:

> ✔ **When a release or scheduled maintenance is under way:** These events are announced ahead of time through the Ning Blog and also through a broadcast message to all members of the Network Creators network. In the course of the maintenance or release session, the Status Blog is the first place for you to keep an eye on because it contains all the detail you may need to be informed yourself and keep your members current about things. When the activity is over, the Status Blog will let you know with a post titled something along the lines of "Tonight's release is complete!"
>
> ✔ **When some or all networks on Ning are experiencing issues or are offline due to some technical issue:** In times like these (which are *very* rare), you learn to appreciate the Status Blog very much. The Ning folks keep it updated with the status and the extent of the situation. They also normally include a time by which you should expect to see a new update. Finally, after the issue has been resolved, you should see a post titled something like "All networks are online and speedy" to let you know all is back to normal.

Index

G

• T •